MOTHERHOOD ACROSS b

White
flight
started
to become
a prob

Motherhood across Borders

*Immigrants and Their Children
in Mexico and New York*

Gabrielle Oliveira

NEW YORK UNIVERSITY PRESS
New York

NEW YORK UNIVERSITY PRESS
New York
www.nyupress.org

References to Internet websites (URLs) were accurate at the time of writing. Neither the author nor New York University Press is responsible for URLs that may have expired or changed since the manuscript was prepared.

Library of Congress Cataloging-in-Publication Data
Names: Oliveira, Gabrielle, author.
Title: Motherhood across borders : immigrants and their children in Mexico and
New York / Gabrielle Oliveira.
Description: New York : New York University, [2018] | Includes bibliographical references
and index.
Identifiers: LCCN 2017054993| ISBN 978-1-4798-7462-0 (cloth : alk. paper) |
ISBN 978-1-4798-6646-5 (pbk : alk. paper)
Subjects: LCSH: Immigrant children—Mexico—Social conditions. | Immigrant children—
New York (State)—New York—Social conditions. | Mothers—Mexico—Social conditions. |
Mothers—New York (State)—New York—Social conditions. | Women immigrants—New
York (State)—New York—Social conditions.
Classification: LCC HQ792.M6 O45 2018 | DDC 305.23086/912072—dc 3
LC record available at https://lccn.loc.gov/2017054993

New York University Press books are printed on acid-free paper, and their binding materials are chosen for strength and durability. We strive to use environmentally responsible suppliers and materials to the greatest extent possible in publishing our books.

Manufactured in the United States of America

10 9 8 7 6 5 4 3 2 1

Also available as an ebook

For all the families that live separated,
may your stories be told.

2 questions

CONTENTS

Introduction

I lived on Manhattan's Upper West Side when I started this book and my neighbor was a busy mother who had a nanny helping her to take care of her two-year-old toddler. One day my neighbor asked what my research was about; I told her I wanted to learn more about maternal migration and how it influences children and youths' lives. "Well," she replied, "what kind of migration are you talking about? I live in the same country, city, and house as my daughter and she is not being raised only by me. Sara, my nanny, is from Mexico and she has a kid there, you should talk to her." As the US media debates whether women can "have it all"—that is, a successful career and a family—migrant women like Sara wonder how they can care for them all: for their children in Mexico, children they have brought over to the United States, children who were born here, and (in some cases) children they care for professionally.

Sara, a Mexican migrant from a small rural town in the state of Hidalgo, became my first interviewee for this book. One day I saw her and told her I was headed to Mexico that summer to do research with children whose mothers were migrants in New York City. Sara told me she had a son, Agustín, whom she had left in Mexico seven years ago. I asked if she was willing to talk to me about her experiences of mothering from afar and her relationship with Agustín. She did not hesitate, as she seemed excited about the prospect of me taking some gifts to her son on my upcoming trip to Mexico. Sara instructed me to come to her house in the following days to meet her US-born son, Felipe, who was the same age as my neighbor's child, whom she cared for professionally.

A day later I went to East Harlem to visit Sara in the one-bedroom apartment that she shared with her husband and Felipe. As we sat in the kitchen, enjoying some very spicy guacamole, I asked Sara about her crossing. Like all other mothers who participated in this study, Sara is undocumented. She crossed into the United States by foot via the Arizona border, from which point she reached the city of Phoenix.

From there, Sara and many others were put into trucks and vans that took them across the country to destinations such as North Carolina, Chicago, New Jersey, and New York City. As it was for other women in this research, her crossing was difficult and painful, something that she hopes never to have to do again. Sara became dehydrated during her four-day crossing and passed out in the middle of the Sonoran Desert. She recalls members of her group discussing if they should leave her behind and continue their journey. One man, who was a friend of her family, carried her for miles until the group found a place to hide from border patrol. The crossing cost Sara more than $4,000. Sara's sister, Rosa, already in New York City, helped her cover half of the cost. Sara used her savings to pay part of the other half and got the remainder from her other sister, Tami, also in the United States. A single mother, Sara migrated alone, leaving her son Agustín behind with his maternal grandmother, Clarisa. Sara later met and moved in together with Marco in New York City, and together they had a son, Felipe. I asked Sara how she felt being away from her child in Mexico, but also having a child in New York City. She responded: "One feels divided, you are here, but your heart sometimes is there. I know I left him with the best care I could ask for and . . . now I have a child here, with another man. It's hard . . . but I think it's better this way."

As Sara talked to me, she also checked her phone, only to find a text message from her 14-year-old son Agustín in Mexico that read: "hi I want to go out with my friends." Sara paused. She took a deep breath and typed a response while uttering the words out loud: "It's late already, what did your grandmother say?" Agustín texted back: "She said it is ok as long as you allow me to go." Sara responded: "You can go, but you need to text me when you come back home. It can't be after 9 p.m., tomorrow you have school." Agustín responded: "Ok, thank you." A couple of hours later Sara sent a text message to her cousin to confirm Agustín's whereabouts. Agustín did not come back at 9 p.m. and his grandmother, instead of calling Agustín on his cell phone, called Sara in New York and asked her to call Agustín, because she was worried.

In between the exchange of text messages and my interview with Sara, Felipe showed up in the kitchen, crying, because his cousin did not want to share her Spiderman toy with him. Sara tried, unsuccessfully, to convince him that he had so many other toys to play with that he did not need his cousin's action figure. When he kept insisting and crying, Sara told him, "Felipe, if you keep being like this I will send you and your cousin to Mexico to be with your *abuela*." At that moment, I observed one of the many daily actions related to "care" that constituted what I began to call a *transnational care constellation*. In the few hours I spent at Sara's house during my very first interview, the small town in Hidalgo and the reality in East Harlem were intrinsically connected. The constant communication among caregivers, children, and mothers regarding everyday decisions and daily discipline made the physical border between Mexico and the United States more fluid. In a split-screen moment, I was able to visualize Agustín going to school in San Nicolás, a town in Hidalgo of 300 residents, and Felipe getting on a bus to attend a public school in New York City. During my fieldwork I was able to accompany both Felipe and Agustín as they got up and went to school. They both woke up before 6 a.m. and ate breakfast before they left. They both complained on the way to school and wished they could have slept another ten minutes. Agustín received money from Sara every week and all his school costs were taken care of, but he wanted to drop out of school as soon as he finished junior high school. Even though Sara did not want Agustín to drop out of school, she felt she had no control over the matter. Alternatively, with Felipe, Sara was confident that dropping out of school would never be an option as she felt completely in control. I reflected: When and where was school important? How did Sara's absence influence or shape Agustín's choices? Conversely, did Agustín's choices influence Felipe?

Sara took center stage in her care constellation because of her decision-making power. This power was attributed to her by her sons and her mother, but at times she claimed it for herself. Her role as the biological mother, or, as she described it, "the one who birthed him," was celebrated for better or for worse. She was the one who got asked for permission, she was the one who sent financial support, she was the one who bought gifts, and she was the one who made decisions about school-related activities. However, when she did not deliver on the activities related to care that were expected from her, she was criticized; she was blamed for everything that went wrong; she felt guilty and at many times helpless. Sara and other mothers interviewed played a large role in the academic and educational lives of their children. Though mothers and children frequently had a tough time communicating about feelings, love life, personal desires, and dreams, when the discussion was about schooling—homework, classes, teachers, uniforms, books, summer classes, field trips, grades, parent-teacher conferences—the mothers were able to communicate their desires and assert their authority by giving children orders. Providing a better education was the topic that participants in the care constellation thought to be the most important or the reason behind familial separation. The act of talking about school, according to another mother, "made everything worth it."

Agustín and Clarisa shared a relationship that Sara respected and did not compete with. As Sara said, "I left him with my mother. I can't fight with my mother and tell her off . . . If she lets him do things that I do not agree with, sometimes I have to let it go. I know at this point he loves her more than he loves me. But that's all right. She is the one that *takes care of him*." At the same time, in my interviews with Clarisa in Mexico, she seemed concerned about not "going over Sara's head" with regard to Agustín's life. She stated: "Whenever she is ready, she should come back to enjoy her son . . . they are only young for a certain period in their lives . . . and those are the most beautiful years. She should really enjoy him."

This book explores the ways in which maternal migration shapes the lives of the children of immigrant women who are in New York City and in Mexico, with a specific focus on children's education experiences. It focuses on the care arrangements and family relationships that follow maternal migration, specifically by examining how these changes shape children's lives in Mexico and the United States. I argue that the influence of migration cannot be understood by looking at only one side of the border; understanding how mothers in one location negotiate their care for children in different spaces requires a methodological approach that entails transnational multi-sited fieldwork. Children's lives are an important, yet often overlooked, part of the story of what feminist scholars have referred to as "global care chains." I show that caregiving practices regarding decisions about education that derive from maternal migration shape and influence children's experiences of education in a broad sense. Schooling, achievement, and education experiences differ for separated siblings in Mexico and in New York City. Moreover, the self-identified gender of the child plays a role in how these experiences unfold.

Mothers often justify their decisions to migrate by stating that their goal is to *provide a better education for their children*, and indeed much of their transnational mothering is focused on that goal. But to stop at this statement would be a mistake. By focusing on the relational dimensions of maternal migration as experienced by members of what I refer to as a transnational care constellation, this research contributes to existing scholarship on how transnational migration and people's mobility shape the lives of children and youth "left behind," "brought over," and "born here." By arguing for the importance of attending to children's lived experiences of familial separation and participation in care constellations, this research provides a nuanced analysis of migration's many faces.

Even though I was looking for transnational practices of families' everyday lives, I was puzzled by how the concept of care worked across transnational boundaries and also by the shifting nature of kinship relations in the context of global political economy, increased migration, and gender hierarchies that are characteristic of a highly integrated and globalized world. Although I am not arguing that maternal migration necessarily provokes a shift in familial power structures, I am describing a shift in familial dynamics, through transnational care constellations and the structures of care that influence the lives of children involved, especially regarding their education trajectories.

In this book I argue that, in order to understand how maternal migration affects children on both sides of the border, one must understand how they are cared for and how caregivers and mothers share child-rearing practices. Although the ideal of care within the relationships in transnational migration oriented the initial steps in my research, throughout my fieldwork I became fundamentally concerned with how these arrangements influence sibling relations across borders, as well as their schooling, and gender roles. Thus, this book aims to answer these two overarching questions: How do mothers with one (or more) offspring living in New York City and one (or more) children in Mexico negotiate care, educational support, and investment in their children's education? And how do high levels of Mexican maternal migration influence the education, migration aspirations, and social opportunities of the children in Mexico and their siblings born in or brought to the United States?

This book aims to answer other questions as well: How do ideas and practices of motherhood shape mothers' attitudes toward their children? How do children on both sides of the border imagine and describe "the other side"? How do the educational experiences and social opportunities of children in Mexico compare to those of their siblings living in the United States? And, how might maternal migration influences vary by the gender of the child?

Mexican Migrants in New York City

Since the 1960s, Mexicans have been the largest group of Latin American immigrants in the United States. Mexicans in the United States are also the largest group of unauthorized immigrants in the country. Since the time of the Bracero Program (1942–1964), which brought significant numbers of Mexicans to the United States as manual laborers, Mexicans only began to experience a reduced rate of overall population growth after the 2007 economic recession. In 2011, 11.4 million undocumented Mexicans were estimated to be in the United States (Stoney & Batalova, 2013). Compared to other immigrant groups, Mexicans have the lowest chance of legalizing their citizenship status by becoming citizens or lawful permanent residents, or receiving refugee status from the government (Dreby, 2010). It is important to note that families are, for the most part, separated not by distance but by immigration status. If they had the ability, they would be going back and forth and so would their kids. Immigration status is a crucial factor for mothers in this study as it constitutes a tangible physical barrier to physical closeness.

US-bound Mexican migration has changed dynamics since the mid-1990s. Militarization of the border combined with stricter immigration enforcement activities and legislation interrupted a long-standing tradition of circular migration. Dreby (2010, 2015) has explained that there are virtually no pathways to citizenship available to Mexican migrants, and this factor changes the configuration of families separated across borders that had enjoyed more flexibility in the past.

According to Gomberg-Muñoz,

> But for people who have entered and lived in the United States unlawfully, whom I call unlawful entrants, the road to a green card is neither

smooth nor easy—even for those with spouses who are U.S. citizens. This is because when they attempt to gain legal residency, two parts of the U.S. immigration system collide: The first part makes them eligible for a green card but requires them to leave the United States to get it. The second part then bars most of them from returning for 10 years. The only way they can return lawfully is if their U.S. citizen petitioner can prove he or she would suffer "extreme hardship" in the event of a 10-year separation. (2016: 340)

Mendoza (2008) explains that the interruption of this circular migration changed trips that in the past averaged 38 months to 72 months. The status of being undocumented, thus, has been created by a number of different factors, including militarization of the border, failed trade negotiations, economic recession, and specially the inability of the American government to pass a comprehensive immigration reform. In addition, issues arise when mixed-status families in the United States experience fear of deportation and detention of parents who are undocumented. According to Rojas-Flores and colleagues (2017), the chronic risk of arrest, detention, and/or deportation contributes to anxiety and tension within families. Enforcement by the government knows no bounds sweeping through residences and workplace. According to Passel, Cohn, and Gonzalez-Barrera (2012), during the five-year period from 2005 to 2010, a total of 1.4 million Mexicans immigrated to the United States, down by more than half from the 3 million who had done so in the five-year period of 1995 to 2000. In the meantime, the number of Mexicans and their children who moved from the United States to Mexico between 2005 and 2010 rose to 1.4 million, roughly double the number who had done so in the five-year period a decade before (ibid.).

Data from the Pew Hispanic Center show that there were 210,000 Mexican-born people living in New York City in 2011 (compared to Los Angeles, the largest immigrant epicenter in the United States, with 1.4 million Mexican-born residents) (Gonzalez-Barrera & Lopez, 2013). The Latino Project developed by the Center for Latin American, Caribbean & Latino Studies at the City University of New York's Graduate Center also estimated that there are around 600,000 Mexicans living in New York City, with the largest concentration in Brooklyn, Queens, and the Bronx; and more than one million Mexicans in the tristate area (Saiz-Álvarez, 2016).

Women constitute 40 percent of all Mexican migrants in New York City (nationally, 47 percent of Mexican migrants are women) and they head approximately 22 percent of Mexican immigrant households. According to the US Census Bureau, in 2011 the median income of Mexican women who are head of household was a little more than $22,000. Estimating how many children migrant mothers leave in Mexico proved to be a daunting task. Fragmented statistics allowed me to only guess that this phenomenon was relevant and significant enough to be studied (Nobles, 2013).

Theorizing Migration

Migration has historically been a topic of study of different disciplines. In this book I draw primarily from an anthropological, transnational approach. Rather than prioritizing nation-states and assuming that people "assimilate," transnational approaches focus on how mobile populations make decisions in relation to social, cultural, political, and economic conditions both at home and in the new location.

In an article entitled "Approaches from Cultural Analysis in Anthropology to Latin@ Immigration," Renato Rosaldo (2014) discusses key perspectives that distinguish anthropological research on migration. He describes how "studies of migration lead scholars to extend the spatial scope of the units of analysis. These works study collectivities, such as binational families [and] networks, rather than seeing the migrant as a discrete unit to be counted as she or he crosses the border" (p. 148). These studies include a focus on transnational family networks and community, and how those in the sending community are affected by the absences of those who leave. Second, anthropological studies of migration consider how immigrants represent their own experiences to themselves and to others. Third, cultural studies of Latin@ transnationalism consider how gender and sexuality shape the lives of immigrants. Young boys and girls face new and sometimes distinct risks and vulnerabilities. For example, boys may display their masculinity through involvement in gang activity; gay and lesbian teens may find that sexual discrimination compounds their marginalization. Fourth, Rosaldo (2014) explains that the association of "immigrant" with stereotypes about Mexicans rests on a racial bias that underlies immigration policy. He also discusses the criminalization and deportation of undocumented Mexicans and the militarization of the border under the Obama administration. This book is situated in the historical moment described by Rosaldo. Militarized borders, high deportation numbers, and the influence of transnational family networks on children and mothers are all central to the stories told in this book. I focus on the everyday lives of separated families and especially how children in the present generation adapt and respond to the present reality.

In her book *Guadalupe in New York: Devotion and Struggle for Citizenship Rights*, Gálvez (2010) presents an argument that discusses the agency of those who are excluded from "first-class citizenship" or the idea of "good citizenship" (p. 16). This juridical definition of citizenship is "impoverished" according to the author. For Gálvez, Mexican immigrants in New York City make space in their new city while they negotiate notions of self-worth and belonging. Citizenship, according to Gálvez, "has been more rigorously defined in legal terms in the last decade" (p. 17).

Dreby (2015), in her timely book *Everyday Illegal: When Policies Undermine Immigrant Families*, makes a poignant argument for how concepts of being an immigrant from Mexico become conflated with being a criminal. Thus, the illegality, which Dreby refers to as an administrative status, becomes a salient part of immigrant families' identities. Her comparative work shows how families in Ohio and New Jersey deal with the everyday anxieties that come with being undocumented. The author, a sociologist, points to the micro-complexities of each family and children in both locations by showing how nonlinear and determined these pathways are.

Building on this argument, I utilize a theoretical approach that allows for a nuanced understanding of immigrant experiences. Children's trajectories are not as "linear" as described by dominant US-based sociological assimilation theories, and micro-contexts on both sides of the border influence each other in real time, every day. In order to build my argument and show the diversity of experiences within the same generation (in both countries), I use transnational care constellations as my unit of analysis. There are millions of people living in the same situation, divided and separated, but the ties they keep and the ways in which they act out these ties play an important role in their trajectories.

As I will show throughout each chapter, a theoretical concept premised upon looking at mobility within generations in the same country does not account for and cannot accurately describe how immigrant families and children live their lives transnationally (Coe et al., 2011; Dreby, 2010; Boehm, 2011; Schmalzbauer, 2004, 2008; Smith, 2005; Grasmuck & Pessar, 2005; Gamburd, 2000).

Anthropology of Migration and Transnationalism

In anthropology, as in other disciplines, scholars have long argued that the social and economic lives of migrants are not always bounded by national boundaries or physical borders. Fredrik Barth (1969) pointed out that boundaries are not necessarily territorialized and that group membership is under constant negotiation. Thus, the concept of transnationalism has been a central anthropological frame since the 1990s.

Glick-Schiller, Basch, and Szanton-Blanc (1995) have convincingly argued that transnationalism is part of an effort to reconfigure anthropological thinking so that it will reflect current transformations in the way in which time and space are lived. As in the United States, caregivers and children in Mexico are actively creating new arrangements to keep their status as members of the same group. Just as (for Barth) the idea of an ethnic group or a community becomes unbounded, parenting—and more specifically mothering—becomes an unbounded practice, where mothers do not necessarily live in the same household but are very much present and involved in the everyday lives of the children they have left behind.

The questions that have traditionally shaped studies of migration in anthropology have focused less on migration flows and more on how individuals respond to these global processes. Culture, which includes the study of the interaction between beliefs and behavior and social relationships, has resulted in an emphasis on adaptation, culture change, identity, and ethnicity (Brettel & Hollifield, 2000, 2008). Historically, the discipline has articulated migration studies as belonging to two analytical approaches: the first was rooted in modernization theory, and the other was rooted in a historical structuralist perspective based on concepts of political economy and the effects of global capitalism.

Modernization theory included a bipolar framework of analysis that separated and opposed sending and receiving societies, which brought attention to the well-known push and pull factors of migration. Push and pull factors are economic, political, cultural, and environmental forces that can either induce people to move to a new location or encourage them to leave their place of residence. According to anthropologist Michael Kearney (1986), this concern with push and pull factors and modernization is rooted in the "folk-urban continuum" formulated by Robert Redfield in 1941. Redfield's model contrasted "traditional" folkways and "modern" urban life. The idea was that modernization theory marked the movement from country to city as people searched for more opportunities (or pull factors). This paradigm dominated much of the discussion regarding migration, linking people's movement (urbanization) to hopes for economic development. Modernization, however, did not mean increased salaries and less poverty; quite the contrary. Many urban centers became characterized by the presence of shantytowns and significant poverty. In addition, this model of looking at migration did not describe international migration. The historical structuralist perspective, with its intellectual roots in Marxist political economy and world systems theory (Wallerstein, 1980), posited that capitalism was responsible for the unequal distribution of economic and political power among developed and developing countries. Thus, countries considered "underdeveloped" were trapped at a disadvantaged position causing people to move because of cheap labor and unequal terms of trade (Haas, 2008). For historical structuralists, people do not have free choice; instead, they are constrained by larger forces. These forces compel them to migrate to another country or region to fulfill globalization's demands.

These theories failed to explain why some people migrate and others do not. As the world became more globalized, migration scholars took up the notion of transnationalism to rethink territories and notions of culture (Appadurai, 1996). Migration forced anthropologists to move away from studies of bounded communities and develop new forms of ethnographic work (later multi-sited ethnography) to account for people's movement and the bonds they maintain with their countries of origin. Transnationalism appeared as a concept to describe a process that could account for these practices developed by migrants. As Kearney (1986)

commented, "A heightened awareness of the magnitude and significance of migration among other things caused anthropologists to turn away from community studies in the 1950s and 1960s, when it became widely realized that such work was suffering from terminal myopia" (p. 332). However, Vertovec (2007) points out that even though transnationalism in anthropology meant that scholars would take on ethnographic work that went beyond geographical boundaries or "tribes," "interrelations between multiple groups have not become the subject of anthropological inquiry as much as one might have expected" (p. 965). Dissatisfaction with how migration was always framed within a macro approach of push and pull factors led to a new form of migration theory. Critique of the bipolar model of migration culminated in a theoretical construct that proposed a transgression of geographic borders and a focus on how relationships and identities are maintained across terrains. Because the concept of transnationalism was developed through different disciplines simultaneously, it remains a complex interdisciplinary idea.

As early as 1979, in a piece for the *International Migration Review*, Elsa Chaney described a certain category of immigrants as having "their feet in two societies" (p. 209). Even though she never used the word "transnational" to describe this type of immigrant, Chaney described the process in which migrants kept practices from their country of origin very much alive in the new land. In addition, according to Brettel and Hollifield (2008), "the roots of transnationalism within anthropology can be found in earlier work on return migration that emphasized links with the homeland and the notion that emigration did not necessarily mean definitive departure in the minds of immigrant themselves" (p. 17). Though not a new phenomenon, transnationalism gained traction in the 1990s with multi-sited ethnographic studies.

Transnationalism is described by some scholars as a "catchall notion" (Ebaugh & Saltzman Chafetz, 2002) or, as Portes, Guarnizo, and Landolt (1999) put it, a "highly fragmented field" (p. 218). The term, however, is central to the understanding and analysis of multiplicity in the daily lives of the families and individuals featured in this book.

Scholars agree that transnationalism is a notion that captures a process that goes beyond geographical borders in the form of political organizations or family relationships. Basch, Glick-Schiller, and Szanton-Blanc defined transnationalism as

The processes by which immigrants forge and sustain multi-stranded social relations that link together their societies of origin and settlement. We call this process transnationalism to emphasize that many immigrants today build social fields that cross geographic, cultural and political borders. (1994: 7)

Whether or not a transnational approach might be an outcome of ethnographic research, or, rather, a lens through which ethnographers have come to see the world, transnational ethnographies of Mexican families like those written by Robert C. Smith (2005), Dreby (2010), Schmalzbauer (2009), Boehm (2011), and Hamann and Zúñiga (2011) have contributed to developing a methodology that is transnational in approach and enhances our understanding of ways in which migration, in association with processes of globalization, transforms everyday life such that people might sustain connections across time and space despite their mobility. A focus on care also allows us to point out the shortcomings of transnationalism. Not only do individuals have their "two feet" in two different worlds, but they also have hands, embraces, and kisses that are disembodied by the separation. Technology may mediate relationships, but it is simply not the same. I use this working definition of transnationalism to allude to the social field created through care. Instead of focusing primarily on political and economic links between the societies being studied, I emphasize "care" as a concern that both unites and divides families across borders.

Another development of anthropological research related to migration occurred when transnationalism came to be closely linked with postmodernism and feminist theory, which conceptualized space and place in new ways. Gender and migration are important components for the analysis of data collected in this book as I focus on maternal migration, care, and children's educational trajectories.

Gender and Migration

More than half of the migrants in the world today are women (Population Facts United Nations, 2013). As the principal wage earners for themselves and their families, many women are driven to migrate in search of a living wage, leaving their families and children behind

(Castles, 1999; Forbes Martin, 2003). Gender, historically, has not been an important piece in the dominant economic and sociological theories of migration (Cerrutti & Massey, 2001). Ethnographic research challenges this notion as it shows how gender reveals power differences within households and families. Cerrutti and Massey have found that most female migrants have left their country of origin to follow a husband or a parent (p. 196).

The reality is that an increasing number of Mexican female migrants migrate to the United States alone, leaving their children behind in the care of relatives or friends (Fernández-Kelly, 2008). Although mothers leaving children behind is not a new phenomenon, the number of years mothers stay separated from their children has increased due to longer periods of settlement stemming from the need to reduce the risks of exit and re-entry to the United States. Although some women migrate to reunify with family, Hondagneu-Sotelo and Avila (1997) found that 40 percent of their sample of undocumented mothers were working to support children left behind in the country of origin. Studies suggest that transnational migration challenges norms and ideals of family life that involve gender hierarchies (Coe et al., 2011), especially gendered roles and the division of household labor. However, women's roles in the household and outside of the home vary tremendously according to social and geographical locations (Dreby & Schmalzbauer, 2013). Only recently have scholars begun to examine the life experiences of children of migrant parents, especially children of migrant mothers, in their home country (Bernhard et al., 2005; Dreby, 2010; Boehm, 2011; Hamann & Zúñiga, 2011; Fresnoza-Flot, 2013).

Mexican women's migration to the United States has always been relevant, but it was not until 1986, with the passage of the Simpson-Rodino Act, which prompted entire families to move to the United States, that scholarly work on female migration developed. The "feminization of migration" (Dwyer, 2004: 36) reflects a global demand for low-priced labor that led women from poor countries to migrate to prosperous countries for jobs.

Undocumented immigration has been, and continues to be, a complex issue of enormous sociopolitical and economic consequence for Latina women who migrate to the United States in search of jobs.[1] Single women's migration is increasing relative to total female out-migration from Mexico and Central America (Valdez-Gardea, 2009). Compared to earlier generations, single women leave their countries with several objectives in mind and under vastly different social and economic conditions. This mobility has prompted interest in "transnational motherhood," the practice of mothers living and working in different countries from those of their children, thus resulting in a "care deficit" in many nations in the global south (Hondagneu-Sotelo & Avila, 1997; Ehrenreich & Hochschild, 2002: 8: Yarova, 2006). In addition, the lack of immigration status contributes to low salary and lack of accountability of employers. Scholars are examining the impact of transnational mothering on children and partners or spouses, as well as on mothers themselves, asking how earning a wage affects women's engagements with gender hierarchies (Parreñas, 2005a, 2005b: 103; Gálvez, 2011).

Maternal migration may economically benefit children, as mothers may be more regular remitters even though they typically earn less than male migrants (Abrego, 2009). However, the emotional costs of "transnational mothering" may affect children differently when compared to the absence of fathers (Hondagneu-Sotelo & Avila, 1997; Ehrenreich & Hochschild, 2002; Parreñas, 2005a). Because the mother is a nurturing and caring figure in Mexican society and her role is socially valued, mothers are often primary caregivers (Hondagneu-Sotelo, 2003; Hirsch, 2003; Paz, 1985; Lewis, 1959); hence, the consequences of maternal absence may be significant. Maternal migration may prompt changes in traditional understandings of gender, motherhood, and caregiving.

Mexican migrant women, in contrast to Mexican migrant men, reportedly continue to remit and stay in touch with children even after long periods of separation, yielding new transnational parenting and shared child-rearing practices that have been largely omitted from the literature on transnationalism and migration (Dreby, 2010). However, ideologies of motherhood are slow to change. In her studies of transnational Filipino families, Parreñas (2005a, 2005b) found that the care children received from relatives or other caregivers became obscured because it was not performed by their mothers. Parreñas (2005a) argues that the resulting "gender paradox" harms "children's acceptance of the reconstitution of mothering and consequently hampers their acceptance of growing up in households split apart from their mothers" (p. 92).

Women in developing nations often resort to migration as a means of family survival (Schmalzbauer, 2005), and transnational mothers struggle with the paradox of having to leave their children in order to care for them. Members of their society call their maternal role into question when Mexican women migrate, and grandmothers, aunts, sisters, elder daughters, or friends assume the role of caregiver for their children. Transnational Latina mothers find themselves negotiating the closeness of family through remittances, gift sending, and various transnational connections.

Although women migrate to provide for their families, the question of how much remittances and migration help migrant families in Mexico is a matter of debate. Remittances can exacerbate economic inequalities in the sending society (Smith, 2005). Families with migrant members enjoy economic advantages (Kandel & Massey, 2002; Cohen, 2004). Children with a US migrant parent have better grades than children in non-migrant households; this trend is assumed to be associated with an increase in overall financial resources for families with a migrant parent (Kandel & Kao, 2001). However, parental migration exerts a heavy emotional toll. Suárez-Orozco and Suárez-Orozco (2001) find levels of depression to be higher among immigrant children in the United States who experienced separation prior to migration than those who migrate with their parents. Others find that in states with a long-standing tradition of US migration, the migration of a caregiver, including the mother, is associated with academic or behavioral problems and emotional difficulties among children (Carling et al., 2012; Heymann et al., 2009; Lahaie et al., 2009).

Childhood and Migration

"Children left-behind" is a term used in the literature to refer to children of immigrant parents who are in the country of origin while the parents are in the host country. The idea of "leaving a child behind" has bothered many scholars, as it is sometimes viewed as synonymous with a negative act, that of abandonment. Mothers who have migrated to the United States discussed openly the difference between "leaving" and "abandoning": as one mother told me about her daughter, "la dejé, pero no la abandoné" [I left her, but I did not abandon her]. Other scholars feel the term "left behind" is negative; they prefer the term "stay-behind children," which alludes to the idea that children "remain" in the same place though other members of the family have departed. During the three years I conducted research with mothers in New York City, they referred to their children in Mexico as "*los que están*" (the ones who are) or "*lo que está*" (that which is) in Mexico. All mothers interviewed used the verb "*dejar*" (to leave) when referring to their departure. In this analysis, I adopt the term "to leave" as a way to capture the differentiation mothers made regarding where their children were located.

"Transnational mothering" has different consequences for children living in societies where the biological mother is socially valued for her provision of care and nurturing, as in Mexico (Hondagneu-Sotelo, 1994, 2003; Hondagneu-Sotelo & Avila, 1997; Ehrenreich & Hochschild, 2002; Hirsch, 2003; Parreñas, 2005a, 2005b; Horton, 2008; Dreby, 2010). Author Garcia-Zamora (2006), with the help of a 2006 UNICEF-UNDP (United Nations Development Project) field office survey of Zacatecas, Jalisco, and Michoacan (three Mexican states), reports that one-third of households with children in each state were without both a father and a mother. Studies on the lives of children born in the United States to Mexican migrants or brought to the United States by Mexican immigrants are better known, especially with regard to educational attainment. Thirty-six percent of first-generation and 11 percent of second-generation Mexican Americans aged 16 to 24 do not have a high school diploma (or its equivalent) (Brick et al., 2011: 9). College enrollment rates of Mexican Latinos are lower than their peers: among children of Mexican migrants, 33 percent had completed only high school in 2010 (ibid.). Indeed, the 2000 Census showed that more than 40 percent of foreign-born Mexican immigrants living in New York City had less than a twelfth grade education, with no diploma. Children of Mexican immigrants face significant educational challenges: 30 percent of Hispanic public school students report speaking only English at home, and 20 percent of second-generation students report speaking English with difficulty (Fry & Gonzalez, 2008: 11). Further, 28 percent of Hispanic students live in poverty, compared with 16 percent of non-Hispanic students (p. 13). Given the correlation of socioeconomic status, parents' education level, and English-language ability with academic success, these indicators should give us pause.

The situation becomes even more challenging for mixed-status families. Suárez-Orozco and Suárez-Orozco (2001) showed how special issues arise in families that have a mix of documented and undocumented children. According to these authors, in some cases the undocumented child may unconsciously become the family's "scapegoat," while the documented child may occupy the role of the "golden child" (p. 35). This inequity creates tensions and resentments, as well as guilt and shame. Suárez-Orozco and Suárez-Orozco state that one of the most demoralizing aspects of undocumented status is its influence on the educational aspirations of immigrant children. Yoshikawa and Kalil (2011) have found that children of parents without documents tend to live in poverty and overcrowded spaces while facing significant financial issues, including difficulties paying rent or bills.

My research adds a third component of many family structures—children who stay in Mexico. With that in mind, I turn to the idea of transnational care in anthropology.

Transnational Care in Anthropology

Maternal migration is shifting gendered notions of care. Baldassar (2007) and Parreñas (2005b), among others, address the gendered nature of "kinwork," the routines carried out to reproduce and maintain the transnational social space across the family network. Parreñas's ethnography of Filipino migrant mothers who leave their children reveals how the issue of their gender comes to the fore as they negotiate the dual roles of transnational breadwinner on the one hand and absent mother on the other.

Further, both roles are dependent on information and communication technologies (facilitating remittances and motherly contact, respectively). Baldassar (2007) observes that email has had the effect of making kinwork less gendered, as male family members with email access are more likely to take the initiative to contact other relatives individually, "thereby reinforcing and sustaining stronger and broader kinship networks" (p. 22). According to Baldassar, as a consequence of their absence and separation, migrants and their children long to be with each other. According to Rhacel Pareñas:

Contemporary transnational households have a different temporal and spatial experience from the binational families of the past. New technologies heighten the immediacy and frequency of migrants' contact with their sending communities and allow them to be actively involved in everyday life there in fundamentally different ways than in the past. (2005a: 317–318)

However, while transnational migrants may adopt new information and communication technologies to suit their networking needs, the influence of these technologies on social networks, daily life, and community is largely contested. There have not been many studies concerned with how communication technologies affect the lives of children left behind in Mexico by their migrant mothers. Scholars do not automatically assume that increased use of the Internet, mobile phones, or other information and communication technologies makes individuals feel more connected or leads them to become more community-minded.

No doubt women and their children in this study longed to see each other. Longer periods of separation, however, did not necessarily reinforce kinship ties; instead, longer periods of separation allowed relationships to change over time. Mothers were still viewed as central in the children's lives, but they also understood their role as a co-parent with caregivers in Mexico. Youth in Mexico had no problem asking their mothers for presents and money, but they also had a sense of loyalty to their caregivers. Thus, though children, youth, and mothers in this research all had cellular phones and participated in some sort of social network, communication was complex and did not always lead to feelings of longing for each other. Fights and discussions would erupt and communication was often cut off.

Transnational Care Constellations

To conceptualize care, I develop the notion of transnational care constellations. Dreby (2010) first developed the approach of looking for constellations of migrant parents to more accurately describe changes in family dynamics. Keeping in mind Dreby's work focused on the parent-child-caregiver constellation, I further develop the concept by putting the mother in the center and focusing on how care crosses transnational terrains and how it influences the different groups of children in Mexico and in New York City. Some scholars of citizenship similarly use the concept of constellation. Author Rainer Baubock (2010) proposes that the study of citizenship move to a more systematic comparative approach. He suggests the term "citizenship constellation" to denote a structure in which "individuals are simultaneous(ly) linked to several such political entities, so that their legal rights and duties are determined not only by one political authority, but by several" (p. 848). In the same vein, I propose that these individuals are linked and that the relationships they develop are determined not only by interactions between them and the people they live with, but also by people who are away from them, whom they imagine to be a certain way.

In astronomy, a constellation is a recognizable pattern of stars that has official borders and an official designation. The International Astronomical Union explains that throughout human history and across many different cultures, names and mythical stories have been attributed to the star patterns in the night sky, thus giving birth to what we know as constellations. Transnational care constellations became my unit of analysis for examining how everyday life happens across borders. My focus is on the relationships between mother, children, and caregivers. I use this unit of analysis as I seek to shed light not on the entirety of a family system, but on a recognizable pattern of who is involved in caregiving, as well as the everyday teaching and educating of children.

Herein, a transnational care constellation is a recognizable pattern always composed by the mother ("the one who gave birth"), children (in both countries), and caregivers in Mexico. In addition, teachers and fathers have sporadic roles that change according to time, emotional proximity, and physical distance. In the model I propose as a frame of analysis (figure 1.1), the mother is in the center in a larger circle—not because I assign her greater importance, but because she mediates the relationships that occur around her. Financially she is also the one who contributes the most. The other members of the constellation put the mother in a position of power, and she takes on the position of primary decision-maker for many issues regarding parenting, schooling, education, travel, curfew, and finances. In short, transnational separations cannot be viewed solely as affecting mothers and children as isolated

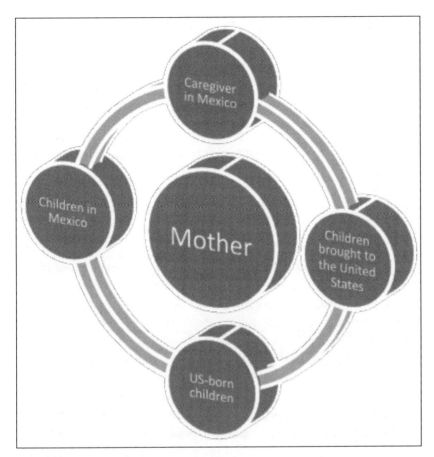

Figure I.1. Transnational Care Constellation.

individuals; rather, transnational separations shape the intimately experienced bonds between mothers and children (Horton, 2009). I use the term transnational care constellation as a spatial concept that references how care and familial bonds travel across geographic and imaginary spaces.

Methods

A transnational project that focuses on the experiences and consequences of care constellations requires multi-sited ethnographic fieldwork. In the mid-1980s, George Marcus (1995) explained that even though the most common mode of ethnographic research was intensively focused upon a single site of ethnographic observation and participation, there was also a second mode. Marcus described the second mode as a "much less common" mode of ethnographic research associated with the wave of intellectual capital labeled postmodern, which moves out from single sites and local situations of conventional ethnographic research designs to examine the circulation of cultural meanings, objects, and identities in diffuse time-space (p. 79). Marcus (1998) explained, "for ethnographers interested in contemporary local changes in culture and society, single-sited research can no longer be easily located in a world system perspective" (p. 82). He explains that multi-sited research is designed around chains, paths, threads, conjunctions, or juxtapositions of locations in which the ethnographer establishes some form of literal, physical presence, with an explicitly posited logic of association of connection among sites that in fact defines the argument of the ethnography. Marcus proposes that the ethnographer can: follow the people, follow the thing, follow the metaphor, follow the story, follow the life, or follow the conflict.

Data for this book derive from a multi-sited ethnographic study that seeks to "follow the people" and their stories (Marcus, 1995: 106). As Abu-Lughod wrote, "by focusing closely on particular individuals and their changing relationships, one would necessarily subvert the most problematic connotations of culture: homogeneity, coherence, and timelessness" (1991: 476). Thus, all chapters in this book present findings, insights, and reflections on my engagement with members of transnational care constellations made up of mothers, their children, and their children's caregivers. Although this study prioritizes the experiences of children with migrant mothers, I found that the interactions between children and caregivers, children and mothers, mothers and caregivers, teachers and children, and sometimes fathers were major parts of the experiences of the folks I studied. I used multi-sited methods to be able to more fully explain the social phenomenon of transnational motherhood. As such, I traveled between New York City and different states in Mexico numerous times over a 32-month period in order to capture the dynamism of communities who are both "here and there." In Mexico, I conducted research in the states of Puebla, Hidalgo, Vera Cruz, Mexico State, Morelos, and Tlaxcala. I spent most of my time in the state of

Puebla. In the United States, I conducted research in the New York City neighborhoods of East Harlem (Manhattan), Sunset Park (Brooklyn), Jackson Heights (Queens), and the South Bronx.

Drawing on ethnography as well as surveys, I examined transnational caregiving practices among women with mixed-status children in New York and Mexico. After recruiting 20 families to participate in my study (see appendix A for a detailed description), I established three levels of engagement with participants. Eight transnational care constellations constituted the center of my qualitative research. I spent time with them in Mexico and in New York and tracked half of them for more than two years. The second level of engagement happened with the other 12 families, whose members I interviewed and observed in New York City but visited fewer times in Mexico. From the transnational care constellations, I interviewed and observed 30 children in Mexico (15 female and 15 male, ranging in age from seven to eighteen years) and 37 children in New York City (20 female and 17 male, ranging in age from four months to eighteen years).

Finally, participants who belonged to the third level of engagement included 40 mothers in New York City, as well as fathers, caregivers, and more than 60 children and youth in Mexico who were not matched. In addition, I surveyed 225 children between the ages of seven and sixteen in three schools in Puebla to understand the ways in which maternal remittance influenced school achievement. Specifically, I compared the educational experiences and social trajectories of children who stayed in Mexico, undocumented children and youth brought to the United States, and children born in the United States. The children and youth in a "care constellation" share the same biological mother who has migrated to New York City, but their lives differ dramatically in terms of education experience and familial support.

Criteria for inclusion in the study were that the candidates were female Mexican migrants who have been in the United States for at least one year but no more than 15 years, were mothers, and had at least one school-age child in New York City and one in Mexico. I found participants for my research in New York City through three strategies. My first strategy included three sampling methods. Sara was my neighbor's nanny and the first participant in my research. She introduced me to different women; they, in turn, introduced me to more potential participants. This sampling technique is what Bernard (2011) calls chain referral or network sampling (p. 147). My second strategy was snowball sampling, in which research participants were asked to identify other potential subjects. My third strategy was respondent-driven sampling (RDS), which involved asking each participant to identify two or more potential subjects, and then expanded through each of those social networks. Snowball sampling and RDS are approaches used for studying hard-to-find or hard-to-study populations. In this study, participants in Mexico were scattered throughout several locations, and in the United States many of my potential subjects were reclusive and "actively hiding" because their most common status of undocumented puts them at risk of deportation. The status of undocumented also infers a "catchall" term referring to multiple complex statuses. According to Bernard (2006), when well used, RDS methods help the researcher avoid the following problems that sometimes occur with snowball sampling: (1) the people whom a participant names may be less anxious to grant an interview; (2) the recruiting process specifically deals with the likelihood that the target population was potentially reluctant to be interviewed; and (3) RDS methods may produce samples that are less biased than traditional snowball samples (p. 194). I looked for a balance in gender of the children "here and there." In addition, I looked for families with comparable socioeconomic status so I could generate cohesive conclusions about this specific population.

My second strategy to find participants for my research in New York City was through volunteer work in selected organizations that I knew served immigrant Latino populations. They were the Union Settlement in East Harlem and the Center for Family Services in Sunset Park, Brooklyn. In the South Bronx I visited a Mexican grocery store and restaurant where my husband had lunch every day because it was near his workplace. I became close with the owner, Doña Dora, who allowed me to "hang out" in the space, talk to her employees, and leave my business cards on the counter. Through Doña Dora I met four of the core transnational constellations in my research.

My third strategy to find participants for my research in New York City was to ask fellow researchers and friends who worked with immigrant populations if they knew anyone who would fit the criteria. Recruitment for this research would not have been possible without the help of others who introduced me to my participants. The nature of the topic is such that it was not easy to gain access into the lives of women and their children.

I conducted interviews and observations with several mothers and their children in the United States and then went to Mexico to meet their children and the caregivers of these children. I identified and recruited additional participants in Mexico through art workshops run by Universidad Iberoamerican in Puebla. There, I met children in two Puebla towns who had one or both parents living in the United States. I conducted interviews and observations with that group. Caregivers put me in contact with the mothers in the United States, whom I later interviewed. Through these many interactions, I collected five kinds of data: (1) structured, semi-structured, and group interviews conducted in Spanish with 68 children (36 female and 32 male, ranging in age from three to eighteen years); in-depth interviews with 31 caregivers and 60 mothers; and informal interviews with 36 family members, 21 teachers, and nine fathers; (2) participant observation documented through field notes with 20 transnational constellations; (3) surveys and drawings of 225 children in schools in Puebla regarding maternal remittances and education aspirations; (4) 88 children's pictorial representations of what family, home, and the United States look like; (5) correspondence in the form of text messages via cell phones and Facebook messages via computers. Following a well-established tradition in anthropology, I changed all the names of my interviewees to protect their privacy. Table 1.1 is a compiled description of the two sides of the transnational care constellations in this study.

Recruiting participants did not come without significant rejection and suspicion. The undocumented status of participants put them in a tough spot, as they wondered what I would do with the information given. The fact that I am Brazilian and I was on a student visa studying in the United States helped put them at ease. My knowledge of soccer and Spanish was also beneficial to establishing long-lasting relationships with these families. Because I moved back and forth from New York City to Mexico, families trusted me to cross the border with small gifts, pictures, and letters for their families on the other side. They asked me to take pictures or short recordings of their sons and daughters at birthdays and celebrations. My position as a "bridge" for their communications

Table I.1. Description of Transnational Care Constellations

20 Transnational Constellations

New York Side of Constellations	Mexico Side of Constellations
Mothers have been in the US for 3 to 16 years	Children have been separated from their mothers for 3 to 16 years
Age range of mothers was 24 to 51	Age range of caregivers was 48 to 86
Age range of US-born children was 3 months to 12 years	Age range of children in Mexico was 3 months to 18 years (26 girls and 19 boys)
Age range of undocumented children was 15 to 18 years	
Mothers were employed as domestic workers, laundry employees, restaurant workers, and caregivers	All but 1 caregiver were grandmothers
Marital status: three were single mothers, two were separated, and 15 were married or re-married	Education status: eight children (out of 45) were enrolled in school; seven dropped out (six boys and one girl)
Household income ranged from USD17,000 to 35,000 a year	Household income ranged from USD100 to 600 a year, not including remittances. Remittances ranged from USD 0 to 1,500 per month.

also helped me build trust. Doing research in Mexico, although dangerous at times, proved to be a simpler task than doing research in New York City. Schedules and time were more flexible in the small towns in Mexico, where I was able to live with each family for a few weeks at a time. I went back and forth for three years, and each time I went to Mexico I was there for a minimum of three months, ultimately spending nine months in total in Mexico.

During a three-year multi-sited ethnographic research project with families in Central New Jersey and Oaxaca, Mexico, Dreby (2010) used a combination of snowball and purposive sampling to interview 142 members of transnational families and recruit a total of 12 families for ongoing ethnographic research. In her research over 18 non-continuous months in the Philippines, Parreñas (2005a) interviewed 30 children with migrant mothers, 26 with migrant fathers, and 13 with two migrant parents. Gálvez (2011), in her two-year multi-sited ethnographic research, combined qualitative and quantitative methods in order to understand women's narratives of reproduction and motherhood. She used surveys, medical records, and interviews to combine biomedical data with cultural practices of patients and their narratives. The number of transnational constellations recruited in this research thus fits within the tradition of other scholars of migration and transnationalism who have done multi-sited research.

Organization of This Book

The two main research questions this study addresses are: How do mothers with one (or more) offspring living in New York City and one child (or more) in Mexico negotiate care, educational support, and investment in their children's education? And, how do the educational experiences and social opportunities of children in Mexico compare to those of their siblings living in the United States?

Chapter 1 explores the tensions behind the ideals migrant mothers have of caregiving and "mothering." It addresses the question: How do ideals and practices of motherhood shape mothers' attitudes toward their children? I discuss how ideals and practices of motherhood that may seem at odds are actually adaptations of what mothers consider to be "good" and "caring" mothers. The very act of leaving and migrating represents a "break" in the nexus of motherhood—which includes physical presence but is made and remade in order to fulfill women's ideas of what care should be.

Chapter 2 addresses the question of how mothers negotiate and participate in the educational trajectories of children in the United States and in Mexico. It illustrates how mothers in New York City are central decision-makers in school-related issues in Mexico and in the United States, even when there is lengthy separation from the children in Mexico and language and legal status barriers with children in the United States. I argue that mothers in New York and grandmothers in Mexico go through similar challenges when interacting with teachers and school staff in both countries, as they feel like they have little power or influence to assist children. This chapter shows a "split-screen" format, comparing the experiences I observed on both sides of the border regarding school interactions. I also use data from phone calls and text messages across borders to explore how the reach of mothers in New York goes beyond formal boundaries. Thus, I show how Internet and Communication Technologies (ICT) foster regular interactions between mothers and grandmothers, between mothers in New York City and teachers in Mexico, and between separated siblings when they are doing homework and/or playing.

Chapter 3 explores the perspectives of children and youth on migration and family separation on both sides of the border. Much of the fieldwork for this research was spent with children and youth as they attended social functions, were at home, went to school, and engaged in other activities like sports, dances, and church. From photographs, drawings, poems, and narratives to Facebook messages, text messages, and other tools in social networks, I am able to show how children and youth make sense of migration and how these ideas shape their perspectives about their futures. I focus on two narratives that illustrate the ways young people make sense of migration: The first narrative concerns material goods and socioeconomic status, and the second is concerned with "the other side" or "where the rest of the *family*" is, informed by their interactions not only with family members who are physically close to them, but also by interactions within the entire transnational care constellation. I use drawings and interview data to explore how their understandings are a product of both their interactions with siblings and the information they receive from their parents.

Chapter 4 compares how Mexican maternal migration has influenced the educational experiences and social opportunities of children in Mexico and their siblings living in the United States. I answer the question: How do high levels of Mexican maternal migration influence the education, migration aspirations, and social opportunities of children in Mexico and their siblings born in or brought to the United States? I argue that some of the assumptions about quality of education and social opportunities in Mexico are complicated when compared to the lives of those who are in the United States. Data for this chapter come from interviews and observations with children, youth, and their teachers in school. I also consider the perceptions of mothers and family members regarding schooling experience on both sides of the border.

How might maternal migration influences vary by the gender of the child? Chapter 5 discusses girls' superior educational performance as linked to the following narratives: (1) education attainment as a path to reunification with mothers; (2) over-achieving in school to live up to the expectations of mothers and hoping that academic performance will bring them together; (3) performing well in school with the expectation of receiving material gifts; and (4) school as a space to forget. Finally, I conclude with one story of reunification in New York City and the implications of transnational care constellations as a care arrangement for children, mothers, and caregivers.

The structure of this book represents the trajectory this research has taken over the years. From the starting point, which was mothers, to the growing focus on children, I try to give enough background on families so that the reader can understand the complexities of the stories. The core of the data for this book is based on ethnographic research with 20 constellations. I complement the chapters with data from interviews with 40 other mothers during the course of the three years, as well as with independent surveys with children in Puebla, Mexico. The chapters build on each other in two different ways. Some chapters address the background stories of mothers and their narratives, and other chapters introduce the voices of children and youth, who describe their side of the experience. Second, the chapters attempt to present to the reader the synchronous impact of maternal migration on both sides of the border. As noted earlier, this research required high levels of mobility and flexibility. Even though the constant back and forth and depth of ethnographic observations and interviews with families on both sides of the border can leave one confused, that is precisely how life is experienced by the participants in this study. Thus, I document the experiences of these families as they challenge steady concepts of "host" and "sending" societies, as well as assumptions behind generational mobility and the way in which parenting—especially *mothering*—influences children and youth's trajectories.

INTERLUDE 1

Parallel Lives

As I sat in the small, bright, lime green room in the South Bronx, 20 women around me chatted in a lively way. Some of them breastfed, others drank tea, and a few just stared. This was a regular place for some of my research participants to go. It was one of hundreds of Herbalife[1] offices spread out in the city. This particular one, near the "Intervale" stop on the 2/5 subway line, was run by a family of undocumented evangelical Mexican immigrants. The office space represented a "break" for many of these women. A break from their tiny apartments. A break from their routine of cleaning, cooking, and caring for the kids. A "safe place," as one of them described that February day. Because almost every woman who went there had one or more children, all of the women "took care" of the kids. Aruna, Emilia, and Maya (participants in my research) were regulars. Sometimes they would spend four hours there and only leave after receiving a phone call from their husbands/partners.

During the winter the small office served as a warm space, and during the summer it was one of the few places in the neighborhood with a strong air conditioning system. The women engaged in a daily ritual. I ended up visiting three different Herbalife sites, in the Bronx, Queens, and Sunset Park. Virtually everywhere I recruited a participant she would ask me to go with her to "*la batida*" (the shake). They called the place "*la batida*" because the "ritual" of hanging out involved consuming the company's products. First, "*el agua*" (flavored water) "because it helps the circulation," then "*el técito*" (the little tea) for digestion, and finally "*la batida*," which helps you lose weight. Not just any weight; baby weight. "Un consumo," or this particular sequence of products, costs $5. Many of these women sold Herbalife products door to door, so they would get "un consumo" for free. There was also a big chart on the wall with each woman's name (my name was eventually added to the chart) that followed each one's daily check-in and consumption. After accruing ten stars, you receive a "free" product from Herbalife. Women there discussed everything from relationships with their partners to problems with teachers and schools to families they left in the country of origin. The liveliest discussions had to do with telling each other about their own childhoods and their relationships with their own mothers.

"Una tequilita Gabi?" Candela asked me as we sat in the garage of her home in Puebla, Mexico (Field notes, Mexico, May 4, 2012). Candela didn't drink, but she wanted me to try the handmade tequila her son had brought her a few days before. As we sat there in chairs while I sipped tequila, more women joined us. When I met Candela in 2010, she gave me her "blessing" to do research in her town in the Mixteca poblana. Many of the caregivers of the constellations I was researching came to "hang out" at Candela's house. Candela was known to be the "informal" mayor of the pueblo. She sold everything: flowers; regalos (gifts) for quinceañeras, weddings, and baptisms; tortillas; and all kinds of "agua" (jamaica, horchata, piña). The women who went there didn't just sit around and chat, they bought and sold different products, gossiped, and talked about what "El Norte" (the North) had done with their sons and daughters. A nostalgic tone was predominant in their narratives. Memories of how "it used to be" when mothers could raise their children. Memories of when women had a well-defined place and role in society. As Tami, a matriarch raising grandchildren at 72, wondered,

> How is it that we have become this type of society that allows and, more than that, needs mothers to leave their children and needs children to leave their mothers? It used to be that you could go to the city [Mexico City] and that was that. But in the last 10, 15, 20 years you have to cross the border to have a future.

Sitting around the coffee table fanning themselves, these women discussed politics and injustice and how corrupt the president was. At the end of every conversation, though, were stories and statements about longing for a period in time when their "families" were together. In the back of Candela's house there were cans and bottles and packages of shakes, teas, and powder to flavor water from Herbalife. I asked Candela if she bought those things herself and she told me some of it, yes, but the more expensive products were sent by her daughter-in-law from Sunset

Park, Brooklyn. Almost every house I visited in Mexico had one or more products from Herbalife that were bought in Mexico or sent from the United States.

In almost parallel lives, mothers and daughters sit in completely different physical places. They are indeed divided by a physical, spatial border. However, they share many characteristics and talk about each other. In my quest for understanding the relationship between mothers and children left-behind, I was surprised by a "child-mother" bond that did not include the small children I was researching: the intergenerational relationship between mothers and their own mothers, who were often raising some of their grandchildren in the mother's absence. Out of the 20 care constellations I followed in my research, 17 had a maternal grandmother as primary caregiver of children left-behind. I found that maternal grandmothers' relationships with their own daughters shaped and influenced concepts related to motherhood and care.

1

Ideals and Practices of Transnational Motherhood and Care

Gemma's Story: "Yo la Dejé, Pero no la Abandoné."

I did not abandon Daniela, I left her. Abandoning means that you forgot about the person, that the person doesn't exist in your life, that you cut her out. To leave someone doesn't change how much you take care and love her and the fact that I am her mother.

Gemma had been living in New York for 13 years. Prior to coming to the United States, Gemma, who is from the small pueblo of Tlacuales in Puebla, "se juntó" (got together) with a man named Elías. They had a baby, Daniela, who was 14 years of age when I met her. Gemma was pursuing a career in nursing when she got pregnant with Daniela. She was the only person in her family who went to high school, completed high school, and went on to professional school. Her mother and father did not know how to read and write, but that did not stop Gemma from doing well in school. Her father Rubén has American citizenship because he was in the United States prior to the 1986 Act,[1] which granted amnesty and citizenship for millions of immigrants in the country. Rubén was able to extend his citizenship to his wife and three sons, but not his daughter Gemma. Regarding gaining and sharing citizenship, Rubén told me, "Women should stay and the men should go [to the U.S.]."

When Daniela was two months old, the relationship between Gemma and Daniela's father, Elias, became difficult. He would go home intoxicated and sometimes even bring female company. He was known to be a "ladies' man." Gemma described the situation, "He would never bring home diapers or baby food. The man did not take care of me or my daughter . . . he was always intoxicated and he had many girlfriends. I was in love with him, but I take my children over a man any day."

Gemma moved into her parents' house, "leaving" Elias. In phone conversations, her father, Rubén, would refer to her as a *dejada*, which in this context meant two things: first, even though she was the one who left, the husband is ultimately the only one who can *dejar* (leave) his wife, thus she is the left one or *dejada*; second, her father used dejada to insult her and insinuate that she could not give good advice or "be a good mother" to her own children because she was a dejada. For Rubén, Gemma was socially marked as a woman who could not maintain a family.

Shortly after moving back into her parents' house, another man, Alejandro, began courting Gemma. Alejandro was Gemma's boyfriend during high school; they dated briefly when they were teenagers and he left for the United States to work before finishing high school. A few years later he came back on a break and found out that Gemma was newly single. Alejandro's parents disapproved of the relationship, as he told me, "She was a separated woman with a baby that was not mine . . . where we come from that's not good for the woman. My mother did not want me to be with her and Gemma's parents also thought it was too soon." It was then that Alejandro told Gemma that he wanted her to go to the United States with him. Gemma's first answer was no because of Daniela. But Alejandro promised on "the Virgin of Guadalupe" that they would go back to Puebla to get Daniela when she was a little older. Gemma explained her rationale for making the decision to migrate:

> You come into this world as a woman, because *Diosito* (God) wants . . . you have to have a family, because you were created for that, and when you do, things go wrong and the family falls apart [referring to Elias]. . . . The only way, maybe I shouldn't say the only way, but the way that I thought to be the most effective to try to give Daniela a better future with a stable family was going with Alejandro to the United States. He was good to me, he promised me we were going to come back for her. And Alejandro said [as they planned their trip], "the baby is going to cry the entire way in the desert and the police will hear us and arrest us." I did not want to take a chance.

While Rubén was against his daughter's departure, her mother Emma told me, "a woman needs to be where her husband is. If she had stayed in

Puebla no one would have married her. My daughter needed to be happy and have a chance in life . . . I told her I would keep Daniela, it's the sacrifices you make for your children." Emma provided two explanations for the migration rationale: for one's husband, and for one's children. She explained to me that in order for children to have a stable life, both emotionally and financially, their parents must be together even if they are far away. Alejandro was not Daniela's father, but even so Emma saw her daughter having a husband and being together as critical to Gemma becoming a good role model for Daniela.

Gemma described leaving Daniela for the first time as heartbreaking. Gemma was still breast-feeding and she felt very connected to her baby. "How is it that we find ourselves in the situation of leaving our own children behind? And for what?" Gemma told me as she put her hands on her cheeks.

Gemma and Alejandro did go back to Puebla three years later, but to Gemma's despair it was too late: "Daniela was three when I returned and she did not recognize me. The pain I suffered there and then was so much bigger than when I left her three years before. She only wanted to be with her grandmother and she cried when I held her." Six months later Gemma and Alejandro again left for the United States and this time Gemma did not know if she would or should go back for Daniela. Emma, Gemma's mother, never tried to take over the role of mother; quite the contrary. Emma made sure to remind Daniela every day that her mother migrated so she could actually *take care* of Daniela and ensure that she could "be whatever she wanted to be." Daniela recounted the story of when her mother left her when she was three years old with a nervous laugh.

> I didn't want to go with her, it was really my fault; I just didn't know who she was anymore. The person that *takes care* [emphasis added] of me: feeds me, bathes me, changes me, washes my clothes, braids my hair, and takes me to the doctor is my *mamá* Emma and not Gemma. The way Gemma takes care of me is by sending me money, gifts, and giving me advice. But I know she is busy with my little brother and little sister.

Daniela had a challenging relationship with her grandfather, Rubén. Even though he spent six months of the year in Texas, whenever he was home it was a nightmare for Daniela. Rubén was reportedly an alcoholic and would often get physically abusive with his wife Emma. He got especially angry with Emma when she would, according to him, "treat Daniela like a baby and let her get away with everything." Whenever I was at their house in Puebla, Rubén was intoxicated. Daniela asked me to stay longer because, in her words, "you being here will make him well-behaved, he will be scared of hitting my mamá because he knows you are a *maestra* that lives in the U.S. so you would call the police." Daniela was extremely concerned for her grandmother's safety. At some point during my stay with them, Rubén yelled at Emma, who had just burnt a tortilla, and told her she was "worth nothing" and that he was better off being in the United States. Daniela immediately responded to him, "you are a drunk, and I am tired of you. I can't believe I have to live here with you. . . . The only reason I stay in this house is because of my mamá."

Emma, on the other hand, assured me that Rubén was not being abusive lately and explained to me,

> He is ill, he has been drinking since he was 11 years old. It's not his fault. Daniela is stubborn and she is a teenager. He gets angry because when Daniela was younger she was very depressed, I sent her to the psychologist and all . . . up until she was 11 years old she didn't shower by herself, she didn't make her own food, she didn't help me at all. But then I told her that she needed to be good, otherwise her mother Gemma would not be proud of her . . . she needed to be a good daughter if she wanted to have a good mother.

In the United States, Gemma settled in Brooklyn's Sunset Park and had two children with Alejandro, Yazmin (age 11) and Alejandro Jr. (age 10). In Gemma's words, "The Virgin was giving me a second chance to be a good mother, to take care of my children." Alejandro Jr. was born with a cleft palate, a severe skin disease, and asthma. He went through multiple surgeries and Gemma dedicated herself entirely to him for the first five years of his life. Her daughter Yazmin also helped her take care of Alejandro Jr. At a time when Yazmin and Alejandro Jr. were in school every day from eight in the morning until two in the afternoon. Yazmin was an excellent student and involved in extracurricular activities such as cheerleading. Alejandro Jr. was one year behind in school, due to his multiple surgeries. He almost failed third grade. He had difficulty reading and writing, but he was an outstanding soccer player. Gemma worked as a caregiver of elderly people. Alejandro worked six days a week at a mechanic shop, where he was the manager. He earned between $1,500 and $2,000 a month. Gemma worked three times a week and made between $200–$300 weekly. They lived on the ground floor of an old brownstone building in a two-bedroom apartment.

Gemma was very active in school-related activities and encouraged Yazmin and Alejandro Jr. to participate in groups, teams, and tournaments. Through government assistance, Gemma secured a tutor who went to her house three times a week to work with Yazmin and Alejandro Jr. The tutor, Paula, was Peruvian and therefore able to alternate between Spanish and English. Gemma spoke very little English and her children spoke very little Spanish in the house. "*No te entiendo!*" (I don't understand you) was Gemma's constant reply to her children. On many occasions Yazmin and Alejandro Jr. talked to each other in English; I often heard them saying, "I don't know how to say this in Spanish, it's not my fault." When she called Mexico, Gemma was able to speak more freely in Spanish with her daughter Daniela on the phone and for longer periods of time, whereas Alejandro Jr. and Yazmin would quickly disengage and not pay attention.

Gemma never told Yazmin and Alejandro Jr. that Daniela was their half-sister; they assumed Daniela was the daughter of both of their parents. When I showed Yazmin a picture of Daniela, she commented, "She doesn't look like she is my sister . . . there is something wrong."

Gemma's story elucidates the impact of gendered ideology of motherhood on Gemma, Emma, and Daniela, and foreshadows patterns that will also emerge in the stories of the other women participants in this research. Gender ideology influenced how women reflected and narrated leaving their children, leaving their mothers, and leaving or accompanying their husbands or partners. Once settled in New York, the gender ideology of motherhood was adapted and molded such that women could "mother" children here and there. However, the tension between mothers in New York and grandmothers in Mexico remained as both sides tried to sort through "perceived" identities of being a mother, woman, and wife as they shared and negotiated care.

Second, within the transnational, fluid context of migration, it is easy to think that the idea of family is radically transformed. Both Gemma and Emma made sure to tell the children about the value of kinship. Emma reminded Daniela of who, in her words, her "real mother" was and insisted that Daniela held on to that idea. Gemma hid the truth from her two children in the New York City in order to maintain the idea of "one" family where all children belonged to the same father, even if physical borders divided them. Gemma wanted her children to see Daniela as their sister, not their half-sister. Gemma worried that if her children knew the truth they could potentially reject Daniela and not see her as *family*. In addition, the history between Gemma and Daniela's father was somewhat shameful for Gemma and her family, and she preferred not to share it with her children.

Finally, Gemma's story shows how the different ideas of what a good mother is and does are in constant flux. Emma had always supported her daughter and never wanted to take over the role of the biological mother. This relationship between Emma and Gemma did not come without a price. Gemma felt indebted to her mother and in many ways felt powerless when making everyday decisions. At the same time, Daniela went back and forth with her own thoughts and feelings about her mother and her relationship with her siblings. This constant fluctuation was characteristic of other children in this research who stayed behind. Daniela was protective of her grandmother, who she described as her "caregiver," as she also felt a sense of debt to Emma.

Gemma's story reflects the observations of almost all other constellations and data collected from interviews with the other 40 mothers. Women explained that every day, month, or year that they remained separate from their children in Mexico made their relationship with their own mothers harder and more delicate. They did not feel empowered to overturn decisions made by their own mothers and believe they have a debt they will never be able to repay. Their mothers, on the other side, wanted these women (their daughters) to participate more actively in the lives of children left in Mexico. At the same time, women's expectations for children left in Mexico only grew stronger with time and represented their way of keeping the mother-child bond alive.

Mexican migrant mothers in New York City associated motherhood with the idea of "taking care" of their children (all of them). Gemma and the other migrant women I interviewed in New York expressed a struggle to "leave" children in order to provide for them. For their mothers, who then became caregivers of their grandchildren, there was yet another layer of perceived contradiction: allowing their own daughter to leave in order that she might be a "good" mother. There was sacrifice on both sides of this intergenerational relationship.

Back in Gemma's kitchen, while her two children, Yazmin and Alejandro Jr., watched a movie in the living room, Gemma stood up to get water from the refrigerator. Before doing so, she stopped to stare at a picture on the refrigerator door. She reached for the picture and brought it over to me. It was a picture of Daniela, her 15-year-old daughter who lived in Mexico. I asked Gemma if she had talked to Daniela that week or that day. Gemma looked at me and answered, "I didn't tell you her latest request? She wants a cell phone, *díos mio!*" She continued, "it's hard being here and Daniela being there; she tells me that I forgot about her, that I abandoned her!" She concluded, "*yo la dejé, pero no la abandoné*" (I left her, but I did not abandon her). I asked Gemma what was the difference between the two words "to leave" and "to abandon"?

> I did not abandon Daniela, I left her. Abandoning means that you forgot about the person, that the person doesn't exist in your life, you cut her out. When you leave someone it doesn't change how much you take care and love her and the fact that I am still her mother. I'm still the mother . . . it's just different, and I know she loves her grandmother more than she loves me . . . a different *mamá, es lo que yo soy* (that is what I am).

According to women in this research, "mothering" in and from a different country does not distort their roles as women. I argue instead that women borrow from emblems and symbols present in the ideologies of motherhood in both Mexico and the United States as a way of creating their own practices of care. They also use childhood memories and experiences with their own mothers to inform the ways in which they practice care for their own children. In this chapter, I address two questions: How do women transform their ideas of caring when living in New York City? How do their ideas contrast those held by their mothers?

I explore the tensions around the ideals migrant mothers have of caregiving and "mothering." I also demonstrate how ideals and practices of motherhood constantly inform how women characterize "good mothers" and "caring ones." The very act of leaving and migrating represents a "break" in the usual nexus of motherhood, which includes physical presence. However, women justify this act by explaining that they must leave *in order to be a "good mother" and care for their children.* I address the meanings the mothers in this research attach to the idea of being a "good mother," feelings of guilt and sacrifice, and the importance of supporting their families. To do that I look at Gemma's story in detail, contrasting her experiences with her children and her ideas of motherhood based on her experience. I highlight how she and other women negotiate the ideology of "the good mother" as they maintain transnational families. While most studies of transnational motherhood focus only on women in the host country, I use the transnational care constellation as a unit of analysis to widen the lens of how transnational motherhood has been studied. Instead of just looking at mothers in New York City, I examine at co-parenting and shared caregiving practices that take place across transnational terrain.

In the following sections I address care as defined and practiced by mothers in New York City and caregivers in Mexico, describe the relationship between motherhood and caring, and highlight what women say about their ideas of motherhood and how they adapt and create new forms of parenting. I pay special attention to the tensions that arise between mothers in New York City and caregivers in Mexico. To achieve these goals, I will first review notions of motherhood and caring in Mexico as represented in the anthropological literature. I will also look at the literature on transnational families and more specifically on how motherhood transforms when women migrate and set up transnational families. Finally, I will show that intergenerational tensions between mothers in New York and their own mothers in Mexico are present precisely because both sides have expectations of care that are not always aligned with expectations of motherhood.

Feminization of Migration

The feminization of migration brings to the forefront of migration studies an important discussion regarding everyday care practices. How is it done? Who is involved? And, finally, what do these practices mean to mothers, caregivers, and children? On one hand, mothers have the ideals and the meanings that they attach to motherhood and care; on the other hand, these gendered ideals are transformed and complemented by mothers' interpretations and actions of care. The ideals of motherhood, some have suggested, are challenged when mothers migrate as family breadwinners (Hondagneu-Sotelo & Avila, 1997). In her study of children in the Philippines whose migrant mothers were away, Parreñas (2005a) describes how a "gender ideology" affects the impact of maternal immigration on the children that stay behind. She explains that the ideology of women's domesticity in the Philippines has been recast to be performed in a transnational terrain by migrant mothers, meaning that tasks mothers have at home in the Philippines are performed also in the host country (p. 168). Parreñas's work belongs to an important body of literature that regards women as central actors in immigration. In the contemporary period, "Thanks to the process we loosely call globalization, women are on the move as never before in history" (Ehrenreich & Hochschild, 2002: 2).

Yet, too often, studies have focused only on immigrant mothers, without adequately considering how social networks have influenced their life experiences. In her 2005 book, *Team of Rivals: The Political Genius of Abraham Lincoln*, biographer Doris Kearns Goodwin explains that she had read the dozens of books written about Abraham Lincoln throughout the years. However, she states, "by widening the lens to include Lincoln's colleagues and their families, my story benefited from a treasure trove of primary sources that have not been generally used in Lincoln biographies" (p. xviii). This anecdote shows that previous research in US-bound Mexican migration presented bias as they prioritized male experiences and male breadwinner patriarchal family structures. And today, even as there is growing literature on the feminization of migration and the central role of immigrant women's labor in contemporary capitalist formations in industrialized countries (Chang, 2009), the role of women in migration is still overlooked. Where are they coming from, or being pulled from? How many have children or care for children as their job?

If we are to understand transnational motherhood, we must look not only at the children in the country of origin, but also the children brought to the United States by the same mothers or born in America. Principally, we must look at the pre-migration care arrangements and the arrangements created between mothers in the host society and their own mothers in the sending country. Mothers in the host country are also somebody's children, and they have also experienced separation. This aspect of transnational mothering has not received attention to date.

Previous studies have theorized on the concept of "care chains" (Ehreinrich & Hochschild, 2002; Sassen, 2002, 2010; Yeates, 2005) and focused on the migrant women on one side of the border; some scholars have moved further to also consider the families they left behind (Parreñas, 2010; Dreby, 2010, 2009a, 2009b; Madianou & Miller, 2012; Yarris, 2011). The political economy of care and the feminist critique on which the care chains approach is based have made significant contributions to the literature on migration, with their emphasis on the economic motivations for migration. Yet, the focus on structural factors does not acknowledge the empowering potential of migration for women as it assumes a normative and universal perspective of motherhood that should be performed in a situation of co-presence (physically living in the same household). Ethnographically based studies such as those by Aguilar et al. (2009) and Dreby (2010) demonstrate that both global feminist discourse employed by Parreñas (2001) and globalized ideas about women's responsibilities have to be complemented by grounded studies within countries, which may reveal very different and more nuanced expectations about mother-child relationships.

Ideologies of Motherhood

Anthropologist Claude Lévi-Strauss (1995) argued that "Myth is language, functioning on an especially high level where meaning succeeds practically at 'taking off' from the linguistic ground on which it keeps rolling" (p. 96). Lévi-Strauss breaks down his argument into three main parts. First, meaning is not isolated within the specific fundamental parts of the myth, but rather within the composition and the interaction of these parts. Second, although myth and language are of similar categories, language functions differently in myth. Finally, unlike the constituents of language, the constituents of a myth, which he labels "mythemes," function as "bundles of relations." The idea of bundles of relations becomes important when assessing how mothers in New York City relate to their children "here and there" and thus construct meanings for "caregiving." In any society, Lévi-Strauss maintained, "the purpose of a myth is to provide a logical model capable of overcoming a contradiction" (1995: 99). As he saw it, the human mind tends to organize thought and culture around binary opposites, and tries to resolve the resulting tension through the creative act of mythmaking. Barthes (1972) defined a myth as an uncontested and unconscious assumption so widely accepted that its historical and cultural origins are often forgotten. Ideologies, thus, are born when myths are combined into coherent philosophies and politically sanctioned by the culture.

Feminist scholarship has long challenged myths of family and motherhood that relegate women to the domestic arena of private/public dichotomies and rely on the ideological conflation of family, woman, reproduction, and nurturance (Collier & Yanagisako, 1987: 36). Different scholars, including Chodorow (1978), Ruddick (1983), and Hays (1996), agree that maternal myths perpetuate patriarchy. Scheper-Hughes (1992) explains, "Mother love is anything *other* than natural and instead represents a matrix of images, meanings, sentiments, and practices that are everywhere socially and culturally produced . . . Consequently, mother love is best bracketed and understood as (m)other loves" (pp. 341–342).

Widespread ideologies of motherhood hold that mothering involves the preservation, nurturance, and training of children so they will have a full adult life (Ruddick, 1989). As feminists have argued, mothers are held more responsible for this outcome than fathers. The ideology depends upon biologically and culturally essentialist notions of motherhood that have been critiqued by anthropologists. For example, in her ethnography of motherhood in a deeply impoverished community in northeastern Brazil, Scheper-Hughes (1992) shows that mothers delayed attachment until they saw that their child would survive. Scheper-Hughes insists, "As fatherhood is social, so is motherhood. Motherhood entails a choice. One as a woman is, you might say, existentially thrown into the world as a potential mother. But motherhood begins with an acceptance, an enfolding, a willingness to nurture a child" (1992: 4).

Thus, even the biological is social; that is, humans interpret the biological in sociocultural ways. Hays (1996) termed this the "cultural contradictions of motherhood," the concept of ideologies of motherhood that are often internally conflicting. As Drummond (1978) argues, "the cultural unit of mother is internally contradictory, and it should be emphasized that this means more than simple normative variation in the way particular women in particular societies mother" (p. 12). Hays (1996), in her work with American mothers, explains that women who are working mothers struggle with the demands on their time and also with how they are supposed to behave. Hays argues that the societies in which women live generate ambivalence if women are expected to work outside the home but are also expected to take on child-rearing as a full-time job. She calls this ideology *intensive mothering* and discusses how children become sacred and mothers become the primary responsible parties. In a similar vein, much of the discussion of sacrifice within female migration places tremendous pressure on migrant mothers to succeed and provide for their children. Thus, the very act of leaving their children in search of a better future, for them, goes against much of the discourse regarding what a "good" mother is.

A mother is both a normative concept—the ideal as to what a mother should be—and the experiences of actually being, or having, a mother. What do we mean when we use the word mother? Madianou and Miller (2012) explain, "Moral panics regularly erupt about what constitutes good, or 'good-enough' mothering" (p. 10). In addition, motherhood is a constant trope in ideological debate. As Hondagneu-Sotelo states, "'Rethinking the family' prompts the rethinking of motherhood, allowing us to see that the glorification and exaltation of isolationist, privatized mothering is historically and culturally specific" (2003: 319).

Transnational Motherhood

Rhacel Salazar Parreñas states,

> Transnational mothering refers to the organizational reconstitution of motherhood that accommodates the temporal and spatial separations forced by migration. This arrangement forms new meanings of motherhood and expands the concept of "mothering" to encompass breadwinning. (2010: 1827)

As Hondagneu-Sotelo and Avila (1997) explain, "immigrant women who work and reside in the United States while their children remain in their countries of origin constitute one variation in the organizational arrangements, meanings and priorities of motherhood" (p. 139). While these definitions and descriptions inspired the very origin of my own work, in this research I expand this concept by examining how these women engage with the perceived duties of motherhood. I use the concept of *transnational care constellations* to address the recognizable pattern of who is involved in the caregiving, everyday teaching, and educating of children.

In contrast to men, when women migrate they undertake a journey that may clash with the gender ideology present in their country of origin. This journey may be transformative for women, but it can also reproduce patriarchal structures of their home country. During the Bracero Program, for example, Mexican men migrated to the United States as breadwinners to fulfill that role for the family. Immigrant women, on the other hand, have had to cope with prejudice, gossip, stigma, and guilt (Hirsh, 2003). In part because of gendered stereotypes, women are more likely to find work in the domestic world, taking care of other children. Studies of migrant women who leave the Philippines or Sri Lanka show precisely the difficulties they face when trying to "keep up" with the expectations of the role mothers fulfill in their countries. Pratt (2012) argues that transnational mothering simply cannot overcome distance. She calls the experience of being separated from children "genuinely traumatic" and asserts that "cyborg mothering," or the use of technology to fulfill maternal roles, is an illusion for most poor migrant mothers (Pratt, 2012: 70). In her book *So, How's the Family?*, Hochschild (2013) describes how the concept of an "ideal mother" varied from one ethnic or religious group to another within Kerala (154). However, she states that "migrants from all these groups shared roughly the same vision of the ideal mother as a woman who lives with her children" (154).

Like Scheper-Hughes (1992) and Hondagneu-Sotelo and Avila (1997), I understand motherhood as not biologically predetermined but instead as socially constructed. Even when mothers describe the physical aspects of being pregnant and giving birth, their narratives are socioculturally patterned and expressed. Transnational mothers are embedded in transnational families. The definition of family, according to the *Oxford*

Dictionary of Sociology (Scott & Marshall 2009), is "a group made up of individuals who are related by bonds of blood, sexual mating or legal ties." Family, as conceptualized by feminists, has been described as a gendered system of reproduction and cultural transmission or a space for gendered social relations (Sørensen, 2005: 3). In migration studies, the identification of family with a domestic, bounded group is problematic.

Portrayals that equate migration with family disintegration are sometimes founded on ethnocentric bias (Zentgraff & Chinchilla, 2012). Parreñas (2010) describes the backlash against mothers who have chosen to migrate and are "vilified in the news media and local communities" (p. 1830). Transnational families, "being here and there" (Hondagneu-Sotelo & Avila, 1997; Dreby, 2010), are more fluid; they do not belong to only one nation or place. This fluidity influences the ideals behind caregiving. Women find themselves struggling between what is expected from them as mothers versus what they want and can do for their children. Thus, to analyze how members of families negotiate obligations and care for each other—especially the children involved—across borders, I take as a starting point the separation of kin, where biological mothers are physically separated from some of their children (see Baldassar, 2008). Duties such as taking care of children and parenting do not end when people move from one nation to another; instead, these concepts shift and adapt. I look at the practices and processes of transnational caregiving that are mediated by both mothers and caregivers, as well as cultural notions of obligation that appear through negotiated commitments within but not restricted to migrant female mothers in New York City, their children, and their children's caregivers in Mexico (Baldassar, Baldock, & Wilding, 2007).

The constellation in this chapter represents patterns in intergenerational relationships as well as in caregiving practices. The first pattern is that women struggle with a range of ideologies of motherhood as they make sense of their choices. They discuss the concepts of abandoning and leaving family members behind. Mothers and caregivers shared an understanding of the decision behind the biological mother's departure. The decision to leave was described by mothers as fundamentally linked to the idea of being a good mother. The second pattern is that the decision to migrate was fed by other equally complex ideas such as "being a good wife," leaving a violent and "shameful" social situation, and seeking a "better life" for themselves. Third, these women carry an emotional burden: mothers carried the guilt of abandonment and were more financially than emotionally present in the lives of their children left in Mexico. Fourth, at the same time, mothers established very high expectations for children left in Mexico. These expectations were expressed through weekly money transfers, phone calls to schools, and constant insistence that the migration "has to be worth it," meaning that their migration to the United States has to have a visible payoff. Thus, the idea of motherhood is a blend of moralities; a set of habits that are constantly sanctioned. Finally, changing or adapting these customs was an everyday process, expressed, for example, by the act of leaving. The act of migrating is done in order to uphold and maintain norms of care and motherhood, yet the migration requires constant negotiation of ideologies of motherhood.

Mexican Migrant Mothers

Women in Mexico deal with a range of ideologies of motherhood, which influence their own practices. First, there is a strong tradition, rooted in a Catholic matrix, of *marianismo*. As Maria Fernanda (age 44) answered when I asked her what motherhood meant to her, "It is what God and what the Virgin of Guadalupe want from us . . . to be good mothers and good women." Many of the women I interviewed frequently referred to God and the Virgin of Guadalupe when discussing their responsibilities and duties toward their children and families. References to God and the Virgin of Guadalupe as a "good" role model versus "bad" and/or "disgraced" can be traced to symbols, myths, and models of femininity in Mexico (Paz, 1985; Anzaldúa, 1987).

In Mexico, Mexican mothers' caregiving role is often celebrated and linked to the self-sacrificing characteristics of the Virgin of Guadalupe (Dreby, 2007). According to Gutmann (2007), "certain prevailing notions of maternal instincts are some of the products and reflections of standard Catholic doctrine promoting female domesticity" (p. 64). Anthropologist Antonella Fagetti explains that motherhood is a rare source of prestige for some women:

> Motherhood is highly valued by men and women, because to be a mother the woman fulfills the destiny God assigned for her and they should

implement God's will. The duty of a couple is to care for their children in a relationship where they complement each other: the man should find through his work a way of supporting his family, and the woman should suffer the pains of giving birth, should nurture and raise her children. (1995: 303–304)

Marianismo is a strong, traditional gender ideology that influenced many of the women I interviewed. However, this research was conducted in a context of significant social transformation. Other gender ideologies emerging from Protestant traditions, secular discussions, popular culture, and feminism were also ambient.

Certainly, these women encountered new ideologies as they migrated. Thus, they drew upon a broad repertoire of gender ideologies in their efforts to recast transnational motherhood. Napolitano (2016) in her book *Migrant Hearts and the Atlantic Return* also explores the complex feelings Latin American women have while living in Rome. Even though they are closer to the Catholic religion, they struggle with the lived experience of religion which differs from what is being preached.

Women in New York described their experience as being mothers "here" and "from here," comparing their relationships with their children who were in the United States and in Mexico. These comparisons involved discussions of school, money, curfew, respect, and how to discipline children. Even though most caregivers in Mexico were not actively trying to take over the role of the biological mothers, intergenerational tensions between mothers in New York and grandmothers in Mexico became apparent. I observed mothers disciplining their children in their homes in the Bronx, Brooklyn, and Queens.

Most of them were impatient with the children, constantly putting them in "time out," yelling, smacking them on the top of the head, or threatening them with "no playing today" or "no soda." Caregivers in Mexico were more permissive and affectionate with the grandchildren they were raising. I observed multiple phone calls between mothers in New York City and caregivers in Mexico during which the mother would warn the grandmother to be stricter and the grandmother would imply that strict discipline is for the mother to mete out. For example, in one weekly phone call about everyday decisions regarding her daughters in Mexico, Emilia in the Bronx insisted, "you know you can't let her do that," and Ester in Mexico responded, "well I can only do so much, you are the mother." Emilia then questioned why Ester had been such a strict mother and pointed out how differently she is now raising her grand-daughters. The fact that mothers in New York provided for all their children—through different strategies and choices that included money, gifts, co-caregiving, and single caregiving—created spaces and ways of "taking care" that they had not known could exist.

As much as archetypes in Mexican literature shed light on the phenomenon of transnational motherhood, they are also easy traps to fall into when analyzing women's words. Throughout multiple interviews over a period of two years, I found that the use of the Virgin of Guadalupe and the language of sacrifice also worked as ways to comfort these mothers and help them deal with the guilt they have suffered. For instance, most of the sacrifice language appeared in the first and second interviews as a way to "open up" about their experiences, and perhaps test in the reaction of the researcher as to how they would be judged. To lock the analysis within the symbols of marianismo and the cultural analysis of the role of women and religion in Mexico is to ignore the narratives these women had *after* talking about sacrifice, the duty of motherhood, and God's expectations. They were also women with desires for a better life for themselves. As Sara struggled to verbally express the fact that she also wanted a "chance" to live a better life, she told me, "it's hard to say [it] because it sounds so selfish "I feel bad, but I didn't want to stay in that little town, there was nothing there for me [to do]." She paused and then continued, "you know the things women are supposed to do . . . I didn't want that."

The lines were blurred between the private and public roles of women, the desires of discovering a better life and finding love, and work and caring for children. Symbols and traditional roles presented in the literature help explain women's use of the language of sacrifice, God, and the Virgin; however, they do not determine or fully explain women's practices of care. Horton (2009) points out that current scholarship on transnational mothers has focused on gender constructs and ideologies. I do not disagree. My contribution through this research is to show that, beyond analyzing migrant women's roles from the point of view of gender ideologies, research must focus on what parts of this "ideology" are used, when, and with what purpose. As Brianna, a mother in Queens, told me:

Of course my instinct is to think about my children first . . . they are my heart. But I also think the husband-wife relationship is very important and I wanted to be with Ronald, that's why I came with him and left my three girls. Is that a crime? I don't think so. But people talk.

In another interview in the Bronx, Aruna (A) told me (G):

A: Can I be honest with you? Are you not going to get offended?
G: No, go ahead.
A: You . . . your type . . .
G: My type?
A: Yes . . . *blanquita* (white lady) like you . . . don't be hurt by my comments, ok?
G: Ok, I won't.
A: You come to this world and you get to choose . . . *felicidad* (happiness) for you is not having a million children, you want to explore, travel, meet people, go to school, learn . . . you know? We are here to have children.
G: Who is "we"?
A: My type of people . . . you know . . . darker, poorer . . . we come to this world to have children. It is a good sign when we get pregnant; it's good to give children to one's husband . . . but [your husband] he doesn't care if you have children now or if it's only one.
G: You are right, he doesn't care right now, or at least he is not telling me!
A: [laughter] What I want to say is that you have time . . . time to choose different things, you have opportunities, you travel, you explore . . . and we have to cook and care for our children . . . but it's ok, because it's what we do . . . I don't want you to pity me, because it's what we do . . . and it's ok.
G: But when you left Mexico did you think about that?
A: I thought I needed to get out . . . to immigrate also meant trying a different life for me. I convinced myself it would be good for my girls, but I knew I was trying to find my opportunities. Sometimes I think I'm being punished because of my choices . . . but then, look at me now. *I feel like I was pulled back into where I belong* [emphasis added] . . . not exactly like it was in Mexico, because

> I have grown and I have more responsibilities now . . . here and
> there. But I am again a wife with three *muchachos*. I'm telling you,
> God has a plan.

This excerpt from a much longer conversation illustrates the point
that I am attempting to make. Most immigration/migration research
has focused on gender ideology and the roles women have "here and
there" and how, through migration, these roles can transform and em-
power women (Hondagneu-Sotelo, 2001) or simply reproduce the roles
from the society of origin (Parrenãs, 2005a). I argue that the issue is
more complex and less localized than this debate suggests. One of the
interesting things about the interview above is that the mother allowed
herself to speak about her own ambitions: she recognized the potential
selfishness of acting on her own ambitions but also acknowledged that
class and race ultimately collapse into distinct forms of personhood for
different groups of women (*blanquitas* and "my type of people").

As women establish transnational arrangements of familial ties,
their roles become more fluid as they are constantly negotiating everyday decisions regarding children in Mexico and children in the United
States. To say that their roles are completely transformed and that these
women become "empowered" through the process of migration because
of their breadwinner status is to disregard the constant connections they
make with what they have learned while growing up about what a good
mother and a good woman "should" be. At the same time, to state that
women only reproduce the gender roles present in the host society is to
ignore the active and creative ways in which mothers care "for them all"
here and there. In addition, theoretically, if the very decision to leave
was purely informed by *marianismo* and other symbols, leaving would
be synonymous with being a "bad" mother. Instead, women used the
social space of our interviews to discuss stereotypes and symbols of what
it means to be an "absent" mother. Several had also begun to explore the
possibility of freedom from at least a few of the expectations they face
in their hometowns, sometimes by giving precedence to one traditional
value over another.

Among the constellations in my research, when the mothers had originally departed from Mexico the average age of their children was seven
years (though this ranged from eight months to thirteen years), and the

mothers and caregivers' average ages were 23 and 42, respectively. Before migrating, women were living in one of two conditions: with their partners but close to their mothers; or with their mothers. In all cases children were left with kin who had directly participated in their care prior to migration. Women already relied on the help of kin in order to work and support their families. However, the role of the biological mother, the one who gave birth, was recognized as the most important and sacred role. This does not mean that children "love" or "respect" their biological mothers more than their caregivers; in fact the contrary is closer to the truth. What it means is that caregivers keep biological mothers as co-parents at a distance and mothers feel it is their duty to maintain and in many cases to attempt to strengthen bonds with the children they leave behind.

When women gave birth to children in the United States or brought them to this country, they saw the opportunity as a "second chance" to be a good mother, and described it as a moment where they could fulfill their mission in the world. In order to understand gender ideology and ideologies of motherhood, which are associated with sacrifice and child-care, it is important to look at pre-migration structures, shared caregiving or co-caregiving, and the caregiving practices adopted by women so they could care for their children left behind as well as their children brought to or born in the United States.

Sharing and Negotiating Caregiving Obligations

Mothers and caregivers in this research rarely discussed migration plans prior to mothers' departures. They may have been living in the same house and already sharing child-rearing tasks, but when it came to the decision to migrate, mothers who participated in this research did not communicate or "prepare" their children prior to departing. This pattern is contrary to other studies, such as that of Zentgraf and Chinchilla (2006), who report that mothers did do their best to prepare children for their departure. In the case of the 20 focal families in this study, all mothers described the time preceding their departure as a struggle. They described their decisions as "quick" and "sudden." One mother said it was "like ripping off a band-aid." There was no preparation or talks prior to parting. The first reason was that children were young, so mothers did not see the need to explain. The second reason was similar to what Dreby (2006) found to be true among migrating fathers: fear of upsetting the children. Finally, the mothers described the process to be too painful, and felt that constant discussion of leaving may have cast doubt on their decision.

Even though caregivers were raising the children who remained in Mexico as if they were their own, the children do not seem to lose sight of their migrant mothers. The different simultaneous dynamics (intergenerational) present within these constellations show that care is a complex and ambiguous concept. Care as a semantic field covers different meanings: to care for, to care about, to take care of (caretaker), to give care (caregiver), or even to be caring. This corresponds with different ethic and normative notions of care. As mentioned previously, most immigrant mothers left their children with maternal grandmothers as primary caregivers. According to Dreby (2010), "Migrants believe maternal grandmothers to be the most logical caregivers for their children during their absences" (p. 149). However, in my research it was not uncommon to see paternal grandmothers who have lived with the children before migration taking care of them. Many women reported leaving their children with their own mothers because they were already living together and shared a house. Thus, in a sense, their perception was that there was no "complete rupture," as the physical home of the child remained the same. Despite strong emotional ties that grandmothers have with their grandchildren, grandparents rarely question biological parents' attachments to their children. Caregivers, however, sometimes faced a paradox. They did not question the claim that biological parents held over the children, despite their own deep attachment to them. Further, they did not question the decisions their sons and daughters made to move north and reunite with their husbands or wives, which they considered proper, but they sometimes resented being left behind, especially when resources were insufficient to take on the responsibility of raising a child.

Care is the single most important aspect that keeps a constellation together. As women crossed the border, contrary to common perception, their sense of responsibility and duty toward not only their child or children but also toward the mother they left behind is intensified. Neither Gemma nor her mother, Emma, envisioned a life where they would share caregiving obligations transnationally, as they did not create this plan together.

Thus, for both of these women the constant worry about not overstepping boundaries as mother and daughter contributed to the tensions that arose from the everyday practice of parenting. As grateful as she was for her mother taking care of Daniela, Gemma struggled with the fact that her daughter "loved" Emma as her own mamá. Emma, on the other hand, did not want to "take over" the role she understood to pertain to the biological mother. Gemma, like many of the mothers interviewed, was conscious about the limits of her role in caregiving. If children in Mexico were young, the relationship between mothers in New York and caregivers in Mexico tended to align without much disagreement. It was when children were in their teenage years that the duties of caregiving and the obligations became more salient. I observed multiple occasions when mothers in New York and caregivers in Mexico discussed on the phone everyday decisions related to curfew, freedom to come and go, health needs, and above all schooling. The ideals of motherhood described in the beginning of this chapter were re-conceptualized by both mothers and caregivers; in almost every case in my study the latter were maternal grandmothers. Kin-related obligations and obligations expected to be performed by mothers happened across transnational space, and mothers in New York and caregivers in Mexico actively created ways to "take care" of each other and the children involved.

Gemma's particular story sheds light on a pattern I found in relationships between caregivers and mothers. The first component had to do with Gemma's past; she was once with a man whom she left. That fact created a source of anxiety for both of her parents, who wanted to see her married with children. Her mother, Emma, supported her decision of leaving Daniela because she understood Gemma to have a need to be formally married, given that she was known as a dejada. Thus, her commitment to her daughter's need to be seen as a "good" woman and wife trumped one of the basic concepts of "good" mother for Emma—physical presence. Second, after taking care of Daniela for a few years, Emma was emotionally attached to her but ready to hand her over when Gemma returned to Mexico. The decision to leave Daniela a second time was made with support from Emma. Gemma felt she had "lost" the *mother love* she once had with Daniela. Both women also worried about safety during border crossing and made a decision that was different from what they had agreed on a few years back. In that moment, together they created an alternative way of caring for Daniela. All caregivers and grandmothers interviewed conveyed one particular feeling over and over: preoccupation. Caregivers worried about their own daughters, they questioned how good they themselves had been as mothers, and in many ways they described their shared responsibilities with their daughters as second chances to be "a good mother." On the other side, mothers worry about their children and their own mothers. Thus, the "hierarchy of responsibility" was not only challenged, but constantly reversed. In a mirrored way, mothers in New York City also saw their US-born children as giving them a second chance to be good mothers. Therefore, caregivers and mothers in New York City had very similar preoccupations regarding to whom they were good mothers and, above all, if they could indeed "care for them all." The idea of good mothers as discussed by women reflects care, and emotional and financial support are part of the puzzle as well. Children and youth also had their expectations of the contact with their mothers to be one that reflected support above all.

Working one or more jobs was a reality to these migrant Mexican women. They often compared the amount of work they now had with how much they worked in Mexico before leaving. As soon as they became mothers in Mexico, the majority of their time was spent at home. Even if they worked outside of the house it normally involved making tortillas, selling chicken, or working at the small family stores that were usually attached to their homes. Some women, however, had held jobs as housekeepers in towns that were farther away from their pueblos. Even women with those jobs felt like they had more time to dedicate to their children, and that was synonymous with "good mothering." In New York, women found themselves facing three different mothering realities. For the children they left behind, they became the breadwinners who cared for and supported them financially; transnational mothers are not replacing "caregiving" with "breadwinning" in their definitions of motherhood, but they are expanding their definitions of motherhood to encompass breadwinning and they recognize that this may require long-term physical separations as the ultimate sacrifice (Hondagneu-Sotelo & Avila, 1997). For the children they brought over to the United States, women discussed guilt as well as a sense of sameness. Maria Fernanda, a migrant mother, told me, "Florencia [daughter she brought with her from Mexico] is illegal and so am I. She helps me take care of my younger children and now she has a baby herself, so in a way we are both illegal mothers." Finally, for the children born in the United States, migrant mothers were the primary caregivers *and* main economic supporters, as working mothers; however, they often felt an emotional distance from one another because of language and cultural barriers (detailed in chapter 3).

When I asked mothers if they planned to ever go back to Mexico, their responses were mixed. Sara explained:

> Felipe, my son, has asthma. The center where we go is right in front of my apartment. The government pays for it and I have help . . . in Mexico I would have to take a truck and go three hours to find a hospital for my son. Is that fair to him? No. But is it fair to Agustín that he is left there in Mexico?

It is interesting to note the notion of illness that exists in Mexico and in the United States. In many instances mothers discussed how allergies and mental illnesses were not as prevalent in Mexico when compared with the United States. Thus, even though New York City was considered a better source of treatment, they were not always sure that their children would actually need that treatment if they were in Mexico.

When Sara first migrated, her mother, Clarisa, supported her decision because Sara was a teenage mother whose boyfriend just disappeared. Clarisa wanted her daughter to find love and happiness. But then Clarisa began to feel that Sara was missing out by being away from her son, Agustín. Sara had recently separated from Felipe's father, so Clarisa said, "she is not caring for a man anymore, so she should now come back and enjoy her son." Sara found out that her husband had impregnated another woman. She told me that when she confronted him, he hit her and forced her to have sex with him. She confronted him again, threatening to kill him with a knife. Her sister, Rosa, told me she came downstairs from her apartment and tried to calm Sara down. The two of them got into a fight as well, and Sara stopped talking to her sister. Sara's husband told her that he had recorded her threatening to kill him and that he would have her arrested. Sara's boss could not understand what was going on, so I helped by translating and then going to the lawyer with Sara and her boss to translate the conversations. In the end, Sara's husband was bluffing—he had not recorded. Clarisa could not understand how Sara could still stay in New York and provide for Felipe and Agustín if she was a single mother now. Even though this story made me reflect on the way men abuse women in these situations, it was also clear that there were moments when clashes between grandmothers and mothers' understandings of care and motherhood were at the forefront of the relationships.

Conclusion

While child-rearing patterns vary widely from one society to another, in most it is primarily mothers who are expected to perform this vital function. Yet in many families in developing societies, many mothers are physically absent. In the majority of the countries in the world, women engage in domestic internal migration prior to international migration. In the United States there is a strong tradition of quantitative studies that link child development with mothers' physical presence. For the past several decades, hundreds of thousands of women, many of them mothers, have been migrating from poorer countries to wealthier countries in search of employment. Contrary to ideas that they are abandoning their children (Parreñas, 2005a) or turning them into "Euro-orphans" (Lutz, 2012), these "transnational mothers" believe they can fulfill their maternal responsibilities by earning much-needed cash for better food, clothing, shelter, and—above all—improved chances for an education (Segura, 1994).

In addition, a less discussed subject pertaining to why women migrate has to do with their own desires to follow a husband or to attempt to start a new life in a country with more perceived opportunities. Even though migrant women do rationalize their departure as a sacrifice, there is more to their stories than much of the literature cares to analyze, as illustrated in this chapter. Narratives about desires, personal "realization," and fate are lost in the notion that justifications beyond "providing for children" are deemed inappropriate and unfitting to the moralities and ethics of motherhood. These narratives emerged later in my interviews with women and are not discussed as being part of the "myths" and "symbols" of motherhood used and created by mothers and grandmothers. They are instead part of an idea of womanhood that may not be connected to the idea of motherhood.

This chapter demonstrated how ideals and practices of motherhood that may seem at odds are actually adaptations of what mothers consider to be "good" and "caring" mothers. The dualism of "good and bad" mothers is part of the narrative of women, however the reality appears to be more nuanced. The very act of leaving and migrating represents a "break" in the nexus of motherhood that includes physical presence. However, for many this act is justified by the very reason of trying to be a good mother and care for one's children. I addressed the meanings mothers attach to the idea of a good mother, feelings of guilt and sacrifice, and the importance of supporting their families. The issues at play are more complex than discussions of empowered migrant women versus migrant women reproducing the reality of the host society. An analysis that focuses solely on dichotomies loses sight of the shifting gendered ideologies of motherhood within the migration context. Gemma's story complements the results of more than 40 interviews and observations with the other constellations: intergenerational relationships between women contribute to constructions of the ideals behind caregiving and transnational motherhood; personal desires feed motivations to migrate, but are quickly suppressed beneath the perceived duty of how a mother should care for a child; and women are not contradicting ideas of motherhood learned from their mothers in Mexico, they are using those concepts to create new forms of mothering from afar. They struggle to deal with the guilt that stems from the sacrifices associated with their decisions just as much as they crave the idea of family.

When Caregivers and Mothers Don't Get Along

After spending time in the South Bronx for a few weeks I befriended Dora, the owner of a small restaurant and grocery store called Mercado San Marcos. Dora was from a town in Puebla I had visited before. I told her about my research and that I was hoping to speak with mothers who had children in both Mexico and the United States. Dora told me about Aruna. I left my business card with Dora and told her to give it to Aruna when she had a chance. The next day I received a phone call from Aruna. She was the first mother to voluntarily get in touch with me. We arranged for me to go to her house and meet her. She said her sons would be in school, so she had a few hours to talk to me. The next day I went to see Aruna's house, where I pressed the buzzer and she let me in. I walked up three flights of stairs and could not help but notice that there were 20 apartments per floor. I could hear loud music coming from the different apartments and a strong smell of marijuana. I heard loud men's voices. I heard young children's loud voices. I heard arguments about how loud the music was. I heard dogs barking. I finally arrived at Aruna's door and knocked. She opened the door slightly to see who it was. I smiled and greeted her. She closed the door quickly and unlocked a few locks in to let me in. I walked into a one-bedroom apartment with a small living room, a kitchen, and a bathroom. The apartment was 550 square feet. Marco, Aruna's husband, slept on the couch in the living room. Aruna slept in the bedroom with her three sons: six-year-old Carlito, four-year-old Kiki, and four-month-old Pablo. There was also another person living with them named Tami. Tami rented a bed and paid $200 a month. She was only there for the weekend since she was a live-in housekeeper for a family in the Upper East Side of Manhattan. Tami also had left her children behind in Mexico, but they were now aged 30 and 33. She was a transnational grandmother.

As we started talking in the kitchen, I asked Aruna to walk me through her life from the time she was born to whatever she knew about her own mother and father's life history and her decision to migrate. Aruna got nervous and her eyes filled up with tears. Aruna was 26 and looked even younger. She was rocking Pablo's bouncer with her left foot as she began to tell me her story:

> You know . . . my life was hard, but now I have been blessed. I can't com-
> plain. I don't know from where to start because some things make me feel
> really sad. I have been depressed and anxious and I didn't want to get out
> of the house. I cried for no reason and I didn't want to work. Some days
> are still bad, but I look at my precious miracle, my baby and try to get
> on . . . move on, you know?

Aruna told me that her life before moving to the United States had been difficult. Aruna's mother, Clara, lives in Catlas, south of Mexico City, and Aruna lived with her mother until 2005 when she moved to the United States. Her mother was an immigrant herself and spent eight months in California when Aruna was seven years old. Aruna described those eight months as "sad in the beginning, then I got used to it." She explained to me that while her mother was gone she forgot her mother's face and that felt sad. She remembered making an effort to visualize her mother's face and all she could see was a blurred image. During that time Aruna stayed with her aunt, who lived across the street. She didn't remember speaking to her mother much during that time, but she did remember receiving gifts. When Clara returned, they went back to living together and Clara quickly found a boyfriend. "El Señor," as Aruna described, "was nice to me in the beginning." After a few years Clara and her boyfriend broke up. She began going out frequently and bringing home different men. Aruna described their relationship as turbulent because Clara always criticized Aruna, calling her names and being aggressive.

During her teenage years Aruna began seeing a man called Vicente. At sixteen Aruna got pregnant and had her first daughter, Elvira. While she was pregnant she married Vicente because, according to her, "if you get pregnant and the father is there, you have to get married, you can't be a single mother . . . it doesn't look good." One year later Aruna gave birth to Kaia. She was seventeen years old and had two babies. Aruna worked at her mother's grocery store where they sold chicken and tortillas.

Aruna told me that Vicente began to drink heavily; she would ask him to go buy diapers or milk and he would come back empty-handed and smelling like alcohol. Aruna described herself as someone who speaks her mind. I agreed. She told Vicente that he was a "bad" father and that he didn't care about her or their two daughters. Aruna told me that from that day on she began to suffer regular beatings. Vicente slapped and punched her in her face, arms, and legs. "He never touched my babies, never!" she told me. After a few months of ongoing violence, Clara told Aruna to bring her children and move in. Aruna packed her bags and went back to her mother's house. Vicente began a campaign to get Aruna to move back with him. He asked her for forgiveness, spoke to Clara, got a better job, and stopped drinking. Aruna went back to live with him. She moved out again a month later and did that three more times. Clara was fed up with the constant back and forth and finally threatened Aruna, saying that if Aruna left her house again she would keep the girls and raise them herself. Aruna decided to leave Vicente for good and moved to her mother's house permanently. Clara had gotten back together with "El Señor," her former boyfriend. Aruna got along with him at first. However, after a few months living together, Carlos started to drink. He would come home intoxicated and harass Aruna. She told me, "If I was cleaning the floor or cooking he would try to touch me and say stuff like 'you are so pretty' or 'I want you.' I told my mother and she got mad at him and he promised to stop. He told her he was just joking around." After that happened, Carlos stopped harassing her for a while, until one day:

I was in the shower and my daughters were in the bedroom. One in the crib and the other in the little walking chair. My mother had given me specific orders not to give that idiot the truck keys because she knew he would be drunk. He got home drunk, that dog. He was so drunk he couldn't stand up. I got out of the shower and went to my mother's bedroom to get her conditioning cream. I had a towel wrapped around me and I was putting cream in my hair. He walked in the room and started harassing me . . . "I want you" . . . "you are so young and I know you haven't had sex in a long time, I know you want it too." I started screaming at him telling him to get out . . . he started to call me names, "*puta*," everything you can imagine. Then he said "give me the truck keys" and I said no . . . he started saying "you better give me the truck keys" and I felt like if I didn't give him the truck keys he would do something to me. So I grabbed the keys and threw them at him and screamed "*chinga tu madre, pendejo*" (go fu** your mother, you a**hole). And he left.

When her mother returned home, Aruna told her what had happened, and Clara told her that Carlos would not be coming back home ever again. Aruna told me, "I felt protected by her. She held me and said that nothing bad would ever happen to me." A few days passed and Aruna saw the truck in the driveway. Carlos was back in the house and her mother said she wanted to have a conversation with Aruna.

Clara told her that if Aruna wanted to continue living with her, they would have to establish certain boundaries. Carlos and Aruna were not to be in the same room of the house together at the same time. This included the living room, kitchen, bathroom, and patio. Clara also said that Aruna was to stay away from Carlos because she "provoked" many of their encounters, so it was better for both if they stayed away. At that time Elvira was three and Kaia was about to turn two. Aruna described feeling abandoned, lonely, and with no prospect of a "better life." That was when her cousin Ana came to her with an idea: Why not go to the United States? Her cousin told her she had been in touch with a guy who was living in New York and he was also from Catlas. Ana said that this guy, Marco, could help them financially to get to New York and find work. Ana said he knew the right *coyotes* and had work ready for them as soon as they arrived there. Aruna asked to speak to him on the phone. Marco and Aruna started to talk on the phone for hours every day for the next two months. She told him everything that had happened in her life, about her mother, Carlos, Vicente, her daughters. Marco was against her going to the United States because of her daughters. Marco told me, "I didn't want her to leave her children, so I told her not to come." Clara had no idea that Aruna was talking to Marco or that she was considering going to the United States. Aruna convinced Marco to help her cross the border and find work. She did that by repeatedly telling him how hard it had been for her to live in the house with her mother and boyfriend and how she couldn't walk around freely and felt that she had no one. Marco sent her the money and they arranged for her to cross through California and go to Los Angeles. From there she would board an airplane and fly to New York City. As often happens, when people decide to leave, it usually occurs within days. It was no different for Aruna. She received the money and planned to leave the next day. Her biggest concern was her two daughters. She did not want them to stay in that house with her mother and Carlos. Thus, she arranged to leave her daughters with Ana. She packed her daughters' clothes and dropped them at her cousin's house. Clara still didn't know what was about to happen. Then Aruna told her mother: "I will take the girls to have ice cream and I will be back soon." Clara replied with an emphatic no. Aruna insisted and Clara responded: "You never take your daughters for ice cream and you want to do it today?"

Aruna told me she had written a document in which she stated that she wanted to leave her children with her cousin. Clara told Aruna that she knew Aruna was planning something and that she would not let her take her girls. The car that was supposed to pick up Aruna and take her to Mexico City was about to arrive and Aruna saw herself at an impasse. She ultimately decided to go to the car and leave her two daughters in her mother's care. As Aruna tells me this story she can barely complete a sentence. It took me multiple interviews to be able to complete this description, because Aruna was so distressed as she described the last moment she looked at her daughters' eyes and said goodbye.

> My own mother hated me. She despised me. I never wanted my daughters to think that I left them because I didn't love them. Never. My mother was only able to have me, she miscarried many times and in my village we think that God is punishing you when that happens. She got bitter and resented how quickly I got pregnant and can you imagine I have five kids now? So I left her. I left them. I left everything behind and I didn't look back. When people say, "your heart breaks," I think it's true. It breaks and never glues back again. I told my two daughters, "I'll be right back" and it has been almost seven years now. In the beginning I blamed my mother. She resented me, she mistreated me, she miscarried, and she left me. I wanted to break out of that situation. But now I feel divided because if I hadn't come here I wouldn't have had my three boys. But now the consequence is that my daughters think I am their older sister.

Aruna's journey to cross was hard. She told me it took her more than
45 days to arrive in Los Angeles. She walked 10 hours almost every day,
only resting during the day when border patrol was doing their search.
Aruna became close to an older man who was bringing his grandson
with him. She took care of the child during the crossing and the man
protected her. She also cooked for the men in her group (36 men and
4 women). The other women were married and crossing with their husbands. When she got to Tijuana there was a van with clean clothes and
they drove to Los Angeles. She called Marco and he told her he would
fly her to New York the next day. Aruna told me she didn't feel "ready":

> I knew that the moment I arrived in New York I would have to be with
> him. And he is such a great man, but I didn't feel ready. So the man
> I met in the crossing had two nephews and one of them was married.
> They all lived together in an apartment and the woman [nephew's wife]
> cleaned houses . . . she said I could go with her to clean and she would
> give me $20 each time. She also said I could live there with them. So I
> lived there for one month. I cooked for them, cleaned, and did every-
> thing around the house. But then the other brother wanted to have sex
> with me . . . and I didn't want to. I called Marco and told him I wanted
> to get to New York.

Marco was working when Aruna landed in La Guardia airport in New
York City. He sent someone to pick her up and take her to his apartment.
When she arrived at his apartment, as she described it, "there was a
towel on his bed with a toothbrush and toothpaste, new clothes, a cold
beer, and a pack of cigarettes." She took a shower and changed. Marco
shared the apartment with three other men, but each had his room.
After she showered and changed, she sat on the bed and drank the beer.
Marco soon entered the room, greeted her, and asked her how her trip
went. Aruna and Marco talked, drank, and smoked for hours. Marco
was expecting them to sleep together and they did. Aruna told me
that she was shocked at how ugly he was, but that he was very nice. A
couple of weeks later Aruna found out she was pregnant with Carlito.
She called her mother to tell her the news and her mother responded,
"you went there to work not to have babies." Marco has helped Aruna
send remittances to Elvira and Kaia; they sent toys, money, and clothes.

Aruna's relationship with Clara deteriorated further. Aruna called her daughters but Clara would lie and say that they were not home. Clara started telling the girls that she gave birth to both of them. Clara told me she showed them pictures of them as babies and pointed to her belly, affirming that they came from her. Aruna sent toys but Clara would intercept them and gift it to the girls saying that she bought them. When I visited Clara and the girls for the first time, I was not allowed to tell them Aruna was their mother or say "I'm a friend of your mother." Clara told me it was the best thing she could do for Elvira and Kaia. I was only allowed to take the girls to a McDonalds and hang out with them during the day. I went to a Mother's Day event at their school and the girls wrote beautiful cards to their grandmother. They asked me about their "big sister" and about the boys: Carlito, Kiki, and Pablo. I showed them pictures, but always under Clara's supervision.

As I sat in Aruna's kitchen for the sixth day in a row listening to the story of how it all began, Carlito came home from school. When he entered the house he saw his mom crying and said, "is she talking about the 'bad grandma' again? She always cries when she talks about the bad grandma." Clara has said that it is too late now for Aruna to go back to being a family with her daughters. But Aruna was adamant (like all of them were) that there is a bright and happy future ahead of her.

To make things worse, Aruna was evicted for a second time and had to move to a new apartment a few blocks away. Her new apartment was a two-bedroom, and Tami, her weekend renter, shared a room with the boys. Tami was about 60 years old. I arrived at Aruna's house to see the new place and she had a friend visiting. It was a hot summer day and they were having watermelon and chatting. After about an hour at the apartment we went to pick up Carlito, age six, from school. Her friend Irma held Pablo, aged four months, the entire time. Irma told me that Aruna was too rough with the kids and that she needed to be more loving with them. On our way back from school, Aruna told me about a big fight she had with her mother on the phone just a day before:

> I was talking to my aunt and asked her if the amount of money I was sending my mother was enough. I found out that my mom was saying that ever since I left I ruined her financially. She said she paid the police a lot of money to look for me when I went to the US. So I called my cousin

to ask him how much money did my mom actually pay because he was the police . . . and he said "*mi hija*, I didn't ask your mom to pay me or to give me any money." So when I was on the phone with my mom I told her that and she got upset with me and said that she had to sell her car and *polleria* because of me. And I told her, that's not true; you ruined yourself because of Daniel. You wanted to have him in the house as a *papi chulo* (sugar daddy) and now you blame me.

When we returned to Aruna's home, she called her mother in Mexico. Clara did not pick up the phone. Aruna called her four times in a row. An hour later Clara called back and Aruna put her on speaker phone so I could hear. Clara said, "Elvira wants to speak to you." Aruna got excited for a second and then immediately became concerned.

Clara put her Elvira on the phone. Clara prepared Elvira to tell Aruna how she felt about Aruna. Elvira started saying "*yo no te quiero, tu me abandonastes*" (I don't love you, you abandoned me). Then Aruna lost it, "I did not abandon you, I didn't leave you in the street with no food. I send you money and gifts, abandoning is different, it means I forgot about you and I didn't." Elvira gave the phone back to Clara, who told Aruna, "Are you happy now? We have to go." Clara hung up. Aruna was really upset during the phone call and sobbed. Carlito, who was there too, started crying and told me: "*yo lloré porque Elvira no quiere mi mamá*" (I cried because Elvira doesn't love my mother). I asked Aruna if her mother was bitter about her departure; Aruna responded:

> She is bitter for something and not for other things. She makes my daughters not like me and she put her on the phone because she didn't want to talk to me anymore. Nothing I ever send is good enough for my mother, she thinks the store Children's Place is terrible, and she demands brands like Nike. *Yo atraso mis niños en la escuela* (I delay getting my children to school) when I have to deal with her demands.

When I met Elvira in Mexico, Kaia and Clara they were very suspicious of my presence. Because I was Aruna's friend, Clara thought I had some hidden agenda that included telling the girls about Aruna and how much she loved and missed her daughters. Clara agreed to be interviewed after a few days. She told me she was teaching Aruna a lesson on life: "She should have never left her *nenas* here. And now she is off having more and more children with another man. Why? I wasn't good enough mother for her?" Clara complained constantly about the lack of financial support and gifts from Aruna. I asked Kaia and Elvira if they wanted me to bring anything back to the United States for the boys. Both girls asked me to take pictures of them and show them to their *hermanitos* (little brothers). The statement caught my attention, as I had been instructed not to refer to them as their brothers. Clara quickly corrected them: "your little cousins."

Aruna's story shows us that not all mothers in this research had a positive relationship with their own mothers prior to leaving. Aruna's story elucidates how a negative relationship with the caregiver can harm the relationship between the mother and children.

Transnational Mothers and School-Related Decisions

Brianna lived in Jackson Heights, Queens with her husband Ronald and her newborn baby, Junior. She had three daughters in Puebla, Mexico. Brianna had been in the United States for four years, and since getting pregnant with Junior she had not worked. Brianna called and sent text messages to her daughters and her own mother in Mexico several times a day. She sent them pictures and uploaded images onto her page on Facebook throughout the day. Brianna's second daughter, Ashley, was in fifth grade at the time we met. She was an excellent student and always received great grades. In the last few months before finishing fifth grade, Ashley began complaining to her grandmother, who she called "Mamá Leila," about her teacher. During my first visit to Puebla, Ashley talked to me about her teacher José. She said, "He points his finger at me all the time, everything is always my fault for him. I hate him, he is rude." School was out of session during the time of my first visit, so I did not meet José until my next visit. I spoke to other teachers in the pueblo and to Ashley's grandmother, Leila. Leila explained to me, "[José] is one of those teachers that is very rude . . . he doesn't like when girls do well. But who am I to say anything? I didn't even go to school." Lilia, Brianna's cousin who also taught at the school, told me, "he is . . . *traditional* . . . it's hard because he has been at the school for so long." Eventually I did sit in on a few of José's classes at the public elementary school he attended, and he had no issue sharing his complaints. He explained to me, "Kids nowadays have this sense of entitlement. I don't know if it's more freedom, more money from parents, more TV or more El Norte talk. They need to be put into their place."

This situation was not restricted to Ashley only. I have found that teachers in schools in other states of Mexico criticized familial arrangements where mothers were not present to "take care" of their children. A teacher in Vera Cruz openly told me in front of children with migrant mothers, "for them it will be harder for them to learn . . . without the mother it will take longer."

A few weeks later, after I returned to New York City, I was at Brianna's house one afternoon when her phone rang. It was Ashley. She said, "Mamá, I am not going to school anymore, I hate my teacher." Brianna tried to calm her down and immediately asked her if she had asked "Mamá Leila" to intervene. Ashley said she asked Leila, but Leila said that there was nothing she could do and that she did not feel comfortable going to the school and fighting with anyone there. Brianna told Ashley she was going to talk to Leila about it and she would take care of things. After they hung up the phone Brianna told me, "These are the times I have to control myself and not jump in the plane and go back. My daughters need me to take care of their lives. It's the one thing I want them to do . . . the one thing, you know? Go to school, get an education and get a good job. Have a chance in life! And then I am not there! Ay! Me pongo loca (I go crazy)!"

Later that day, Brianna called Leila and asked her to speak with a cousin who worked at the school as a teacher. "Talk to Lilia, she will help you," Brianna told Leila. Leila was in her seventies and she complained about feeling tired.[1] Leila told Brianna, "Why don't *you* solve your children's problems, *hija*? I do the best I can, but I tell them you are their mother, you know?" Brianna responded that she would. An hour later, as I sat on Brianna's bed holding her baby, she called the school's principal: "Is Fidel around? This is Brianna . . . Brianna Osorio . . . Ashley's mother." She looked at me and pushed the speaker button so I could hear. I put Junior in his crib so I could take notes. After about one minute a man came back to the phone: "Yes, can I help you?" Then Brianna began:

BRIANNA: I am calling you from New York. Do you remember me? We met before.

FIDEL: Yes, I remember, yes.

BRIANNA: Listen, you will have to do something for my daughter. This teacher is causing her a lot of trouble and I am getting very upset.

FIDEL: I know . . . I know *señora*, but what do you want me to do? We have one fifth grade class and only four months left of classes.

BRIANNA: You have to do something. Move her. Move her from this class . . . *No me importa!* (I don't care!)

FIDEL: And put her where? If I have to move every student that complains, señora . . . then there is no more school.

BRIANNA: Mr. Fidel. You know my family owns land around the school. We help you with parties and everything . . . that's how you know me. You don't want me to talk to my cousins and my uncle there, do you? We are Osorio . . . my dad was the president of the town 20 years ago!

FIDEL: Listen, I will see what I can do. This is a difficult situation. . . . There are only a few months left. Can you talk to your daughter? We have to be fair with students.

BRIANNA: I will call you every day until you solve this problem . . . *sale?* (Ok?).

FIDEL: Let me see what I can do [very frustrated tone].

They exchanged greetings for each other's families and finished the conversation. After they hung up, Brianna called Ashley and told her not to worry about the future because she had spoken with the principal. Two days later, after continued pressure from Brianna, the principal called and told her they had found a solution. They were going to have Ashley sit in the classroom with sixth graders, but her homework and tests would be the same as fifth graders. Lilia, the teacher and cousin of the Osorio family, had come up with the solution and Brianna was happy about it. She felt accomplished as she told me, "this is to show people that it doesn't matter how far you are from your children, *la mamá es la que hace las cosas para sus niños, punto* (the mother is the one that does things for her children, period)."

Making decisions at a distance may not be anything new for most people, since many families around the world live apart. However, undocumented migration presents an additional challenge to families because mobility across borders is highly restricted, costly, and dangerous. The prospects of reunification are minimal and all members of the constellation feel the emotional toll of separation. All of the women in this research had started families in the United States and found it really complicated to commit to going back to Mexico now that they had US-born children. Part of their justification for staying in the United States was the idea that US-born children would have a better social outcome because of their education opportunities in America. In light of the transnational care constellation as a means to understand how migration reorganizes familial ties, this short vignette illustrates the centrality of mothers in education-related decisions—a responsibility that travels with mothers across borders.

Gender has been a key to understanding dynamics in transnational families. In her study of Filipino left-behind children, Parreñas (2005a) notes that mothers who migrate are expected to perform the caring and emotional work typically associated with their maternal role. In the case above, even though Brianna's bottom line, as she explained herself, was to make sure Ashley stayed in school and had a positive schooling experience, she took on the emotional of work of "taking care of things" for her daughter and honoring her role as the mother. The facility with which Brianna could call her daughter's cell phone, her mother's house, and the school adds a layer to caring across borders that allows mothers to "solve" issues and problems in real time. When Leila told Brianna "*you* solve your child's problem," she directly communicated that expectations do travel across borders and do not diminish or become less important because of physical distance. Brianna understood that because she had a cell phone with competitive service rates, she could call Mexico pretty frequently and there was no excuse for her not to resolve this issue promptly. It was astonishing to witness, in one day of field work, three different phone calls (to Ashley, Leila, and Fidel the principal) and the hopes for a solution develop. If Brianna had tried to move her daughter to a different classroom in their school in Jackson Heights, the response may well have been quite different.

Out of the 20 constellations I observed during this research, 15 mothers had had experiences intervening in school-related activities in Mexico. However, only half were successful in changing or influencing the local reality of the schools in their towns in Mexico. Nancy, a mother in the Bronx, grew frustrated with the fact that her son Marcos did not feel safe going to school in a small town in the state of Vera Cruz. Nancy told me she tried calling the principal of the school with no success: "It's hard because I know who the principal is and he is friends with my cousin, but he makes empty promises. He told me he was going to call the police to say that kids were being mugged on their way to school, but I don't believe him!" Two other mothers complained about safety concerns: Camila, whose three daughters complained about safety when walking to school in the state of Vera Cruz, and Mayra, who was convinced that her son Rodrigo, who lived in Pachuca, Hidalgo, was being targeted by others in school because they knew he received remittances. Both Camila and Mayra persisted in trying to solve their children's issues in Mexico. Camila explained to me, "Here everything is taken care of; there is the police, the social worker, the teachers, the nurses. Everyone is involved in making decisions for your children. In my town in Mexico, if we don't pressure teachers and school staff, who knows what will happen."

Communication across borders resembled everyday conversations parents have with their children who are physically close to them. I witnessed many transnational discussions about curfew, boyfriends and girlfriends, illnesses, and separated sibling rivalry in which mothers performed the role of "counselor" and "friend" to their children in Mexico. However, when the issue was schooling and education, the authority of mothers became prominent. Yet, as I show in the next section, mothers had more difficulty asserting their influence over the schooling of their children in New York City. Since this research was multi-sited and I traveled back and forth between Mexico and New York City multiple times over the period of three years, my approach will be to describe the parallel experiences of the women in these constellations.

* * *

Constellations are split across physical and emotional borders. Relationships across borders are accompanied by distortions of perceptions, roles, ideas, and morals. In order to understand the implications of migration and physical familial separation for mothers, caregivers, and especially children, one must look at how care constellations organize, divide labor, and co-share tasks transnationally.

One central feature of transnational maternal labor entailed engaging with the educational opportunities and experiences of the children in Mexico and in New York. The mothers interviewed often justified their decision to migrate in terms of providing a "better life" for their children; this better life depended in part on what the mothers perceived to be a better education. Though this is a normative response, and though the women eventually revealed myriad [what they consider to be] less noble reasons for migration, it is clear that, for the women, *providing an education* made the process of "leaving" legitimate and thus acceptable for the members of the constellations. This chapter exemplifies how transnational motherhood both in practice and in ideas crosses borders when the subject involves the care and well-being of her children. In addition, I show how caregivers in Mexico and mothers in New York City have parallel experiences when trying to actively participate in children's lives.

I argue that mothers in transnational care constellations have a central role as decision-makers in school-related activities "here and there." Even though the ways migrant mothers undertake their duties and their levels of comfort and confidence vary as they perform tasks in the United States and "virtually" in Mexico, they both take on and are assigned the authority role in the lives of children on both sides. School-related discussions about academic performance, homework completion, respect and politeness in classrooms, aspirations to continue in school, and so on, are central to the communication that takes place across borders.

Maintaining this transnational role of authority was not always easy. Mothers struggled to maintain the position of authority and central decision-maker with their children in New York City. They described feeling particularly vulnerable given their legal status, lack of English language knowledge, and limited knowledge of how the school system works in the city. Further, caregivers in Mexico, who often had never attended school, described their role in helping their charges as limited and potentially damaging; they expressed concern about not knowing how to help children with homework and not feeling competent to interact with teachers during parent-teacher conferences.

Members of these constellations are not connected "neatly" or "evenly"; nonetheless, they are connected. To demonstrate, I will first discuss how mothers in New York City are central decision-makers in school-related issues in Mexico and in the United States, even when there is a lengthy separation with the children in Mexico and language and status barriers with children in the United States. Second, I will argue that mothers in New York and grandmothers in Mexico experience similar challenges when interacting with teachers and school staff in both countries. Third, I will show the critical role Internet and

Communication Technology (ICT) play in transnational mothering, particularly as mothers make education-related decisions. ICT fosters regular interactions between mothers and grandmothers, between mothers in New York City and teachers in Mexico, and between separated siblings doing homework and/or playing. To understand the implications of ICT on both sides of the border is to understand the parallels between separated lives.

Mothers as Central Decision-Makers in School-Related Issues

Mothers in this study understood their central role in school and education issues as both imperative and expected of them by other family members. In their own way, the mothers in this research project sought actively to be engaged in the education of their children in order to, in their words, secure a better future for them. In doing so, they constantly and actively shared tasks and duties with caregivers in Mexico, relying on those caregivers for enforcement and feedback.

Much of the literature on mothers' educational achievement asserts that mothers' school involvement and children's academic performance are heavily correlated (e.g., LeVine et al., 2012; Sawyer, 2010). Even though physical presence of mothers is a well-known argument for better school performance of children and youth, Mexican migrant mothers' central role in the education decisions of the children they left in Mexico is celebrated and expected. Grandmothers and children in Mexico expect the participation of New York–based mothers in their schooling activities. In New York City, even though mothers shoulder the responsibility of education and school-related decisions of their sons and daughters, they experience hardships when it comes to participating in local school activities. This chapter builds on the previous one to examine how members of these transnational constellations face struggles, and in many cases overcome them, when trying to make decisions about schooling, which for them means making decisions about the type of education their children will receive.

Valdez (1996) observed in her study of Mexican immigrant families in the Southwest that husbands were providers and wives were responsible for the welfare and education of the children. Bhandari, Mullen, and Calderon (2005) found that parents who belong to minority groups, were from the lowest economic strata, and were immigrants, particularly those with limited English language skills, were often perceived by educators as being less involved in their children's education, despite the fact that they held educational aspirations for their children that paralleled the aspirations reported by other parents.

These studies do not discuss how immigrant mothers (or fathers, for that matter) actively seek ways to participate in children's education in their country of origin and how that contrasts with the results they achieve when interacting with teachers in the receiving society. In fact, I found that Mexican migrant mothers in New York participate more frequently in school-related decisions in Mexico than in the United States.

While *educación* is a goal migrant mothers have for their children, it is in the process of decisions and actions related to *schooling* that those aspirations get translated. Throughout my fieldwork I found that mothers and caregivers associate the concept of "a good mother" with the idea of "providing an education" and of children who are *educados*, or well-mannered. The cultural model of *educación* in Latin America encompasses not only academic achievement, but also behavior of children and youth. Prins (2011) calls this behavior "social competence." *Educación* goes beyond the formal walls of schools as it involves child-rearing at home, within families, and in communities.

Thus, education or *educación* (or the Brazilian version of *educação*) has a double meaning that covers school achievement as well as manners and respect (Bartlett, 2007). In this research mothers were adamant about being able to keep their children and youth in formal schooling. For them, if children and youth stayed in school and performed well, they found their migration decision to be somewhat worth the sacrifice. Even though most children and youth in this study were attending public schools, field trips, and after-school activities, and receiving books and materials for school, that was all possible only because of parental remittances. Mothers described school as a place where children could also learn about discipline and ethics. Thus, even though report cards and good grades were the ultimate indicator of success, mothers expected their children and youth to be well mannered, knowledgeable, and respectful young people.

When I inquired what "providing an education" meant, mothers overwhelmingly emphasized the importance of providing financial support for schools or school fees as well as money to buy books, uniforms, and food at school. Results from surveys with 225 children in schools in Puebla showed that 90percent of children received some sort of remittance from a family member in the United States. The children that received remittances in the form of physical gifts from their migrant mothers listed them as: backpacks, pencils, pens, notebooks, English language books, pencil cases, and undershirts to be worn with uniforms during school days.

Mothers also described a good mother as one who provides emotional support, is available to help with homework at home, makes sure children learn, makes sure children are polite and respectful, and makes sure teachers treat the children right. Women explained that the role of a "typical mother" is compromised when there is lengthy separation with no possibility of reunification. They work with caregivers in order to find ways to be present in education and school-related decisions. The goals of *educación* with regard to comportment or behavior and the goals of *educación* with regard to schooling were in tension. Mothers leave to get resources for schooling but must abdicate being the one to provide children with the daily discipline that addresses the comportment part.

Mothers interviewed often contrasted the role of the mother with the role of the father. As one mother named Camila explained,

> You have to understand the following: the man is the "head" of the family . . . ok . . . you understand? Now, the woman is the neck, the arms, the body, the everything. And the fact that I am not physically there with my *nenas* (little girls) does not mean I am not important to them, you understand? I am still the one that puts them through school the same way as I put the ones here through school. In my heart there is space for each one of my children. I love them all equally.

Caregivers in Mexico are frequently themselves mothers. When their daughters migrate, they also play an important role in deciding on school and education issues. However, caregivers do not actively attempt to "take over" and "claim" children as their own, with rare exceptions like Aruna. As explained by Tami, a grandmother and caregiver,

My daughter gave birth to Pilar. I raise Pilar as one of my own, but she is my daughter's daughter, she [Pilar's mother] is the one that has to make the decisions about everything. . . . God didn't make me to take over as Pilar's mother . . . when my daughter returns, it is her right to take Pilar with her. I try to do what I'm told and Pilar must respect her mother's wishes.

Grandmothers and caregivers aid mothers in New York in their attempts to establish legitimacy as a transnational parent. They do so by reminding children and youth on a daily basis about the "hardships" their mothers had gone through and still go through in order "to provide" for them. It is not just within kinship circles that the role of the biological mother or "*la que dió a luz*" (the one who gave birth) is linked to decision-making in children's lives. The teachers interviewed in Mexico also described the role of biological mothers as central to children's academic performance, attributing to them the responsibility of success or failure. In contrast, teachers in New York City complained that sometimes migrant mothers who worked too many jobs and did not speak fluent English could not assist their children "properly" at home and thus had "little understanding" of teachers' notes, school activities, opportunities for after-school activities, and report card notations. Teachers on both sides of the border held biological mothers responsible for children and youth's actions (*educación*) and performance in school.

Through the story of this constellation, Brianna, a mother in New York City, not only acted as the authority in an important decision regarding her daughter's schooling, but also used the available limited resources she had to push for what she believed to be the best outcome for her daughter. Their story illustrated the importance of looking at the interactions across borders in order to understand who is making decisions and the roles of each member in these constellations. Parent-teacher conferences were yet another example where decisions crossed borders.

Parallel Experiences: Parent-Teacher Conferences

SOUTH BRONX, NEW YORK CITY. The day had come for Violeta to go to parent-teacher conferences for three of her four US-born children in the South Bronx, New York City. A few days earlier, Violeta had asked me to accompany her to the meetings since, as she explained to me, she had a difficult time communicating with the teachers in English. Violeta told me she did not understand when they spoke in English, because they talked too fast and it made her nervous to stop them and ask them to repeat themselves. She also described her reticence about her eight-year-old daughter Leah's second grade teacher. "She is a black woman . . . she hates Latinos and doesn't speak Spanish. You will see how awful she is, that whore. I get pissed off with that *hija de puta* (son of a bitch)." While acknowledging the racism in these comments, it is important to explain that much of Violeta's anger was influenced by her view of the context of her home in the South Bronx. In her building alone, there had been a number of incidents of Latino men and women getting into physical fights with African American men and women. Like other mothers interviewed in the South Bronx, Violeta expressed concern, fear, and insecurity when describing her relationships with her children's teachers and school staff. Her fear and anger stemmed from feeling uncomfortable speaking in English and also feeling uncomfortable with her undocumented legal status. Still, Violeta, like all mothers interviewed, understood and described her duty as a mother to "take care" of school-related things. Nancy, another mother in the South Bronx, explained, "It comes down to you, the *mamá*, to register children in school, get the paper work, transfer them, complain, get their uniforms, sign their homework . . . check every child's notebook; and tell me if there is ONE father that has ever signed those."

It was a cold morning in March when I met Violeta at her apartment. She lived in a two-bedroom apartment in the South Bronx with her husband Silas and her four children: Ramiro (age 10), Leah (age 8), Nicole (age 5), and Kimberly (age 3). They had been living in that apartment for two weeks when I met them; the management company moved them from their previous residence for health and safety reasons.[2] While they were in their previous apartment, the police knocked on Violeta's door almost every day looking for different people involved in selling and using crack cocaine and heroin. In that one-bedroom apartment, the children slept in the bedroom and Silas, Violeta, and her brother Samuel slept in the living room. In the old building, her children developed allergies and severe coughs due to the constant smoke in the building.

Even though their new apartment was only a few blocks from the old one, it was an improvement. The two-bedroom apartment gave the family more room and allowed more space for the children to play inside. Their new building was located in front of a park that had a baseball field, benches, and a small playground; however, the children were not allowed to go there often because members of gangs "hung out" there and caused problems from time to time. Often, Dominican and Puerto Rican gangs would fight African American groups in the neighborhood, and vice-versa.

The children's school was a 20-minute walk from their home. Silas dropped off the kids at the school every morning, but he never spoke to any of the teachers, did not know their names, and was not interested in participating in school activities. Violeta worked four times a week and was the one in charge of helping the kids with homework, as well as securing food stamps, child support, health insurance, and any school-related activity.

These activities included the dreaded parent-teacher conferences.

VISITACIÓN, MEXICO. Back home in Mexico, Tatiana took care of Andrés (age 14), Violeta and Silas's first born. Tatiana is Violeta's mother and Andrés's grandmother. Parent-teacher conferences for Tatiana in Mexico were also difficult. Tatiana never went to school herself and her four kids, including Violeta, had all migrated North when they were teenagers. Tatiana never learned how to read or write, and she had a tough time helping her grandchildren with homework and school assignments. At the time of our interview, Tatiana was 66. She was very active and rode her bicycle everywhere. She took care of three grandchildren because their mothers were in the United States. She cooked, cleaned, and dealt with teenage drama. The house where Tatiana lived with Andrés and Carmen (another grandchild) was a two-bedroom home they owned. Anair (the third grandchild) had just moved to a small house with her boyfriend. Tatiana's home had a backyard with chickens, turkeys, and a donkey. Their house was in front of a plaza where children played and listened to live music. Lately, Tatiana confided, the whole town was getting more dangerous, as cartel members were buying property and there were an increasing number of kidnappings and murders. Although I could not find exact numbers that exceeded the national average and reflected the violence Tatiana described, other family members in the town told me different stories about where dead bodies were hiding and how they were able to detect a car that belonged to one of the cartels because it had a specific logo on the rear window.

In an interview, Tatiana described herself as feeling left behind and abandoned by all her children, including Violeta. She had very little money and depended on remittances and on her animals. She would sell a valuable animal whenever Andrés really wanted something. For a while Violeta did not send money. She could not find a job that paid well and quickly grew her family. Then Tatiana told her, "if you don't help your son, he is not going to go to *Secundaria* . . . and I will send him to be with his other *abuelita* because she can pay for his school and I can't." Violeta immediately started sending money: $180 a month to pay for school supplies and other bills. Tatiana and Andrés shared a bedroom and Tatiana called him her *mandante*, meaning that she ordered him around to run errands like buying food, paying the man who brings tortillas, and feeding the animals. Tatiana described Andrés as "very smart." His teachers complained that he finished his assignments too fast and bothered his peers in class. Andrés's school was located ten minutes from their house. After school, Tatiana took Andrés to swimming lessons and soccer practice. Tatiana was proud of her grandson's academic performance. She showed me his report cards and asked me, "Aren't the grades good? That's what he tells me, but what do I know?" His grades were good in a few subjects, but not as consistent as Tatiana imagined. Tatiana did not like to participate in teacher-parent conferences, so she was almost always absent. She said:

> The teachers are nice people, they treat him right, but I don't understand them very much . . . and the person feels bad . . . before it was difficult because I didn't know how to help him with homework . . . but his cousins are older and they helped him. Even though Violeta left when she was 15, she went to school. . . . She almost finished high school, she was smart. Andrés needs to know that . . . that he has his mother's head, he can be someone.

SOUTH BRONX, NEW YORK CITY, CONTINUED. We arrived at South Bronx Elementary School at ten in the morning. As we walked in, we were handed a ticket and an evaluation form that was required by the Department of Education in the City of New York. The lady at the entrance explained, "If you fill out this evaluation, you will get a free ice cream." Violeta looked at me and complained, "These bastards think they can bribe us with ice cream, I am not filling these evaluations . . . throw them out. Garbage."

We started by visiting Nicole's classroom. Nicole was in first grade and her teacher was of Puerto Rican origin. She went back and forth between Spanish and English to talk about Nicole. Leah (Violeta's older daughter) had also been a student of Mrs. Cruz, so Violeta knew her already. Mrs. Cruz started by talking about Nicole's reading abilities. She pointed to the wall where big letters were hanging. "See the letters?" Mrs. Cruz asked. "The best students are reading at level 'O' but Nicole is reading on the 'F' level, which is very, very low, OK?" Violeta sat there in the tiny children's chair looking at Mrs. Cruz, who continued to talk, "Nicole doesn't speak good English and she doesn't speak good Spanish. You need to read with her at home, practice reading with her *mami*, in English please! She is not putting any effort in class, it's hard for me . . . you know *mami*, it's hard!" Violeta kept saying "OK." Mrs. Cruz then described an episode in class where she asked children to draw their families and name family members as in "brother," "sister," etc., and she said that Nicole confused the names frequently. Mrs. Cruz referred to a man that appeared in the drawing. According to her, Nicole described this man differently each time. He would be grandfather, then uncle, then brother. This man was sometimes Samuel (Violeta's brother) and sometimes Andrés (the son/her brother in Mexico). Violeta did not like that Mrs. Cruz implied that Nicole did not know something that seemed basic and in Spanish said to the teacher that maybe Nicole was having a bad day. Violeta wanted to leave and Mrs. Cruz wanted to be done, so we all got up and exited the classroom. As we walked to the next meeting, Violeta told me: "I told you . . . they hate my kids and now they decided that Nicole should be in a class for English as a second language. I don't understand . . . they have moved her three times."

Next we went to Leah's classroom and Violeta continued: "This is the bitch I told you about . . . She is the one that hates the Mexican people." Mrs. Smith welcomed us into the classroom. We sat down and she pulled out Leah's test scores. She also pulled out a model exam.

Mrs. Smith said, "This is what a perfect test looks like and this is what your child's test looks like, you see the difference? This one is good [she mimicked a thumbs-up] and this one is bad [she pointed to Leah's paper, mimicking a thumbs-down] and it's Leah's test." Violeta looked down the entire time we were in the classroom to avoid eye contact with the teacher. I started translating to Spanish some of the things Mrs. Smith was telling Violeta. Mrs. Smith would use basic vocabulary to point at tests and say, "this is bad" or "this is good." The teacher also said at least four times in 20 minutes, "No more Spanish at home, otherwise she will never learn." In the final part of the conversation, Mrs. Smith said that Leah was most likely going to fail the grade and that she had one chance left, so it was up to Violeta to study with her and make sure she learned.[3] She explained that Leah was always late with homework, that she was sloppy and did not put any effort into learning. I translated as fast as I could to Violeta.

She understood what I explained to her, but I do not think Violeta was listening at that point, as she was already closing her purse and getting ready to leave the classroom. We stood up and the teacher shook my hand and said, "Thank you for translating, this is an impossible task otherwise." There was a moment where Violeta did not know if she should shake the teacher's hand, and the teacher also was not sure if she should put her hand out. They finally shook hands and Violeta said under her breath and in Spanish, "She is only doing this because you are here, bastards."

In the hallway we saw other mothers waiting to be seen by the teachers. Two of them greeted Violeta and asked, "Did you talk to the devil yet?" Violeta responded, "I just left hell." We arrived at the final stop, Mr. Okima's classroom. He was Ramiro's fourth grade teacher. Mr. Okima had a projector with Google translator opened on the monitor. He told me he was using this strategy all day to speak to parents who did not speak English. Violeta smiled and said under her breath "*que buena gente* (what good people)." Mr. Okima was different from the other teachers because he seemed concerned about Ramiro's performance and behavior in class. Mr. Okima told me, "Listen, my parents are Japanese and don't speak a word of English. I get it. It's hard." He proceeded to describe Ramiro as a "quick" and an "interested" student. However, he explained that Ramiro "gave up easily" and did not aim to be great. Mr. Okima also told Violeta that Ramiro did not show up to the after-school tutoring sessions he had arranged for Ramiro and that concerned him. Violeta was surprised, as she had no idea where Ramiro was from 2:40 p.m. to 5 p.m. if not in school. "I will kill that boy when I get home!" she told me as we walked out of class. Violeta was livid, "I work to keep these kids in school and this is what I get. Even Andrés [her son who is in Mexico] does better in school . . . Ramiro is lazy, the laziest boy I know."

Throughout the visits Violeta did not ask the teachers any questions. She did not ask for clarifications, and she did not defend her children or agree with the teachers. She listened to the teachers with her head down and talked to me under her breath often. She was mostly angry with the school staff and teachers. She was frustrated with the lack of support and with the "negative" comments about her children's performance. She described the first teacher as an "idiot," the second one as "racist," and the third as "nice, but maybe too nice." Violeta dreaded parent-teacher conferences and her role as the decision-maker and discipline enforcer for school-related issues in New York. All of the teachers complained to Violeta about the fact that she was the one writing down answers on her children's homework, and more often than not teachers said the answers were wrong. I asked Violeta if she did the homework for her children and she told me she did.

Violeta, like other mothers interviewed, grew frustrated with her "failed" attempts of helping the children succeed in school. And the injunction against Spanish pained her: she said, "They say don't speak Spanish at home, but I don't speak English . . . so should I not speak to my children at all?"

VISITACIÓN, MEXICO. I walked to Andrés's school with Tatiana. As we arrived, teachers and the principal were in one room chatting and having coffee. Tatiana stood at the door and kept her head down until they noticed her. "Hello, can I help you?" one teacher asked Tatiana. "Yes, I'm here because my son, I mean my grandson, Andrés, told me the principal wanted to talk about him to his mamá . . . so to me." The principal asked her to take a seat and I introduced myself to him. Principal Leonardo explained that Andrés was very smart, but he bothered other students in class. "He finishes his assignment faster and then he bothers students, he teases them." Tatiana responded "oh" or "ah," but not more than that. The principal then called the other teacher and asked her to give Tatiana examples of Andrés's behavior. Carmo, the teacher, explained,

> He is a teenager and he wants attention. My guess is that he doesn't get attention at home . . . it happens. Also, Andrés likes to talk about his family in the United States and the video games he gets, shoes, etc. I tell the students write a response to this text we just read, he finishes before I am done explaining the assignment and he gets up and walks around, disturbing students with his stories.

Tatiana occasionally looked up to the teacher and principal and finally responded, "I'll tell his mother that." The principal looked at me and said, "I feel bad because families are destroyed because of migration and poor grandma here has to raise teenagers. How unfair!" Carmo, the teacher, then explained that she sent several notes to Tatiana that she did not sign. She also said Andrés missed many visits to museums because he did not bring the release forms or the payment. Tatiana apologized and said she was going to talk to his mom. After a few minutes we stood up and left the school.

Tatiana told me it was not the first time she had received complaints from Andrés's teachers. She said,

> In the beginning, when he was younger, like seven or eight, he would come home crying every day and say "why did my mother leave me?" He didn't want to go to school. He was sick. So he went to a . . . one of those . . . psychologists and he helped him. I feel bad because I feel like I can't help him, I can just love him.

If they could afford it, other grandmothers and caregivers in Mexico also resorted to psychologists when they thought the children were depressed or anxious. It was a common response for grandmothers and caregivers to say they felt they could not help children with school because they were "illiterate" and they needed to use professional help because "the mothers were gone."

PARALLEL EXPERIENCES. Violeta and her mother Tatiana both clearly felt disempowered when assisting children with school-related activities. In New York, Violeta struggled with a language barrier and felt nervous about her undocumented status. Her status never came up during the school visit, but she explained to me that being "*ilegal*" is a cloud you live under and you never know what will happen. Violeta understood her role as central in school decisions; she never questioned the fact that she was the one going to school for parent-teacher conferences and not her partner Silas. However, she felt inferior to teachers and complained that she could not "fully" help her children with homework if she did not understand the instructions. It was not just about the impact of the language barrier on Violeta's ability to perform her role as a decision-maker in school-related subjects, it was about the expectation Violeta, her partner, her children, and other family members held that it was her role as the person who would "take care" of the children's education. After all, she said, their opinion was: *That's why she left.* On the other side, Tatiana did not experience a language barrier but as woman with a low level of schooling, she was uncomfortable in the school and did not always understand the discussion of homework, teachers' notes, or other instructions. Tatiana also had Violeta and Violeta's role in her mind when she responded to the teacher and principal: "I will tell his [Andrés's] mother."

Grandmothers understood their roles as caregivers as an extremely important duty. Some caregivers endured abuse from their partners in order to, in the words of one, "provide a stable home for the children, since their mothers are gone, you know?" Grandmothers encouraged children to attend school and sometimes enforced school attendance. However, school attendance did not mean academic achievement, as some children go home and find no one to help with homework. A schoolteacher told me, "We don't know what to do, because sometimes you see that [the children] are putting effort into learning, but when they go home they have no support, especially if the grandparents run a farm or have a job where they are all day." A teacher in Puebla explained to me, "The mother is the head, the neck, and the body of a family. When they leave it's not just the psychological part that gets affected. Grandmothers also lose their daughters and the whole family feels it. It's serious." Caregivers interviewed who did not know how to read and write felt ashamed. This study shows that caregivers were invested in the school life of children; they had immense pride and great aspirations for the children. However, many did not

feel qualified to assist with homework, go to parent-teacher conferences, or demand better quality schooling.

Caregivers interviewed reported some kind of difficulty intervening
or trying to be part of school-related activities with their grandchildren
in Mexico. I interviewed 31 caregivers and did extensive ethnographic
work with eight of them. Of the 31, six had finished ninth grade, fifteen
had gone as far second grade, four had completed fourth grade, and six
had never been to school. Thus, the feeling of lack of confidence because
of their backgrounds kept them at a distance from any formal education
setting. Caregivers were firm and steady with teachings at home. Cleaning, cooking, feeding the animals, keeping oneself clean, and respecting
the elderly were all part of the duties and knowledge they imparted to
the children they cared for, and they executed this aspect of caregiving
with great confidence. With the exception of Aruna and Clara, caregivers turned to the mothers for input in most school-related issues. There
was a clear divide when the subject was formal education: "*Eso es cosa
de la mamá, yo ya no puedo ayudar con eso* (this subject belongs to the
mother, I can't help with that)." Thus, these grandmothers could help
their grandkids with comportment and social competence, but not with
the formal aspects of schooling. It became clear to me that the perceived
noble explanation for migration, which was tied to providing a better
education, allowed all members of the constellation to "hang on" to this
reality of transnational duty. Cecilia, a caregiver and grandmother, explained to me, "First, my daughter *knows* more than I do about school,
second, that's why she went to El Norte . . . it's her responsibility and she
pays for it."

On the other side, mothers in New York City had less involvement
with decisions in school-related activities in New York City than in Mexico. I observed that this comparative lack of local involvement, reported
by 46 of the 60 women interviewed, was not because they cared less
about their children born in the United States. Their hesitation had to
do with how they understood their place in society.

One afternoon in March, when I accompanied Emilia and her baby
Alondra to the Herbalife office, 13 of the 60 mothers I had come to
know were waiting for me patiently, chatting in the small office. When
I walked in, Nancy screamed to the others: "She is here, let's ask her."

I did not know what they wanted to ask me, but I saw all these women, some with their babies or toddlers next to them, holding papers in their hands and ready to talk to me. Nancy approached me first and asked me to read and translate a document from her son's school. In the document, the Department of Education had denied her petition to transfer her child to another school. Anthony had been diagnosed as having special needs, and Nancy complained that he was being bullied in school and that the teachers did not provide him any support. She never spoke to anyone at the school; she reached out to a social worker who knew someone in the Department of Education who told her to submit some paperwork. When I asked Nancy why she didn't go to the school and try to talk to the principal and teachers, she replied, "Because I don't want to see anyone face to face . . . what if they mark me and target me after I complain and maybe even call the police . . . I can't even understand English. I'll be the clown." Other women followed Nancy's lead, asking me all kinds of questions: "Can my son join summer school?" "How do we get free lunches?" "Who do we call for free tutoring?" "Is there a way to transfer schools?" "My daughter is undocumented, can she get a GED?" "Can you come to a parent-teacher conference with me?" They knew I had accompanied other mothers to school, to the welfare government building, and to the housing management office; they were looking for a close resource. Needless to say, I was in the dark almost as much as they were, but I could find people to talk to them.

Mothers may have appeared not to be as involved in their children's education in New York City as they were with the children in Mexico, but the reason often had to do with fears related to not knowing the language, concerns about legal status, and general lack of confidence that they would be treated fairly. In parallel lives, caregivers and mothers saw their backgrounds and who they were as limitations to how much they could help children.

The description of these parallel lives raises an important point for discussion: the contrast in what is valued in the two educational systems. In New York schools, teachers were very specific about the individual progress of each child. The emphasis was on school achievement and independence. They emphasized the acquisition of English. Test scores, after-school programs, and reading skills were at the top of their list when discussing the experiences of each New York–born child. In the case of Andrés in Mexico, teachers were more concerned with giving feedback regarding social and group interactions. There was very little discussion regarding achievement and performance, but more focus on the idea of *educación*.

Communication

All women interviewed used Internet and Communication Technology (ICT) to maintain relationships and non-school-related practices. ICTs can also be considered as solutions (though difficult ones) to the "cultural contradictions of migration and motherhood and the 'accentuated ambivalence' they engender" (Madianou, 2012: 278). This, in turn, has consequences for the whole experience of migration, sometimes even affecting decisions about settlement and return.

The women in this study used ICT extensively to communicate with their children and impart ideas about *educación*. Mothers in New York City worried about how their own mothers (their children's caregivers) were being treated. Brianna, Gemma, Violeta, Sara, Emilia, Camila, and even Aruna (who did not have a good relationship with her mother) constantly sent text messages or wrote notes on the online social network Facebook that read: "make sure you are helping your grandmother" or "show respect to your grandmother and do as she tells you." Those messages got pushback from youth, especially children on the other side, who responded with emoticons to signal a rolling of the eyes or a happy face sticking its tongue out. Still, mothers often referred to their own experiences, "This is the woman that raised me! Show her respect" (Sara's text to Agustín). The mothers also relied on ICT to help directly with schooling. Of the 60 women I interviewed, 20 reported using social media to help with homework.

Within the 20 constellations where I dedicated most of my research time, I observed ten of them engaging with social networks or other communication vehicles to assist with homework.

As described in a previous interlude, Aruna, a mother in the South Bronx, developed strategies to use ICT methods to get in touch with her daughters and help them with homework and school projects. It was with this argument that Clara, Aruna's mother and her children's caregiver, allowed Aruna to speak with her daughters. "If she is going to help them with homework, great! Because I don't know how to . . . but I don't want Aruna telling these poor girls she will be back, because she won't." Aruna used Facebook and different forms of instant messaging to communicate with her 10- and 12-year-old daughters in Mexico about homework. When I visited Clara and the girls for the first time in Mexico, I was not allowed to tell them Aruna was their mother or even say "I'm a friend of your mother." Both Clara and Aruna asked me not to do that. Clara told me it was the best thing she could do for Elvira and Kaia. I agreed, since that was the condition for me to visit Aruna's daughters. Despite this elaborate ruse, Aruna wanted to participate in her daughters' schooling process. She constantly sent them books, pencils, pens, pencil cases, and backpacks with notes like: "for you to continue to do well in school." She went on Facebook and wrote to her aunts and cousins, begging them to show her pictures on Facebook of Elvira and Kaia. She wrote her status on Facebook as "missing the rest of my family" or "sad not be home for my daughter's birthday" and asked other family members to show those to her daughters. Her cousin Ana did show Elvira and Kaia Aruna's posts and pictures of Aruna's sons in New York City. Aruna constantly posted videos, cartoons with sayings, and motivational greetings for her daughters to stay in school and do well. She hoped that through social networks her mother Clara would not be able to keep her from her *nenas* (daughters).

Aruna also wanted her three boys in New York to be close with their sisters in Mexico. Thus, every week Aruna set up Skype calls for homework help time where her two daughters in Mexico brought their questions and doubts about homework that week. Clara allowed that communication to take place. Aruna also made sure Carlito (age 6) and Kiki (age 4) taught the two girls some words in English. Aruna herself did not always understand the homework questions Elvira and Kaia had. When that happened, she used the Google search engine to find out how to respond to her daughters. During these sessions Aruna did not want to say, "I don't know" to any of the questions her daughters had. ICTs facilitated a kind of interaction that would not have been possible in real time. Aruna also knew that as her daughters grew older there was a risk of them resenting Aruna because she had lied to them their whole lives. "I can't have my daughters wake up one day and only have terrible memories about me . . . they need to know I support them in their opportunities and that I want them to succeed, even if I am far away."

Brianna, Gemma, and Camila also used Facebook to exchange motivational notes for school achievement. Stella, Camila's 14-year-old daughter, took pictures of her homework and posted on her mother's "Facebook wall." Camila printed the pictures and glued them to her refrigerator, just as she did with her children in New York City. Through social networks, mothers received news much faster about school achievements and education experiences of their children on the other side.

Conclusion

Transnational care constellations are unique in a sense that separation exists, but the desire to maintain family ties through this system also exists, as illustrated by the case of the Osorio constellation. Part of the definition of transnational motherhood is the idea women have of "being here and being there"—or not being here and not being there. Brianna, for example, operated outside this dichotomy, fully acknowledging her position within the care constellation and using her resources to fulfill her role of central decision-maker.

I have argued that mothers were sometimes more successful engaging with the school "back home" than with the school in New York City. At local schools in New York City, the mothers in this study mentioned feeling fearful and disempowered due to language barriers and legal status. Furthermore, Hamann and Zúñiga (2011) have argued that expectations regarding the involvement of parents in schools in Mexico versus in the United States is very different. Parents in Mexico paint schools, build desks, make food for the students, and help with celebrations. In the United States, parents are supposed to be educators: they are supposed to read to children, teach them English, and supervise homework. Their roles are considered pivotal for children's academic development. Mothers in the United States are expected to take on more pedagogical roles, and the mothers in this study often felt unprepared for that work.

Despite their presence, parents and caregivers both experienced difficulties communicating with the local school. Violeta and Tatiana went through similar struggles in Mexico and in the United States; they felt powerless to help children under their care with homework and dreaded interacting with teachers and school staff. Other mothers in this research described similar feelings. I have read countless letters from teachers and school administrators in New York City regarding children's behavioral issues, grades, parental participation, transferring from English as a Second Language (ESL) to different classrooms, requests for children to see psychologists, and offers for tutoring that mothers either ignored or did not understand. Teachers in both systems complained about parents/caregivers, using deficit language and assuming the adult did not care about schooling. As I show here, lack of parental involvement in schooling did not mean lack of aspirations for a better education. Education was always the goal of caregivers and mothers. Constellations united over this common goal and gave each other support.

However, the process of schooling and especially homework, extracurricular activities, and reading at home were particularly difficult. Mothers used ICTs to remain active in the education of their children, despite the distance. While I am not arguing that Skype or Facebook are the glues of transnationalism, they do play important roles as tools to remain connected. These tools allowed for real-time updates and interactions that meant more presence for mothers involved.

It is clear that mothers have centrality in the transnational care constellation with regard to schooling and education, especially when topics involve the model of comportment or behavior. Education becomes identified with mothering. It implies both a practical situation where mothers have more years of schooling than grandmothers, so they are better suited to take charge of their biological children's education, and an ideological adaptation to mothering in a transnational setting in which education continues to be a key dimension of child-rearing— all the more so given the broader meaning that *educación* has in Latin America.

Drawings

I used a variety of methods during my fieldwork. I used drawings to elicit narratives from children who were separated from their mothers and/or siblings. I collected more than 65 drawings from children during workshops and 75 through surveys. The figures in this section are examples of how children and youth depicted their families, their thoughts about Mexico, and their impressions about the United States.

Carlito, Aruna's son, drew the picture shown in figure I3.2 when I asked him to draw his family. Carlito, who lives with Aruna in New York City, did not include his sisters Elvira and Kaia or his grandmother Clara in the drawing. When he finished explaining to me who was who in the

Figure I3.1. Workshop in Mexico, August 2012.

Figure I3.2. "My Family" by Carlito (age 6).

picture, Aruna scolded him: "How can you not draw your sisters? How can you forget?" Carlito asked me if he could draw the family again. Later he told me, "I know they are my sisters, but they don't live with me . . . and my mom cries about them all the time. Do you think they are my family?"

Carlito's brother Santino, age four, asked me to help him as he attempted to draw his family. After listening to his mother get upset with Carlito for not including the two sisters in Mexico, Santino told me: "don't forget *mis hermanas* (my sisters)." He drew the characters and asked me to name them for him. Aruna looked at the drawing and told him, "well done!" Mothers like Aruna tried their best to keep their children's memories of their siblings alive. Aruna had the names of her daughters written on the bathroom walls and constantly asked Carlito and Santino to write them and talk to them on phone. Children, on the other hand, were mostly confused by the idea of who belonged to their families and more often than not associated family with the people who lived in the same residence with them.

Figure I3.3. "My Family" by Santino (age 4).

Figure I3.4 shows one of the drawings I collected during workshops in two towns in Puebla. A nine-year-old named Roman created this picture. His aunt and his uncle were raising him as he had been separated from his mother for more than four years. He drew himself, his two dogs, a man, and a woman. He then told me the story behind the picture: "This is my mother Quirina . . . the one in El Norte . . . you know? But the man is Erasto, my uncle . . . because I don't know my father, my aunt tells me she is not my mother and I know that. My mother sends me gifts like backpacks and books . . . she has babies there [in New York City] but I don't know them . . . I guess they are my family." Roman, like other children I encountered in the course of my research, had a hard time making sense of who belonged where in his family. He held on to his mother, as represented in the picture, but his uncle was drawn next to her as part of his family. His cousins and aunt in Mexico as well as his brothers in New York City were not included in the picture.

Figure I3.4. "My Family" by Roman (age 9).

Figure I3.5. "My Family" by Brian (age 7).

Brian, age 7, Allison's son, did not draw his biological mother in the picture, shown in figure I3.5. He drew his grandmother Agustina and his two aunts, Sofia and Luna. Agustina, his grandmother, had been taking care of him for more than three years. She told me, "I raised him like he is my own." Brian did not speak with Allison frequently. One day during the week I was staying at Agustina and Brian's house, Allison called. I was drawing with Brian on the floor while Agustina chatted with Allison on the phone. "*Hijo*, your little brother wants to talk to you on the phone," Agustina told Brian. Brian looked at me, scratched his head "Quien?" Agustina replied, "Your brother, *hijo*, Allison's son." Brian got up and went to the phone, saying "Oh, Allison's son." Allison told me in New York she had given up claiming Brian as her own. She told me,

> The truth is I left because I thought in the long run I could help my mom and Brian by sending her money. Well, things didn't turn out the way I hoped they would. I am losing another child now [referring to the fact

that her ex-husband has custody of her daughter]. I'm scared of seeing Brian now.

When I inquired why, she said, "He might reject me and I understand it." Allison didn't have a job for a while, so she did not send money home for months. She would also not call for a month because, according to her, "it is too painful to talk to my son when he doesn't even care for me as his mother. But I understand. I did this."

The picture in figure 13.6 depicts the family of a young girl named Geraldine. She explained to me that the baby that her mother was holding in the drawing was herself. Geraldine exemplifies how families do stay "frozen" in time when there is migration. Her last memory of her mother was when she was very young. Her mother left Mexico when she was not yet two years old. Geraldine is older than all the siblings pictured in the drawing, but she described herself as her mother's baby. She told me, "I still dream about my mother holding me and singing to put me to sleep . . . I wonder if she still sings for my brothers."

Figure 13.6. "My Family" by Geraldine (age 11).

3

Children and Youth's Perspectives of the Other Side

Ideas of Inequality and Sense of Belonging

Children are both social actors and subjects of social forces; as they experience migration in their families, they have their own responses and opinions. Their experiences are central when understanding the consequences of maternal migration and family separation. In this chapter I explore the perspectives held by children and youth on both sides of the border regarding migration and family separation. I argue that transnational care constellations allow children and youth to imagine the other side of the border, and through that they are able to explore their thoughts and perspectives on material things and inequality, as well as sense of belonging and family. Their imaginaries are the vehicle for making sense of being part of a transnational care constellation. This chapter represents the uniqueness of particular data I was able to capture of dynamics between separated siblings. Within transnational research, separated siblings' relationships have been understudied in part because of the complexity involved in the collection of data, but also because children and youth seem to be constantly learning about where the "rest" of their families are.

Much of my time doing fieldwork for this research was spent with children and youth. Through their photographs, drawings, poems, journal entries, Facebook messages, text messages, and other representations, I show how children and youth make sense of maternal migration and transnational families and how these ideas get translated into two main points: inequality and sense of belonging. I focus on two themes that illustrate how the children in my research make sense of migration. The first narrative concerns the existent inequality on "the other side," which is informed by their interactions not only with family members who are physically close to them, but also by interactions across the entire transnational care constellation. Children inherently contrast their experiences to what they understand about the experiences of the "rest" of the family. Second, I focus on the narrative in which children and youth describe their sense of belonging in the family. Considering oneself part of a family remains a latent desire of children and youth, and the transnational separation heightens the craving for a family unit. Attention to these themes illustrates how children and youth use cultural values they learn and develop to build characters and realities that inhabit spaces far away from them.

Children of immigrants "here and there" change as a result of family movements across cultural and geopolitical borders, and their interface with institutions like schools and neighborhoods changes as well. Orellana (2009) accurately describes this phenomenon: "Children and youth experience juxtapositions of discrepant beliefs and practices made visible by the movement of people" (p. 25). As Coe et al. (2011) remind us, the idea of childhood is culturally specific, and it shifts over time in response to political and social changes. Children and youth construct their own stories about what Mexico and the United States are like, about their brothers and sisters, and about opportunities, which in turn shape their ideas about migration and separation. Coe et al. (2011) bring attention to children and youth, who, as they put it, are at the nexus of family separation. In this chapter, I too focus on children and youth, as they are understudied actors in the context of international migration. Attention to their experiences reveals much about how migration shapes their perspectives of family, of inequality, and of Mexico and the United States.

Mexican immigrant women often form new families as they settle in the new country. Even women who stay married to the same partner may have more children once they settle in the new country. Those decisions yield siblings and half-siblings who are separated across borders. The perspectives and sense-making of children and youth on both sides of the border is not restricted to news of parents; children also imagine how their siblings live and reflect on what kind of lives they have on the other side. Children in this research discussed their understanding of the reasons behind the migration of their mothers and other family members initially in light of economics: lack of employment in the *pueblo*, the need to work, the possibility of stable income elsewhere, upward mobility, and better living conditions. Even though there is support for the claim that employment and economic factors motivate people to leave a country (push and pull factors), children and youth I interviewed also discussed alternative explanations and justifications for parental migration. They engaged discourses they heard in both households—Mexico and the United States—and sometimes agreed with them and sometimes rebelled against them. I found the narratives created by children and youth to be gendered; girls discussed how hard it was to raise children in Mexico and in the United States, while boys talked about the hardships of going to the field and working long hours.

According to Orellana's research on migration, children continue to be mostly invisible outside of families and schools. They are often addressed as baggage that is "brought along," "sent for," or "left behind" by sojourning parents (Orellana, 2009: 15). Explorations of children's actions, contributions, social relationships, and cultures are paramount to understanding the implications of maternal migration. In addition to understanding how children use their power within families (Dreby, 2007), it is also important to look at how children and youth express resentment or appreciation for parents and far-away siblings, and ultimately how migration shapes and influences their worldviews.

Realities across borders may seem distant, but children and youth are constantly "crossing the border" with their imaginaries. Gardner (2012) asked, "what is it like to have a 'home' where close relatives live, but which one has never visited?" (p. 1) and "how is transnational migration experienced by children?" (p. 1). In order to answer these questions, the author describes:

> Clearly, imaginations and imaginings are central to the future shape of transnational social fields. In some instances this may lead to certain places becoming sites for heritage tourism, very much "over there" and conceptually different from "home," but in others it may lead to the distinctions between places becoming increasingly blurred, especially if the children themselves do not make such distinctions, however much state boundaries or (adult) discourses of ethnic belonging insist on them. (p. 12)

This chapter builds on the discussion presented by Gardner but includes the micro-contexts and the specific accounts children and youth give of their transnational experience. In the introduction to *Minor Transnationalism*, Lionnet and Shih explain,

> The transnational designates spaces and practices acted upon by border-crossing agents. . . . The transnational . . . can be conceived as a space of exchange and participation wherever processes of hybridization occur and where it is still possible for cultures to be produced and performed without necessary mediation by the center. (2005: 5)

Can there be a transnational body? If we understand the body as a physical "space of exchange and participation," as stated above, perhaps. More importantly: Can children and youth actively construct this transnational body? Yes, they can. In this chapter I bring children and youth to the forefront of the migration discussion and engage with them as primary sources of thoughts on migration. Concepts like inequality and family, though complex in theoretical discussions, are also everyday discussions for children and youth.

Mirrored Perceptions

When asked why they migrated, mothers almost always responded "to provide for my children" or "to provide a better life to those who stayed." Children and youth responded in similar ways to the same question. Mothers justified their absence as service to others: They explained that the reason they had migrated in the first place was to be able to provide for their children. Even though they offered other explanations and justifications for leaving their children, they did not deem those explanations appropriate for a caring mother (as described in chapter 2). In an almost mirrored way, when I asked the children in the United States and in Mexico, "Why do you think your mother migrated?" the first reaction from children and youth was to explain that their mothers needed to work to support them, to provide them with a better life. Agustín (age 16), whose mother Sara had been living in New York City for almost ten years, told me: "She left so we can have a good life here." In Mexico, caregivers and especially grandmothers reminded children every day that their mothers were away to provide for them. "This sacrifice of [your mother] being away from you,"

Clarisa told Agustín, "it's exactly for you." In another household in Mexico I asked the same question to Daniela, whose mother Gemma had been in New York for 12 years. Daniela (age 14) responded, "I know she works a lot there, I know she is always busy running around, so I think people there work . . . well there is more work there, so you make more money . . . so that's why you go." Daniela's grandmother and caregiver, Emma, also repeated to her every chance she got, "People go North for the ones they love, *hija*."

Hochschild (2013) described the experience of children left in Kerala, which is similar to my findings in Mexico, "managing" their doubts and questions regarding the reasons behind a mother's departure.

> Why, the older children recalled asking themselves, did my mother leave me when the mothers of my school friends did not leave them? Did my mother have to leave, or did she want to? Or did she leave me because I was naughty? Answers to these questions seemed to differ depending on how a child imagined a parent's role as well as that of fathers, grandparents, friends and others . . . As one grown child of a migrant worker put it, "I wondered why she couldn't have stayed back or I couldn't have gone with her. I still wonder." (p. 156)

Research in global migration (Dreby, 2010; Parreñas, 2010) explains this phenomenon as the "sacrifice" mothers and fathers undertake for their children. My interviews and observations revealed a complex picture that challenges the assumption that children and youth accept this rationalization of sacrifice. For both Agustín and Daniela, for example, this explanation about why their mothers left generated confusion. The 37 youth I interviewed expressed frustration with that explanation and pressed their grandmothers for a more detailed account. These moments of frustration were usually preceded by grandmothers telling the children what to do, the children reacting to the orders, and grandmothers resorting to saying something such as, "you are disappointing your mother with your behavior." One morning Monsterrat (age 14) confronted her grandmother: "Did I ask to be born? NO. Why is it my fault that she left . . . let me tell you why she left, *abuela* (grandmother), because she wanted to leave and go make her money and get out of this *pueblo*. It has NOTHING to do with me." Agustín expressed similar thoughts when talking to his mother Sara on the phone, "You made that decision to leave . . . I didn't make you, so don't blame it on me!" Thus, even though the normative response was to say, "my mother migrated for me," children and youth had moments of resentment, and they expressed confusion about the justification for migrating. They sometimes felt that the role assigned to them as the primary beneficiaries of their mothers' migration was unfair.

On the other side, US-born children and youth discussed the migration of their parents in two instances, when they wanted to inquire about "life on the other side" and when they had to discuss legal status, government welfare, school registration, and the possibility of family trips. At Gemma's house in Sunset Park, Brooklyn, her daughter Yazmin inquired: "Why can't we go to Mexico this summer?" Gemma explained that they were waiting for lawyers to figure out the paperwork that would allow the whole family to travel together. Yazmin was not convinced. "Why do you need lawyers to get paperwork? What paperwork?" Gemma did not want to tell Yazmin that she did not have documents and that her status in the United States was actually different from her daughter's. Later Gemma explained to me that she and her husband were asking for asylum from the United States by claiming that there was political and economic persecution in Mexico. Thus, they could not send their children to Mexico for the summer if they were claiming to the court system that the country was dangerous for them. Yazmin told me a few days later, "I always think my parents are speaking fast in Spanish when they want to talk about travel plans, you know . . . they try to do that so we won't understand. But you know Gabi, I'm smart!"

Children and youth carry both the burden and the honor that migration brings. They are dependent on their families and they experience a disjuncture between their symbolic role as beneficiaries of migration and their actual experiences of power vis-à-vis other members of the family. Children and youth in Mexico expected parents to provide for them while working in the United States, as exemplified by Tina (age 7) when she opened the gifts her mother Brianna had sent through me. "She is there all this time and all I get is *one* t-shirt. I thought people went there to get rich!" This is what the sociologist Robert C. Smith calls the "immigrant bargain," which is the expectation that children will work hard in school to *salir adelante* (move forward) to compensate for parents' sacrifice by migrating. Smith (2005) and Dreby (2010) both describe the phenomenon where mothers and fathers in the United States become frustrated when they feel that the expectations are one-sided: expectations that they will make lots of money and will be able to provide. However, children and youth in Mexico understand that their parents' choice to migrate entails them doing well and being able to provide a better life for them. At the same time, children born in the United States question their mothers' commitment to sending money and gifts across borders when they themselves want more material gifts. The responses of children in the United States and in Mexico are thus mirrored in the sense that mothers' very explanation for leaving is reflected in their children's expectations and perspectives on migration. The children at first repeat their mothers' explanation for leaving. In the end, however, frustration, resentment, and doubt creep into children's and youth's responses, which cause backlash.

In their narratives, children and youth on both sides of the border make sense of inequalities between Mexico and the United States. They do so by reflecting on symbols, cultural values, ideologies, employment, and economic status "here and there."

Images of the Other Side: Making Sense of Inequality

Members of these transnational care constellations perceived and understood the other side to have "more" or "less" than what they had. This inequality, perceived or real, created space for children and youth to imagine the other side. Children and youth on both sides made sense of distance and assessed what it means to be in the United States or in Mexico by thinking about work, class, and material things. Children and youth in New York City valued being able to buy items like shoes, clothes, phones, and video games. Sense-making through difference is not an uncommon practice. However, children and youth in this research showed a degree of specificity that not only was part of existing stereotypes of modern and traditional societies, but was also reinforced by their parents. In the following situation I illustrate how children and youth in New York City discussed their ideas about the "other side" through the lens of inequality and distribution of wealth.

G: We are going to draw today. Are you guys ready?

RAMIRO (age 11): Yes!!! What are we going to draw?

G: We are going to draw what you think Mexico looks like. Ready?

As we sat in the living room of Violeta's apartment in the South Bronx in New York City, her four children started painting and coloring, and using glitter and crayons as they began to draw Mexico. After a few minutes Ramiro was very excited to be done. He wanted to explain the drawing to me and make sure I understood every detail and the reasons he had included those details. Ramiro described the picture:

RAMIRO: Here are the people in Mexico . . . you see them? They are at farms with lots of animals, a donkey, a cow, chickens, and maybe a dragon . . . just kidding [about the dragon]! The people in Mexico work a lot, they wake up at 4 or 5 a.m. every day and just work . . . someone told me that some of the fruit we eat come from Mexico and clothes too. There are trees and forests and a big house there . . . but there are no buildings and cars like here. They have to work a lot.

G: Why do you think they have to work a lot?

RAMIRO: Well, because they are poor.

G: How do you know?

RAMIRO: [pause] Because my mom says it all the time, how there is kidnapping in Mexico and she is not letting me go there because I could die . . . People will take your money no matter what . . . they want your Nikes, they want your watch . . . because they can't have it. Here there are so many stores that sell all that, in Mexico there aren't, so they steal.

LEAH (age 8): Gabi, my mom can show you the videos of people without their heads . . . their heads get cut [off]. Women too . . . they take things from you. I don't want to go. I'm scared.

G: Your brother Andrés lives there, right? Do you think he is also afraid?

LEAH: No he is not afraid . . . because he is really old, he is like 28 years old.

RAMIRO: He is not 28!

LEAH: How do you know?

RAMIRO: Because we play video games together and I asked him . . . you are so dumb.

There are several ironies in this juxtaposition. These children live in New York City and their father Silas reported that he had been mugged and beaten twice for being "Mexican"; the children themselves had described not feeling safe playing in the park because of "gangs" of Puerto Ricans. Yet, safety did not come up as an issue at home, only in Mexico. Further, the children hold a perception that Americans are wealthier because of the amount of available consumer goods. Violeta's children believe there is a need to work more in Mexico, because people don't have enough. Meanwhile, Violeta works five days a week and earns only $100 per week. Her husband Silas stays at home and watches television all day. In Mexico, Violeta's mother Tatiana sells animals and food and receives remittances from her daughters and son who live in the United States.

Ramiro has a Facebook account and communicates with his brother Andrés in Mexico and with other family members. Ramiro knew Andrés was 14 years old because they played video games together. Andrés did not have an Xbox or Playstation in his home in Mexico, but he went to a computer/game store a few blocks from his house and played with his brother. Andrés told me, "I wish I also had an Xbox at home like my brother has in his house in El Norte. I have been asking my mamá Violeta but they don't send me, I think they have more money there." Ramiro's perception of Mexico was informed by a combination of the videos Violeta showed them and how she and Silas talked to each other about Mexico. During my observations, I heard them say things like "I will never go back there" or "the government doesn't help you one bit." Both Silas and Violeta sported tattoos on their arms and necks that included the word "death" written inside skulls. There was an obsession with talking about death and Violeta had stated in different moments that she felt a connection with her country when she looked at the skull tattooed on her arm (Lomnitz, 2005). It was not uncommon for them to give elaborate accounts of stories about kidnappings, violence, rape, or beatings at the dinner table while the children were eating their meal. There was sometimes indignation toward their home country, but their descriptions at times also sounded more like the plot of an action-packed movie.

Leah, age 8, showed me yet another representation of what she thought Mexico was. After she was done drawing she picked up her three-year-old sister Kimberly, put her on her lap, and started rocking her from side to side. She made noises that sounded like she was trying to put Kimberly to sleep, patting her back gently and singing her a song. She looked at me and with her sister in her arms told me:

> You know, I was trying to draw mothers and children in Mexico to explain that raising children in Mexico is really hard. Buying a house, even worse! You have to work really hard for your children to put food on the table, to be a good mother. Here in New York there is help and jobs . . . but you must know that is a hard life over there in Mexico.

It took me a few seconds to absorb her short explanation. She sounded exactly like her mother at that particular moment. Leah did not get along with Violeta, and she wrote extensively in her journal about feeling unloved by her mother. During my observations, Leah often disagreed openly with her mother. But when we were talking about what she thought Mexico was like, Leah channeled her mother's narrative to explain the feeling of inequality that exists between Mexico and the United States. In many instances, when the children would complain about not being able to go to the movies or not being able to buy something, Violeta got extremely frustrated, and would give the children a lecture:

> Do you think life is easy? I want you to go to Mexico to see how it is there . . . how people have to *batallar* (fight), to be someone . . . here you kids have it all! You have no idea what it takes to bring up a family and feed you all. I was pregnant riding a bike from one place to another to deliver chickens for your grandmother. Do you think I ever complained? NO. The answer is no. So shut up, now.

In this case, as with other families I observed, the children adopted the mother's narrative about how difficult life was in Mexico.

Another description came from US-born six-year-old Carlito, whose mother, Aruna, had been living in New York City for seven years. Carlito had two brothers in New York who were US-born and

Figure 3.1. Leah with her sister Kimberly on her lap.

two half-sisters in Mexico. When I asked Carlito what he thought Mexico looked like, he explained to me:

> There are cows and chickens, and people work in really hot weather . . . they work many hours a day and don't get paid much, then they can't go to the mall and buy toys. . . . I had a dream the other day that there were two Carlitos: one was in Mexico and the other one was here. The one in Mexico was running outside with the cows and the donkeys and then . . . I don't remember, but I think I remember now he didn't have a house to live [in] or a school to go . . . just a soccer ball . . . then the Carlito here was going to school, eating at McDonalds . . . It was a dream.

As he finished telling me that story, his four-year-old brother joked with him, "you cry, you cry." I asked Carlito if he had woken up from the dream crying and he told me, "I don't remember," and followed up with, "do you think that's how my sisters live?" The week Carlito had this dream was a difficult one for his mother. Aruna did not have a positive relationship with her own mother, who used information about her daughters as leverage to have Aruna send her more money, clothes, and gifts. Throughout the week Carlito heard Aruna describing her worries about what her daughters would eat if her own mother kept on deciding what to do with the money. Carlito showed me a small pot in his bedroom with lots of coins and he told me, "this is for my sisters; they need the money because in Mexico they don't use cars and the schools are outside, not like in buildings." Carlito had an elaborate view of how his sisters lived in Mexico and the level of inequality that separated them as siblings. Children and youth in the United States worried about their siblings in Mexico. Children and youth interviewed in New York City (excluding the three infants) expressed concerns for the safety of their siblings and their living conditions.

At the same time, many of the children I interviewed in Mexico assumed that their families in the United States had a better life than they did, replete with consumer goods. Children and youth made the distinction between Mexico and the United States based on material things that directly differentiated socioeconomic status. Ana (age 18), one of three sisters who lived in Mexico away from her mother Camila and her three siblings, described what she imagined the lives of her siblings to be like:

"All I know is that my mom has her own grocery store and that my siblings wear nice clothes and they always have what they want. In our case I have to ask her to give me things, I know they have more there." Brian (age 1) and Pilar (age 13) also described the "better life" they assumed their siblings had in the United States. They used the phrase "*Viven mejor*" (They live better) to explain how their siblings lived. After doing participant observation and interviews with the 30 children who belonged to the 20 transnational constellations, I observed a pattern in how they responded as to how they imagined the United States to be. The pattern is exemplified by this conversation with Yuri (age 11) in Mexico:

> G: How do you imagine New York or the United States to be like?
> Y: I think it's really big . . . with big, big buildings and a lot of stores where people buy gifts.
> G: What about where your siblings live?
> Y: They live in these big buildings I think, but I think my house is bigger . . . and they shop at these stores and send us nice gifts [she showed me a t-shirt she was wearing]; everyone has money there and they buy the newest bicycles and new shoes and they can eat at McDonalds all the time, right?
> Y: [After a moment of hesitation] they could send us more if they wanted to . . . [very low voice and looking down to the floor]
> G: What do you mean?
> Y: *Maestra* (teacher), you and them have so much more than we have and then all we get are a few things every month . . . why can't they share more?

Children and youth began their answers with broad descriptions of what the United States or New York City looked like, as illustrated in the drawings interlude. But they quickly transitioned to a narrative where they described a sense of inequality based on material goods and money. As they transitioned into a narrative that seemed more resentful, they were not totally comfortable seeming ungrateful. When Yuri's grandmother, Rita, heard him say "Why can't they share more," she gave him a look that showed me and him that she was upset. She said, "How can you say that? After all the effort your mother puts into working and sending you things." Of the 30 children and youth I interviewed in Mexico who were part of the 20 constellations, 27 complained about inequality in the distribution of money and material goods between siblings. This finding challenges assumptions that inform the debate that has long existed in migration studies on the benefits of remittances. Children and youth feel the socioeconomic divide between families "here" and "there." The way children and youth perceive upward socioeconomic mobility is linked to consuming material goods. My analysis reveals that within this transnational context, children create their own versions of the story using inequality as a base for comparison. Thus, they are assessing the economic and political inequalities on the other side of the border.

Suárez-Orozco (2002) argues that the poorest immigrants suffer tremendous adversity as a result of immigration, but in spite of these difficulties they often improve their economic and social circumstances. I cannot affirm that without a longer study. However, many of the children of maternal immigrants in Mexico and in the United States did share that opinion, and as a result came to expect certain benefits from migration. While US children and youth do not think about the migration of the parents as much as the children and youth in Mexico do, the assumption is that by living in the United States they are "better off."

Symbols of development are present in the description of what the United States looks like, but the lack of these same symbols illustrates the narrative toward Mexico. A parallel can be made with the work by Kearney (2004), who argued that basic conceptualizations of the anthropological subject began to change rapidly in the 1970s and 1980s, to deal with the expressions of identity and class in this complex world.

Scholars like Kearney and Roger Rouse (2011), who has also worked in Mexico, explain that the main influence that inevitably demanded and stimulated a theory of a more complex subject than the individual was the ethnography of migration across national boundaries, especially migrations of persons between "traditional" and "modern" societies. Children and youth's imaginaries remain very much attached to ideas of what is modern and what is traditional in the form of material goods.

The "Rest" of the Family: Sense of Belonging

Studies regarding the effects of migration on children suggest that children show some resentment toward migrant mothers and less so to fathers. In her work with children of immigrants in Ghana, Cati Coe argues that children express more pain about the migration of parents than the parents themselves. She points out that children complained about two aspects of migration: the dispersion of the nuclear family, and the care they received from caregivers (Coe et al., 2011, p. 102). I documented children and youth in Mexico complaining about the scattering of the family, but more about not belonging in what many of them called the "new family." Even though children and youth rationalized the reasons behind the migration of their mothers, resentment emerged regularly. The children in Mexico struggled to reconcile their feelings of anger and abandonment with the constant discourse that they should be grateful for their mother's sacrifice on their behalf.

This situation was very much a part of the relationship between Emilia and Esperanza. At the time of our interview, 17-year-old Esperanza lived in a house in a *rancho* called San Felipe, four hours outside of Jalapa, the capital of the state of Vera Cruz. She had two siblings who lived with her in Mexico and two half-siblings who lived with her mother, Emilia, in the Bronx, New York. The first time I met Esperanza, she was waiting for me at the plaza of a larger town close to San Felipe, called Maltla. Emilia told me that arriving to San Felipe was difficult and I would need someone from there to guide me along. Esperanza gave me a warm welcome and was excited to show me around and introduce me to her favorite spots in Maltla. It was a big holiday in Mexico, Mother's Day, so many festivals were under way in the streets and people were cooking their favorite foods to celebrate their *madres*. Esperanza was not alone; her grandmother Enriqueta was there as well. Enriqueta could not contain herself and asked me ten questions at a time about her daughter Emilia. She touched my arm and said, "You hugged my daughter, right?"

As we started to walk, Esperanza's phone rang; it was Emilia. Emilia and Esperanza chatted for a few seconds and Esperanza passed me the phone. Emilia wanted to check if I had arrived safely and if they were going to cook me a big meal. I told Emilia "Happy Mother's Day," she thanked me, and I passed the phone back to Esperanza. During the rest of walk in Maltla, Esperanza and Emilia chatted on the phone. We got in the car to head to San Felipe and the two of them were still on the phone. In the car Esperanza put Emilia on speaker; thus I was able to listen to both sides of the conversation. Esperanza quickly transitioned from an excited mood to a more assertive and impatient mood. Even though that was the first time I had met Esperanza, I observed similar behavior in the days to come. In calmer moments, Esperanza justified her mother's decision to leave Mexico. She said, "Look around where we live. There is nothing here but the family. She had to go and make something of herself, work, send us money, and support herself. Life may be easy for many people, but not for poor people. It was not a choice, she had to do it." However, at that moment, on the phone with her mother, Esperanza's logic fell apart and frustration took over:

ESPERANZA: The teacher at my school told me that I can start teaching kindergarten next year because I'm really good with kids, I'm patient with them . . . I help them a lot.

EMILIA: That's good, but don't forget that you have to finish your studies first, that is what the money is for . . . [baby crying in the background on Emilia's side]

ESPERANZA: *Mamá! Calla la niña* (Mamá, shut her up)! *Hazme caso mamá* (Pay attention to me, Mamá)! That's why I hate talking to you on the phone, all you care about is your new family, the family you have there in the United States . . . I hate your new family!

EMILIA: Calm down Espe . . . the baby is hungry, you know how babies get when they are hungry, *hija*.

ESPERANZA: It's always the same talking to you, you only want to talk fast and ask me about school, then you have to go with your kids from your new family. *Nadie me quiere* (no one loves me).

Emilia continued her attempts to calm Esperanza, but with no success. The phone reception nearing the rancho got weak, until we could only hear every other syllable that came from Emilia's side. Enriqueta told me: "It's always like this. Esperanza thinks that Emilia and her children live in this beautiful house in New York and that her mother doesn't care about her and about her siblings . . . but that's not true. My daughter is a fighter."

After I showed Esperanza and her siblings Yago (age 13) and Juan Pablo (age 12) pictures of her mother and half-siblings in New York City's South Bronx, Yago, who had been diagnosed with Down Syndrome since birth, yanked Emilia's picture from my hand and ran to his bedroom. I followed him and asked if everything was all right. He sat on the bed and started kissing and hugging the picture and repeating over and over, "This is my *mamá*, my family." Esperanza also followed us into the room and took the picture back from him. She stood up as he sat down and, holding the picture, she told him, "We are NOT part of this family [pointing at the picture]. We don't belong with them Yago, they don't even know who we are. Did you know that? They don't care about us. . . . Look at them, they don't even look like you and me." She turned to me and asked, "Do you think they look like me?" I told her I thought they all had the same eyes. She looked at the picture for a few seconds. Then Yago got up again and yanked the picture from Esperanza's hands. "It's my mamá, my family." Esperanza, upset, responded,

> Maybe yours Yago, but not mine. . . . They know nothing about me. Do you know what a family is, Gabi? A family stays together . . . they talk to each other, they know what is going on. What do they know? They are so busy living their life . . . together . . . under the same roof, like a family.

I noticed Juan Pablo standing at the door, watching the interaction between his siblings. I asked him if he had any thoughts about what Esperanza and Yago were discussing and Juan Pablo told me, "I feel like my mamá is my mamá. She is. I don't know her husband there or her kids, so the rest of the family . . . I guess . . . I don't know them. I don't know if they would like me, but blood is blood, right?"

In many regards, children in Mexico respected and appreciated their mother, but moments of frustration brought up really raw feelings of resentment. Children left behind sometimes resented siblings they largely did not know but were supposed to love, that got to live with their mothers. There is no denial that the opposing symbols of beneficiary as well as bearer of the consequence—distance—was a constant thought and struggle in the minds of children and youth in Mexico. As with other children and youth I interviewed, Esperanza could easily explain and justify the reasons for migration. However, they resented the "other family," and the impossibility of reunification fed their resentment. It had been years since the three siblings had seen their mother. They struggled with the idea that they were the beneficiaries of their mother's sacrifice.

Perceptions Grounded in ICT

Children in Mexico and in the United States wondered about how the "rest" of their family lived, if those family members knew who they were, and especially if they looked alike. Back at Gemma's house in Sunset Park, Brooklyn, I was showing Yazmin (age 10), Gemma's daughter in New York, pictures of Daniela (age 15), her daughter in Mexico.

Daniela was Yartitza's half-sister, but Yazmin believed Daniela was the daughter of both her parents. When a picture of Daniela came up, Yazmin looked puzzled. The last picture she had seen of Daniela was when Daniela was fairly young. Yazmin asked: "Is this my sister?" Gemma told her, "yes, *hija* . . . you knew that." Yazmin continued, "That's not how I imagined . . . I thought she would look like me and she doesn't . . . she looks like someone else. It's weird to have a sister so far! Where is she? I always thought she was like older and married [laughter]." When I later asked Yazmin to draw a picture of her family, Yazmin's drawing did not include Daniela. Gemma asked her angrily: "Why are you not drawing your sister Daniela in the picture?" Yazmin seemed confused with Gemma's reaction as she explained: "She never posts pictures of herself on Facebook . . . she only posts pictures of bands and boys. I know she can go out and do all kinds of things because she is old, too. . . . I never see her *mamá*, how am I supposed to know what she looks like? I can't draw her if I don't know her." Yazmin's younger brother Alejandro Jr. (age 10) interrupted her, "You are so dumb, you can see her if you click on the albums . . . I saw her party for graduation, it was so much bigger than mine."

Facebook is a major tool that now, more than ever, connects people around the world. It is no different for transnational families. Because the children in the constellations are generally younger in the United States, they rarely post pictures of themselves and use a parent's Facebook account. In Mexico, youth posted revealing statuses such as, "I am really sad today because he broke up with me" or "This is the worst day of my life," and some allude to supporting illegal activities like consuming drugs and using firearms. For example, Agustín at age 16 posted pictures of himself holding fake guns and wearing masks. They post pictures and videos of bands and type portions of lyrics that sometimes are racy. Grandmothers in Mexico had no control over the content. In

New York City, children were heavily supervised, and mothers worried about their children in Mexico not being careful and unwittingly exposing themselves to danger.

The perceptions Yazmin and Alejandro Jr. had of Daniela's life were largely based on Facebook information. Yazmin complained that the pictures she saw from Daniela were about bands and boys and not of her. Yazmin knew a lot of the songs and bands that were popular in Mexico and asked her parents to buy her the albums. Ever since becoming friends with Daniela on Facebook, Yazmin started to question much of the story her mother had told her about migration and leaving Daniela in Mexico.

Yazmin wanted to know why her parents could not travel to Mexico and what was "wrong" with the life there that they had to leave. She told me, "Daniela has this free life; she is always going to places. Why are my parents not allowed to travel? What did they do wrong? Is it because they left Daniela there that the government wants to put them in jail?" Gemma expended tremendous effort to frame Mexico and life in Mexico positively for her New York children. But constant interactions, especially through Facebook, had this 11-year-old very suspicious about her parents' country of origin. Gemma also did not want to tell Yazmin and Alejandro Jr. that Daniela was not their father's daughter. She was afraid that the children would dismiss Daniela and deem her less important.

Facebook can be a source of stress and tension between families. Emilia, a mother who lived in South Bronx, New York City for more than eight years, had a Facebook account. One of her friends, also in New York City, posted a picture of Emilia, her two US-born children Alonso and Alondra, and her husband Oliver. The caption of the picture was "beautiful family." Thousands of miles away, in the small rural town of San Felipe in Vera Cruz, Esperanza, Emilia's 17-year-old daughter, saw the picture on her own Facebook account. The caption of the picture infuriated her. Esperanza wrote a comment under the picture that read, "There are more people in this family, you don't know us!" The friend responded, "I only know the family in El Norte and her babies are the most beautiful ones in the neighborhood." To which Esperanza replied, "Don't talk about what you don't know, stay out of it." Finally, Emilia intervened, writing: "Stop fighting! We are all family." After that exchange, Esperanza started sending text messages to her mother telling her to "unfriend" or "de-friend" the woman who had posted the picture.

In workshops I held in Puebla and Hidalgo with more than 80 children and youth, and in my interviews with children and youth in New York City, online social networks were often described as the source of much tension that fed into existing resentment between siblings. Henrique, age 15, was upset with his mother Karina because she did not send him a new pair of Nikes, but he saw her picture with his little sister Katarina, age 6, at an amusement park in New York City. Henrique asked, "If she doesn't have money to give me a gift, how does she have money to take Katarina to the park?" In truth, there was a street fair in Sunset Park where many things were free and it was three blocks from Karina's house. All Henrique got was an image that fed his thoughts about the divide between him and his sister and the attention and investments of his mother.

Children and youth on both sides of the border with access to Facebook and computers (41 children total) described *chisme* or gossip as a problem when communicating with the other side. When on the computer or on their phones, they were hypnotized by images and text from the other side and tried to decipher what it all meant. Joaquín, Maria Fernanda's son who lived in Mexico, asked me when I was in Mexico: "My sister Florencia dresses up her daughter with really fancy clothes . . . but I know she doesn't work and I know her boyfriend, the father of her baby, is a bum." I asked him how he knew that and he replied, "She always writes on her wall on Facebook, 'God give me patience because Marcelino is driving me crazy,' and I saw pictures of him and he is covered in tattoos." Marcelino worked at a mechanics shop and was studying to get his GED. I offered that information to Joaquín, but he already seemed to have a story in his own mind.

Children and youth became attached to the information they were able to find. For younger youth and children, Facebook was not as widely used as for the older kids. Madianou and Miller (2012), in their work *Migration and the New Media*, describe transnational communication as asymmetrical in terms of the ratio of inbound and outbound calls, and the urban/rural and class divides in Internet access. I did observe that children and youth in New York City had more consistent access to computers and phones, which allowed them to engage more often with social networking sites. In Mexico, even in the smallest, most rural areas, children and youth carried smart phones and constantly traced places where they could use a wireless Internet connection. From 2010 to 2013, I witnessed a tremendous difference in the number of cellular phones, Internet cafes in small villages in Mexico, and children and youth's knowledge of the latest technology.

Siblings Coming Together

"I want to be like my brother Agustín . . . I don't want to go to school. I want to stay at home and sleep and go out with my friends and get girls [laughter]" (Felipe, age 6). I had known both Felipe and Agustín for more than three years. At age four Felipe refused to talk about his brother Agustín; he would repeat, "My mother is only my mother, she is not his mother." When Felipe was five years old, his mother Sara sent him to Mexico for a month so he could visit his grandmother and meet his brother Agustín. By age six, Felipe had been to Mexico twice and had become his brother's biggest fan. He once said, "Agustín plays video games all day . . . it's the best. He has stuff that I don't have, like Xbox and all the new games and I decided that I don't want to go to school anymore."

Sara sent Felipe with cousins to spend one to two months in Mexico every summer. She saved all her money to pay for the ticket. This was an expensive arrangement that few of the families in the study (3 of the 20) could afford, especially when the mother herself was not authorized to travel. During Felipe's first visit he was very excited about his grandmother's house. It was a medium-sized house that sat on a very large lot. They had sheep, cows, donkeys, chickens, dogs, cats, and turkeys. Felipe played all day outside with his cousins and brother and was in bed by 6 p.m. because he was so tired. I was able to observe them together in Mexico. His second day visiting his brother, he asked Agustín if he could sleep with him in the same bed. Agustín, who was 12 at the time, used to sleep in the same bed as his grandmother. Felipe became increasingly attached to Agustín. They looked alike and both of them knew that. Agustín was proud to take Felipe around the village and show him to neighbors and other family members. Felipe asked Agustín to please come back with him to New York City. Agustín replied, "I can't leave my *mamá.*" Felipe was puzzled. "But our *mamá* is over there in the other side." Agustín stayed quiet as Felipe kept begging him to go back with him. By the end of Felipe's stay he wanted to go back to New York. He missed his mother Sara and wanted to see his friends. He had also gotten sick twice from the food and water, and Sara started to worry about him.

On the one hand, it was incredible to watch Felipe's first visit to Mexico and how he became enamored of the lifestyle his brother and grandmother had there. On the other hand, it was clear that Felipe did not want to stay in Mexico for the long run, especially without his mother. In the following years Felipe grew more independent and so did Agustín. Three years later when Felipe visited, Agustín just wanted to play video games and spend time with his girlfriend. He had dropped out of school and fought with his mother Sara on the phone every other day. She insisted that she would only send him money if he went back to school, and he responded that nothing could come out of high school. "There are no jobs here. And I want to join the army, handle guns and stuff," he told her. Felipe was fascinated by his brother's skills with the games that involved fighting and killing and started to ask Sara for an Xbox with games for him to play. Sara refused repeatedly, but Felipe kept pushing and saying, "Why does Agustín have it, then?"

Agustín also started to use Facebook strategically. He found jujitsu classes (martial arts) that he wanted to enroll in Pachuca, the state of Hidalgo's capital. The classes were expensive and he needed his mother to send him the money. He sent his mother a group message on Facebook that included me. He told his mother he had spoken with me and that I had supported him. Both Sara and I knew that the story was not true.

Felipe heard the discussions Sara had with Agustín about dropping out of school and, like other children and youth in this study, began to question his mother about why he had to stay in school if his brother in Mexico did not. Agustín also started posting Facebook pictures of him wearing masks and making symbols with his hands that suggested affiliation with a group known for criminal activity in the region. Felipe, on the other side, started to imitate Agustín. One day at their New York apartment I was talking to Sara in the kitchen and Felipe showed up with a sweater wrapped around his face and toy gun in his hand.

He looked at us and said, "Everybody down, I'm a Guadalupano!" I asked him where he had learned about the *guadalupanos*, and he took me to the computer and showed me Agustín's page. Those situations were unforeseen for mothers and caregivers. Relationships that were once mediated by mothers and caregivers were now occurring directly between siblings. What did these interactions mean to children and youth's perspectives on their future? In the long term, it's hard to say. But in the short term these interactions fed daily discussions about schooling, jobs, and the prospects of living in Mexico or in the United States.

Children in Mexico clung tightly to the notion of family and resented their exclusion from representations of the family. Kinship, which some have argued has lost its importance in modern societies, proved to be vital and something the participants of this study craved. In a legal environment that promotes and necessitates prolonged periods of separation, the emotional aspects of separation are extremely difficult for family members. The women I interviewed showed great resolve to affirm their maternal ties with children in Mexico, but the children themselves sometimes felt excluded.

Conclusion: Thoughts about the Future

Thoughts of inequality related to material goods as well as emotional support create imaginaries for children and youth on both sides. The idea of family never quite disappears even with distance and prolonged periods of separation. Children and youth take real and perceived inequalities to heart, and this complicates how they come to resent, idolize, love, and miss family members. Children and youth's thoughts and impressions about migration, separated families, and siblings on the other side influence their ideas about inequality within the family and their sense of belonging. Physical resemblance was important when children and youth discussed their siblings, grandmothers, and mothers. In addition to these emotions, children and youth on both sides imagined their siblings in different time and spaces. They started with an economic perspective of how the "rest" of the family lived and used those ideas to build characters of who they are.

Using inequality as a lens to reflect on how siblings live on the other side was a common practice among children. Siblings in New York City worried about the well-being of their siblings in Mexico and had ideas of the country as a "harder" or "tougher" place to live. At the same time, there were examples of children in New York City using the situation of their siblings in Mexico as leverage to ask for different things from their mothers. Children and youth in Mexico sometimes resented siblings in New York City, who they largely did not know but were supposed to love, and who shared the same residence as their mothers. For children and youth in Mexico, being the beneficiary as well as the bearer of the consequence—distance—built frustration and added to the confusion of how they were "supposed" to treat their siblings. Even though children and youth from the constellations said they did not want to move to the other country, in my surveys with more than 225 children and youth in Puebla, those whose migrant mothers and siblings lived away were more inclined to want to migrate than those who did not have migrant parents.

Participants in this research project held on to strong feelings of kinship across borders, though children and youth also wondered about their position and relevance within the family established on the other side. ICT was a form of mediation. The communication between separated siblings, the influence of social network, and the narratives parents present to children and youth contributed to the formation of this transnational space where ideas and kinship travel. What are the implications of these interactions for the future of these families? By the end of my fieldwork I continued to observe increasing social media interactions between siblings. There were signs that many of the narratives that mothers in New York and caregivers in Mexico used were consequently starting to be interrogated by children and youth "here and there."

Giving Birth in New York City

"Gabi, how is she going to give birth here?"

That was the question Ronald asked me not too long ago after I received a frantic call from him asking me to come to a Manhattan hospital where his wife was about to give birth. He felt that something was very wrong. "I don't understand what the doctors are doing and I think she is going to have a C-section, and she has never had one," he said. "Can you come?"

When I arrived at the hospital, a haggard-looking Ronald directed me to a security counter where I could sign in to see Brianna. But Ronald himself kept his distance from the counter and avoided eye contact with any of the security staff. When I arrived on the sixth floor, Brianna told me she was in tremendous pain. She had been admitted the night before, but still was only dilated three centimeters. "They did some tests and there is green fluid. I think it has something to do with my liver," she said.

When I asked the doctors about the green fluid, they said the baby was so stressed that there was meconium in her placenta. I asked one doctor what this could mean for Brianna and the baby, and she said the worst-case scenario was that it could be fatal. "But don't worry," she tried to reassure me, "that's not her case." The main doctor asked me if I were the translator; I said no. I requested one for Brianna, but no one ever came. In the couple of hours that I spent in her room, several different doctors came to check on her progress. With minimal explanation and introduction, they examined her; Brianna was uncomfortable, gripping the sheets as doctors examined her.

The doctors eventually decided to break Brianna's water to induce birth, but it didn't work. Two doctors entered the room and in English and Spanish, alternating, one doctor told her she would do the procedure to help accelerate the birth, since she was diabetic and diagnosed as "high risk" for her pregnancy. At the time I had no children of my own and knew little to nothing about interventions during labor and delivery. So I translated the best I could for Brianna. After the doctor told her they would break her water, he exited the room. She asked me, "do you think it will hurt?" I had no idea. When the doctor returned, she inserted a needle through Brianna's vagina to reach the amniotic sac, which surrounds and cushions the baby during pregnancy. Brianna was caught by surprise when she felt the pain, but did not say a word and just squeezed my hand tightly.

"She handles pain very well, she doesn't scream or complain," I overhead one doctor tell a resident. Brianna had not been screaming or even grunting at all, even though tears welled in her eyes. She had wanted to ask for painkillers, but was too afraid it would hurt her baby. Through it all she had tried to smile at doctors and nurses and struggled to say "thank you." Brianna, who had three daughters living in Mexico, later told me that it was the most painful birth she had been through.

Brianna told me, "I just don't want them to know me . . . I've heard stories in Arizona about women being deported from the hospital to Mexico." Both she and Ronald had done their best to remain "invisible" during this experience. They did not want to draw any attention to their presence, their statuses, and their existence. Both Brianna and Ronald were excited about the prospect of having a child born in the United States so he could travel to Mexico and meet his sisters. "If we can't go, he will be able to spend summers at home and meet his sisters, what a blessing," Ronald told me. Ronald discussed that the fact that they would now be a mixed status family living in the United States. "How weird that he won't know where he is from right away," said Brianna. When I asked her what she meant by that, she told me, "all my daughters have their roots in San Lucas, but he will never know how it is to be born there and experience what we experienced. He will be different." She also told me how with her first three pregnancies she went to the hospital and got sent home because they did not have enough beds to accommodate all the patients. She complimented the facilities in New York City and said that it looked more serious than the clinic that she was used to. However, she felt powerless in her decisions as she did not think she was fully aware or sufficiently informed of what was happening to her.

Brianna gave birth that night, via a C-section, to a healthy baby boy.

There were complications, though. In the recovery room, Brianna bled heavily for hours after the operation and her sheets were soaked red. One nurse came in and checked her blood pressure and said, "it is very low." But she didn't have time to help right away. "I just started my shift, just came from my house . . . you have to wait for the doctor," she said. Ronald opened one of the drawers in the room, found clean sheets, and changed his wife's bed himself and held her hand. He did that over and over for the next few hours.

4

Educational Aspirations and Social Trajectories of Separated Siblings

Maria Fernanda's Constellation

When I met her in 2012, Maria Fernanda had lived in Sunset Park, Brooklyn for almost 11 years. She had three daughters, one son, and two grandchildren. She immigrated to this country without permits and had not been home to Tlaxcala, Mexico for more than a decade. Maria Fernanda, like several other mothers in this study, revealed that she had been in an abusive relationship in Mexico. When Maria Fernanda left Mexico she left one son, Joaquín, who at that time was eight, with his father and took with her a daughter, Florencia, who at that time was seven. According to Maria Fernanda, Joaquín remained in Mexico because he wanted to stay with his father. In less than a couple of months Cecilia, Maria Fernanda's mother, insisted that Joaquín move in with her and the father did not oppose. After Maria Fernanda left with her daughter, her husband served her with court papers that alleged she had kidnapped Florencia and left the country. This situation, Maria Fernanda told me, prevented her from ever getting formally divorced and remarried and from going back to Mexico for her son and extended family. In addition, Maria Fernanda revealed to me that she was in financial trouble in Mexico. She gave money to a friend who told her she would invest her funds and start a lucrative business. The friend needed work desperately and did not have a house to live in. In order for Maria Fernanda to lend her the money, she went into debt with a local small loan business. The friend took off with her money and Maria Fernanda defaulted on her payments. She explained to me that she felt threatened and did not think she would have her family's support since she believed she made a bad judgment call. The decision to migrate was made quickly. She thought that her mistake could have cost the well-being of her children.

In New York City Maria Fernanda worried that her choices of where to live would determine what kind of work she could find, what kind of school her children could attend, and what kind of neighborhood her children would grow up in. In addition, her occupation in the United States coupled with her partner's salary would also determine how much money she could send to Mexico. All these pieces of the migration puzzle had to be in place, as she explained to me, "in order for all children to have a fair chance at succeeding." Centering the responsibility on her own shoulders, she told me, "Your children are the ones that pay for your errors, not you."

At the time of our interview, Maria Fernanda lived in a two-bedroom apartment in Sunset Park with her three daughters, her new partner, her granddaughter (Florencia's baby), and her daughter's boyfriend (the father of the baby). At night the living room became a third bedroom where Maria Fernanda slept with her husband Armando. Upon arriving in New York, Maria Fernanda and Florencia lived alone for almost two years until Maria Fernanda met Armando. They decided to get together, or *juntarse*. It took Maria Fernanda a bit of time to settle and find a job that paid well when she first arrived in New York City. However, as soon as she could, she started sending Joaquín money—through her mother—every month, which supported his schooling. After one year with Armando, Maria Fernanda had Mariana (8 years old in 2012) and then Rosa (7 years old in 2012).

I met Maria Fernanda when I was volunteering at a small organization based in Sunset Park that ran a cooperative for domestic workers. In this cooperative a group of almost 60 women had workshops on cardiopulmonary resuscitation, the developmental psychology of babies, children's language learning, nutrition, and health. According to Maria Fernanda, she learned through those workshops how to be a "better" mother. When I asked Maria Fernanda what it meant for her to be a better mother she explained to me:

> I was not a good mother to Florencia when she was younger. I would get hysterical and I have hit her before . . . one day I slapped her in the face. I feel terrible about it . . . I didn't know what I was doing, I regretted it. I would never do that with my younger daughters now . . . because I learned here in America, through my work at the cooperative.

The co-op in Sunset Park helped Maria Fernanda secure a job as a nanny for a young couple, both physicians, in Manhattan. She took care of baby Victoria. She worked eight to nine hours a day and was able to secure weekly payments of more than $500. At her house Maria Fernanda showed me the different charts she learned to make at the workshops she attended. One, a large, pink, thick piece of paper, featured a reward system with chores on the left, names on the top, and space for stars on the right. On her refrigerator door there was a smaller piece of paper with rules for how to behave at home and in school copied by the girls themselves: "respect the teacher," "respect mother," "do the homework," "study hard to be the best," and "love school." Both Mariana (second grade) and Rosa (third grade) were mostly meeting grade-level expectations in school; their report cards were filled with 2s and 3s (the range was 1–4, with 1 being the lowest possible grade). They both struggled in math and English; one teacher asked that the daughter "please practice writing these words at home." Maria Fernanda's other daughter, Florencia, who at the time of our interview was the seventeen-year-old mother of four-month-old Graciela, had dropped out of school when she got pregnant and was studying for her GED. Her report cards from high school were filled with 9s and 10s (on a 10-point scale), with teacher comments like "she is one of our best students" and "we are always very impressed with her passion for learning." For more than ten years Maria Fernanda continued to send remittances home to Mexico; for five years, she had regularly sent in excess of $1,000 a month to her son Joaquín and her mother. Joaquín had just finished high school (*la prepa*) and been accepted into university to study law.

For Maria Fernanda, as for most mothers interviewed, providing a better education for her children was a principal motive for migration. Maria Fernanda explained to me,

Do you know what a good mother does? A good mother teaches her children. A good mother is patient with her children and shows them that school is the best pathway. When I was in Mexico I could not give my kids the best education . . . I had to leave Mexico because my husband was not a good man. He was violent. And I lent money to the wrong people in the town and ended up owing more money than I will ever have. I needed to make money and a clean break. I was under a lot of stress, you know?

I needed to *care* [emphasis added] for my children . . . that is my role; a mother's role [is] to care. If I can't take care of them I have nothing left. With my son Joaquín I feel guilt. I left him. So I compensated that by putting him through school and now college. I send him money religiously every week . . . I pray to the Virgin and [then] send him the money. He deserves everything. With Florencia . . . ai . . . [tears start to come down her face] . . . I blamed her [referring to the hardships she faced when she first arrived in New York City]. She represented everything that was bad and I argued with her a lot. I hit her for no good reason . . . I hit her in the face once . . . I feel really bad when I think about it.

With her youngest daughters, Maria Fernanda was calm, permissive, and tender. But, perhaps because of Maria Fernanda's work schedule, Florencia spent a lot of time raising her sisters. Florencia woke them up every morning to go to school, walked them to school, went to parent-teacher meetings, helped them with homework, and fed them. She did a lot of the daily care. For example, during one of my visits, Rosa went to the bathroom. From the bathroom she screamed, "Florencia, I need you here to help me really quick." Maria Fernanda looked at me, embarrassed, and responded to Rosa, "My baby, don't you mean your *mamá*?" Rosa contested, "I said Florencia!" Maria Fernanda looked at me and said, "Caring doesn't always mean being there [next to them] physically . . . look at Joaquín and how his life turned out. He needed my care, but not me [pounding on her chest]." Maria Fernanda did not hide the fact that Joaquín's educational trajectory during these last 10 years had been the most rewarding part of her life. She thought bringing Florencia to the United States would give her daughter a better chance of succeeding in life, but in fact Florencia's academic career was put on hold when she got pregnant at age 16. Maria Fernanda told me, "*los errores no los pagas tu, pagan los niños*" (you don't pay for your own errors, your children do). She explained to me that as soon as she was able to find stability in New York City with a paying job and partner who was not abusive, she was able to get back on her feet. Like other mothers, it took Maria Fernanda some time to be able to start remitting money home and "keeping the promise" she once made to her child in Mexico. Economic and emotional stability were, in her opinion, the two most important aspects of her succeeding as a mother.

When I visited and interviewed Joaquín in Mexico, he explained to me,

> In the beginning I did not understand why my mother had left me, but then I understood that she actually respected my wishes when I told her I did not want to go to the U.S. with her, I wanted to stay with my father. And then, she never abandoned me. My grandmother raised me and now I work at my uncle's pharmacy and soon I will start college. Look at everything she has given me. I wish I could have seen that when I was younger.

Joaquín, who was 18 at the time, already had a child and a partner. He worked to support this new family, but he never stopped studying because of his mother's constant pressure and the financial conditions she had imposed. Joaquín was raised by his maternal grandparents, but mostly by his grandmother. Maria Fernanda's mother, Cecilia, supported her daughter's departure as she knew about the relationship Maria Fernanda had with her ex-husband. Maria Fernanda's departure was sudden and Cecilia was quick to take Joaquín in. Cecilia was committed to keeping Maria Fernanda's power over her child alive; as she explained to me, "When you see a mother leaving a child you know she is in pain . . . it's not normal. Some people say, 'oh it's normal' and I say to them 'it's not!'" She continued, "I decided to help my daughter and help my grandson . . . but some people don't take their own family in." Cecilia joked, "I was probably more prepared to raise a boy than she was." All of Maria Fernanda's siblings in Tlaxcala had careers: accountant, pharmacist, and teacher. Both Maria Fernanda and Cecilia agreed that the family surrounding Joaquín heavily influenced him into pursuing a career.

Florencia, on the other hand, felt she had limited options for her future. She described to me, "I am truly the middle child . . . I'm not there like Joaquín, or here like Rosa and Mariana." Florencia wanted to take advantage of the 2012 law passed by the Obama administration that allowed youth who had arrived in the United States at a young age to obtain temporary legal status. One of the conditions of this law was for the minor to be enrolled in school, and she was not. Her teachers at school wanted to help her, as they described her as a very engaged and dedicated student who just got "unlucky." Florencia considered returning to Mexico, but she was nervous about not being very fluent in Spanish, not knowing the country, and not having friends. The situation was complicated by the fact that she had a daughter and a Puerto Rican partner, Marco, who was a US citizen. They considered getting married and applying for her permanent residency. However, they worried that if the government did not grant the status adjustment she could be deported. Undocumented youth living in the United States face difficult decisions with serious consequences that shape their aspirations.

Rosa and Mariana, though young, were aware of their parents' efforts to bring in money, save, and distribute their earnings across members of the family. Maria Fernanda always made sure Rosa and Mariana spoke to Joaquín over Skype, and she used him as an example that her younger daughters should follow. "I want to be like Joaquín and go to college," Mariana told me. "Yes, me too! But I never want to leave Florencia and I don't want her to go to Mexico," Rosa said. The sisters showed me a heavy porcelain pig on the top shelf in their bedroom. They climbed the walls to grab it. When I shook it, I heard the sound of coins. Mariana told me, "this is for us to go to college . . . our parents put some money in there every week." Rosa continued, "Yes, my mom says that it is the only way to guarantee she will not spend the money or send it to Mexico." Rosa and Mariana enjoyed school and during the summer they participated in summer camps in the neighborhood. They both also had access to after-school programs and had many friends in the neighborhood. They loved summer because it meant block parties, *comidas*, and outings with neighborhood friends. Their school was 15 minutes away from their house. Both of their teachers spoke Spanish and English. One teacher, Cassie, explained to me, "if you want to teach in this neighborhood you have to be familiar with Mexican culture and Spanish . . . there are so many Puerto Ricans and Mexicans here that we have figured out ways to incorporate some of their traditions in our activities." Her openness to the students' language and culture stood in stark contrast to teachers at the school I had observed in the South Bronx.

One may think, after reading Maria Fernanda's story, that there are too many factors that may or may not contribute to the different trajectories of separated siblings: gender of children, level of income, neighborhood where they lived, relationship with caregivers, and their mother's and their own legal status. Maria Fernanda placed the burden of care on her shoulders, as she felt responsible for the trajectories of each of her children. Maria Fernanda's constellation faced adversities in terms of legality, but they were also positioned well above the average income of the constellations that participated in this study. Having substantial income to spare allowed Maria Fernanda to support Joaquín, but that only happened because her partner also earned money and allowed her to save some of her earnings. Joaquín went on to university in part because he had his mother's constant motivation to finish his degree. Money was also attached to his achievement. Legality for Florencia worked against her as she pursued a high school diploma, but she also became pregnant and dropped out before she could finish. Rosa and Mariana, who were American citizens and were fortunate to be born when their parents had more income and were more stable, did not spend much time with Maria Fernanda, as she worked long hours. The point here is that a multitude of factors influence children and youth's life experiences, especially education experiences. I argue, however, that the stability of mothers, which I define below, allows mothers to try to provide and care for all of their children, wherever they are.

* * *

Media portrayals demonstrate implicit assumptions about children who stay behind when parents migrate. These portrayals refer to children of migrants who are in the home country as "orphans" or "abandoned" children. Generally, such portrayals assume that children who stay behind are vulnerable and disadvantaged by the mother's absence. When they do admit that migration might be in some way positive, media portrayals generally focus solely on how remittances alleviate the strain on household budgets. For example, one UNICEF publication, *The Impact of International Migration: Children Left Behind in Selected Countries of Latin America and the Caribbean* (2011), maps out the "negative" effects on children: psychological, economic, education, safety, and health. Obviously, there are plenty of negative consequences for children and youth when a primary caregiver leaves to migrate. However, there are unforeseen experiences, related to schooling for example, that such reports rarely include. In order to make sense of patterns related to more complex and nuanced observations, one may have to spend more time with children and youth.

The influence of parental migration and remittances on the educational attainment of children in migrants' countries of origin and host countries remains an important and open debate. Research on the education of children of immigrants in the United States is more established; various studies address the school performance of first- and second-generation students (e.g., Suárez-Orozco et al., 2008), patterns of acculturation (e.g., Portes & Rumbaut, 1996, 2001; Portes et al., 2011), and language acquisition and academic achievement (e.g., Bartlett & Garcia, 2011). Apart from US-based research, which Thomson and Crul (2007) have described thus: "in some ways, this reflects the growing disparity between, on the one hand, immigrant youth who are performing well, and, on the other, the relatively high numbers dropping out of school and failing to find secure employment" (p. 1032), the authors also point to the experiences of immigrants in Europe. They critique the assimilationist model by stating that it homogenizes ethnic groups and fails to recognize how groups of migrants may be different even within the same nationality. They contend, "It also fails to bring to light clear ethnic and religious differences within migrant communities in Europe, like Syrian Christians or Kurds" (1034). Significant questions remain about the experience of schooling and education of children in their home countries.

I compare how Mexican maternal migration has influenced the education experiences of the children left behind in Mexico and their siblings living in the United States. I use *separated siblings* as a way to refer to siblings who are not in the same home and country and do not share the same residence. I argue that these micro-contexts where siblings live and how they live in Mexico and in New York City present us with a somewhat surprising picture of the different education experiences of separated siblings. It is inaccurate to assume that children left behind are automatically at a disadvantage. My analysis reveals that the contrary is possible. I present the story of Maria Fernanda and her children to illustrate concerns about the schooling of separated siblings. I draw from all other constellations involved in this study to highlight the major findings regarding separated siblings.

While we often assume that the quality of education and social opportunities is better in the United States, data in this research suggest this is not always the case. Based on my research on separated siblings and schooling, I discovered two major patterns: (1) the emotional and financial stability of mothers in New York City allowed for more emotional and financial support of the children in Mexico, but not necessarily for the children in the United States; and (2) schooling experiences for children and youth in New York City varied a great deal depending on residential location. As with chapter 3, I consider children and youth primary sources as I attempt to provide another split-screen description of how separated siblings fare in the two countries. Ultimately, I argue that within these constellations, children of immigrant parents in the United States are not always "better off"; this study exemplifies the importance of looking comparatively at the educational experiences of children from transnational families in different locations.

Children of Immigrants in the United States

Mexico, like many other countries in the world, is home to a number of children with immigrant parents. In the United States an estimated 15 million immigrants entered the country during the 1990s (Capps & Fortuny, 2006). The same report indicates that immigrants from all countries comprise more than 12 percent of the US population, and their children, more than 20 percent. One in every five children of immigrants is foreign born, thus immigrant families in the United States are characteristically mixed-status, with children and parents who are citizens and non-citizens. As different studies have shown (see Suárez-Orozco & Suárez-Orozco, 2001), mixed-status families affect the well-being of children. Socioeconomically speaking, children of immigrants live in lower income families than US-born children (Capps & Fortuny, 2006). Thomson and Crul (2007), Crul and Schneider (2009), and Barban and White (2011) all agree that in Europe, children of immigrants do experience a better trajectory overall in terms of education and occupation than their parents.

The schooling experiences of children and youth attending schools in the South Bronx, as I will show below, are influenced by waning support for bilingualism and bilingual education as well as by an economic context in which immigrants continue to be relegated to low-paying work. It is important to consider the complex interrelationships among school, community, history, and economy, including the ways in which social class and previous educational experiences set up students to pursue certain pathways through school. In addition, it is essential to engage a transnational perspective, as the siblings and mothers often do.

According to Zong and Batalova (2014), Mexican immigrants accounted for 28 percent of the country's 41.3 million foreign-born. The Mexican population in the United States more than tripled since the 1980s, and even though there has been some decline following the 2008 crisis, large-scale immigration shapes how families organize across borders. Academically, children of Mexican immigrants have performed below other groups of children in New York City. In 2011, writer Kirk Semple published a piece in the *New York Times* entitled "In New York, Mexicans Lag in Education" that referred to census data indicating that more than 40 percent of all Mexicans between ages 16 and 19 in the city have dropped out of school. No other major immigrant group has a dropout rate higher than 20 percent, and the overall rate for the city is below 9 percent. Among Mexican immigrants aged 19 to 23 without a college degree, only 6 percent are enrolled in tertiary education. Laird Bergad, director of CUNY's Center for Latin American and Caribbean Studies, disputed the Community Service Society's report on dropout rates in the Mexican community, arguing that the way they calculated the dropout rate was erroneous because they included non–high school age adults in their findings. Also, many scholars have noted that migration is an "emancipatory event," so, if migrants finish *secundaria*[1] and migrate to the United States to work instead of continuing study before the age of 18, it is not the same as a young person who drops out of compulsory schooling in the United States before the age of 18.

Research has shown that 36 percent of first-generation and 11 percent of second-generation Mexican Americans aged 16–24 do not have a diploma (or its equivalent) (Brick et al., 2011: 9). College enrollment rates of Mexican Latinos are lower than their peers: among children of Mexican migrants, 33 percent had completed only high school in 2010 (ibid.). The children of Mexican immigrants face significant educational challenges: 30 percent of Hispanic public school students report speaking only English at home, and 20 percent of second-generation students report speaking English with difficulty (Fry & Gonzalez, 2008: 11). Further, 28 percent of Hispanic students live in poverty, compared with 16 percent of non-Hispanic students (p. 13). Indeed, the 2000 Census showed that more than 40 percent of foreign-born Mexican immigrants living in New York City had less than a twelfth grade education, with no diploma. Given the correlation of socioeconomic status, parents' education level, and English language ability with academic success, these indicators are not encouraging.

The situation becomes even more challenging for mixed-status families. Suárez-Orozco and Suárez-Orozco (2001) showed how special issues arise in families that have a mix of documented and undocumented children. In some instances, the undocumented child may become the family's scapegoat, while the documented child may occupy the role of "the golden child" (p. 35). Children in mixed-status families may experience tension and resentment, as well as guilt and shame. The authors state, "One of the most demoralizing aspects of undocumented status is its effect on the educational aspirations of immigrant children" (p. 34). Parents' attitudes toward education are expressed to their children. The same authors found that attending school and getting a degree are high on the priority list of Latinos (Mexicans included). In my study, three families within the transnational care constellations studied had mixed-status siblings living in the same home. My observations were similar to the authors' findings on the motivation immigrant children had about gaining an education. In one constellation where the family was mixed-status, the undocumented daughter in New York City suffered with the reality that she may not be allowed to go to college. That particular situation caused Maria Fernanda, her mother, to reflect on how much she would invest in her daughter's education given that she herself could only get as far as high school.

Children of Immigrants in Mexico

There is reason to suspect that maternal migration has mixed effects for the education of the children left behind. Cohen (2004) has discussed a "culture" of migration where the act of migrating is associated with the desire for upward mobility. But does this upward mobility take place? If yes, does it travel back to Mexico? I found that, financially, an upward mobility sometimes does take place. But in order to travel back to Mexico there is a need for emotional stability in the United States. Even though children and young people spoke about not being privy to explanations for their parents' migration, this fact did not always negatively influence their education experiences.

The correlation between migration and remittances on families and children in the host country has been widely studied. Different conclusions emerge from these studies. Parental migration may produce economic benefits but also emotional costs. Asis and Ruiz-Marave (2013) argue that, based on their study with young children in the Philippines, "economically better off families are in a better position to enhance the children's academic performance. Should children need tutoring, for example, this will not pose a problem for families with more economic resources" (p. 14).

In terms of development in an economic sense, remittances are known to benefit families who have been left behind economically (Asis, 2006). However, what happens with the money and how it is spent leaves doubt about the real efficacy of remittances. Cortés (2007) discusses how remittances can create dependence on the receiver side and even contribute to children's disinterest in school. Kandel and Kao (2001) found that children of migrant parents, particularly boys, may have a greater propensity to drop out of school than children of non-migrants. In her research, Dreby (2007) found that more than 40 percent of children interviewed in Mexico who had immigrant parents dropped out of school in the middle of their studies. However, Dreby and Stutz (2012) argue that children's scholastic success depends on their experiences after a parent migrates and not on their migrant parents' hopes and desires.

In the field of economics, scholars have assessed the causal impacts of remittances on children's education. In Mexico, remittances totaled US$21.7 billion in 2010 according to the National Bank of Mexico, making remittances the second largest source of foreign trade after tourism. How much remittances help migrant families in Mexico is a matter of debate. As research has shown (Sawyer, 2010), remittances allow families to meet expenses they otherwise might not be able to afford. Jensen and Sawyer (2012) point out, though, that remittances may actually exacerbate inequalities within families and come at the high cost of separation. Regarding these potential inequalities in the host society, Robert C. Smith (2005) uses the term "remittance bourgeoisie" to describe those who live more comfortably because of the flow of dollars. The flip side is the existence of a "transnational underclass" that receives no remittances. This new reality in the host society causes this underclass to participate in a "dollarized" society (Smith, 2005), having negative consequences for the population of towns with intense out-migration.

Economic remittances represent only part of the reality of separated families. For many of the families in this study, income did increase when they received remittances. However, constant interruptions related to changes of jobs, birth and death of family members, and separation heavily impacted the socioeconomic status of these families. Even though there have been numerous studies on the impacts of remittances, none have uncovered how constant interruptions of financial support affect children here and there.

Emotional consequences of maternal migration are another core concern. Children and youth in this research described feeling anxious and sad during periods of time since their parent/s departed. The psychological literature on the effects of migration has looked at "levels of acceptance" or tolerance of children depending on their cognitive development (Carandang and Sison, 2007). Battistella and Conaco's (1996) findings show that children of migrant parents experience higher anxiety and loneliness. Thus, children and youth do remain attached to images of their parents on the other side. According to Parreñas (2005a), "the strength of family relationship, particularly the children's closeness to their parents, is reflected in the children's choice of their parents as role models" (p. 11). The emotional attachment Parreñas refers to is exemplified by the fact that children want to follow their parents' footsteps (60 percent of the children would like to work abroad). Añonuevo and Añonuevo (2002) in their study of female workers abroad have pointed toward a reality in terms of children's aspirations to work like their parents. They conclude that children and youth feel they could earn a higher salary abroad without considering going to school.

As stated in the opening paragraphs of this chapter, the reality is that children and youth's experiences with education and social opportunities are more nuanced and deserve a critical look. Building on data from previous chapters, this study uses the transnational care constellation to show how emotional and financial stability coupled with place of residence largely contributed to the type of experience separated siblings had in Mexico and in the United States. The literature presented above is extensive in its attempts to document the lives of children who have migrant parents. More often than not, these distinguish between children on each side of the border in attempts to quantify the impacts or effects of migration, remittance, and parents' level of education on the educational attainment of children and youth. Remittances on their own don't always result in higher academic performance in Mexico, and studies looking at paths of upward or downward assimilation for the sons and daughters of migrants neglect myriad factors that influence and shape the experiences of children and youth in New York City. This research is based on the idea that ideologies of care and motherhood, schools, teachers and principals, social networks, and relationships hold these constellations together as their everyday interactions take place.

The story of Maria and her children—Joaquín, Florencia, Mariana, Rosa, and Cecilia—makes clear the fact that the social and education trajectories of the children both in Mexico and in the United States depended on both the support of their mothers and their own decisions. It is important to keep in mind that the separated siblings had obvious differences in age. In New York City, the US-born children's ages varied from newborn to 12 years old; undocumented youth's ages were between 15 and 18; and children in Mexico were aged between 9 and 18 years.

Mothers in New York City

After two years of participant observation and interviews, I found that Mexican migrant women in New York City were able to provide for children in Mexico and in the United States only if they were able to experience stability in their homes. As I went back and forth looking at women's income numbers, occupation, and number of years living in New York City, stability was always associated with all of these factors. Thus, stability derived from three key factors: living in a secure, stable home with some physical space that was not crammed with different extended family; having stable occupations and financial stability that allowed them to save money and keep homes in the United States and in Mexico afloat; and finally, having a supportive, nonviolent partner who contributed financially or with childcare. The combination of these factors provided mothers with resources to be financially and emotionally present in the lives of all children here and there.

Housing and Sharing Space

The four transnational constellations in the South Bronx had an imminent fear of housing displacement. Violeta moved twice because of issues in the building such as bed bugs, drug trafficking, and poor construction. The structure of the building where she lived had been compromised by leaks and had multiple rat infestation incidents. Emilia lived with her family of four in a two-bedroom apartment that she shared with six other people. Her family stayed in one of the bedrooms while the other six people lived in the living room and second bedroom. Sharing the rent was paramount to making ends meet. The people who lived in the apartment generated stress and were a source of constant gossip. Her son Alonso had nightmares at night and sometimes urinated in the bed. In their living room two men alternated sleeping in a makeshift tent and screamed when Emilia made noises in the middle of the night or early in the morning. This dynamic resulted in Alonso's bed being wet for longer periods of time, and the bedroom's smell bothered Emilia, her husband Alonso, and their one-year-old daughter Alondra. Aruna, also a South Bronx resident, changed apartments twice because they lost their government rent subsidy and her family was evicted with only three hours' notice. These living arrangements left women and their families in a constant state of fear of being evicted or robbed by outsiders or by the very people with whom they shared their homes.

Micaela, a mother in Sunset Park, Brooklyn, lived in an apartment with her seven-year-old son Dino and her husband Orlando. It was a two-bedroom apartment above a grocery store. Dino had been diagnosed with autism and Micaela was very active in getting him the help he needed. Through the New York City Department of Education she was able to find a tutor who came after school to help Dino with his homework. Dino was happy when Kristin, his tutor, came to work with him. They worked in his bedroom, which had a desk and a laptop. Dino told me one day after Kristin left, "I like that I have my bedroom to do my work and Kristin says that it's very good I have my space, right mamá? Not like my cousins." I followed up with a question about how his cousins lived and Dino replied, "One on top of the other." Micaela smiled at me and told me it was not always like that, they had lived in the South Bronx before with six other people, and she had especially struggled with the lack of tranquility for Dino to sleep. She told me, "When you have a son like Dino, with autism, the teachers told us it's better to have a home that is calm and spacious so the child doesn't lose control, you know?" These families and women valued space and children struggled when they had to live with more people.

Both Maria Fernanda and Gemma had partners who held steady jobs that paid well. Both households earned more than $3,000 a month. Paying rent consumed a third of their joint income. Maria Fernanda was a nanny and Gemma cared for the elderly. When they had to work while children were out of school they could rely on neighbors and friends to look after their own children. These mothers' expectations for the education future of their children were extremely high. Both families enrolled their children in after-school programs and summer camps. They found tutors for their children that the city subsidized and took advantage of any other programs available. In addition, Sunset Park had a small but organized public library where Gemma and Maria Fernanda took their children constantly. Gemma's Yazmin (age 11) and Alejandro Jr. (age 10), and Maria Fernanda's Mariana (age 8) and Rosa (age 6) always had books in their homes and constantly discussed with me what they had learned by reading. Maria Fernanda's oldest daughter, Florencia, also described having had an inclusive positive experience with peers and teachers while she was in school. Teachers spoke Spanish and were in tune with many of the Mexican traditions. Teachers in one school in Sunset Park organized a celebration for *Dia de los Muertos* (Day of the Dead) where parents were welcome to come in and tell stories about how the party is celebrated in their hometowns in Mexico. They allowed children to write holiday or festive cards in whatever language they preferred and encouraged the children to share new words in their own languages.

The positive outlook and positive experiences within the neighborhood's schools did not guarantee high academic achievement. All of the children mentioned performed with average grades, except for Alejandro Jr., who had to repeat third grade and performed below average. They all struggled to do homework as they faced language barriers with their parents. Maria Fernanda had help from Florencia, who spoke English better than Spanish and explained instructions to her little sisters. Gemma depended entirely on the tutors or on me when I was doing home observations. Children in both of these households would speak in English with me, but as soon as their mothers entered the room they switched to Spanish. As Yazmin (11) told me, "I want her to understand me . . . I need to include her . . . I feel bad if she doesn't, because she feels bad." Both Gemma and Maria Fernanda asked for help from neighbors and friends who could speak English and also used the Center for Family Services as a source of help and assistance.

In comparison with the transnational constellations that lived in Sunset Park, Brooklyn or Jackson Heights, Queens, the income of families in the South Bronx was significantly lower. Latinos represent half of the population in both the South Bronx and Sunset Park, but Sunset Park had a larger Mexican population, with many Mexicans from Puebla. Though the median rent in Sunset Park was $1,035 compared to $831 in the South Bronx, the homes of the participants were more spacious in Sunset Park and less crowded. The number of reported crimes in Sunset Park was 1,206 in 2013 compared to 1,760 in the South Bronx (NYPD Crime Statistics, 2012) and the median household income in Sunset Park was $41,912 compared to $20,867 in the South Bronx (WNYC Median Income NYC Neighborhoods, 2010–2012).[2] All families in this research study that lived in Sunset Park did not share their apartments with extended family or friends, as was the case in the South Bronx. Children in Sunset Park experienced more quiet time when they did their homework at home.

Occupation and Financial Stability of Mothers

Caregivers and children in Mexico experienced the difference when women had more stability in terms of housing and occupation. Caregivers described the ebbs and flows of remittances as worrisome for the well-being of their daughters and grandchildren, which corresponded directly to difficult moments described above. When mothers in New York City enjoyed financial stability through constant and consistent income, their top investment was to hire tutors and psychologists to help their children in Mexico and in the United States. However, when faced with decisions between whom to "help" first, mothers struggled with their priorities. Maria Fernanda was the only participant who was always able to "keep the promise" to help her son, Joaquín. Other women in this study went back and forth, first prioritizing the children in Mexico and sending any extra money they received to their children there, then switching attention and investment to children in New York City. Their rationale was that in New York City, if you had absolutely no money, your children were still US citizens and the government would assist you with food stamps, child support, and public schools. In Mexico, on the other hand, women worked on the assumption that their families could not count on the government for assistance, and guaranteeing school supplies and money for school fees was a requirement for children in Mexico to have a shot at obtaining an education. This idea was enhanced by the guilt many mothers felt. However, this strategy was in some ways perverse. In Mexico, even when mothers were not able to send money, most of the families were able to eat. Most of them raised chickens, turkeys, and donkeys, and knew enough people in their community they could turn to if necessary so that the children would not go hungry. Caregivers would accumulate debt if they needed to in order to acquire school material and uniforms. In New York City, the lack of financial resources affected the living arrangements of children, which in some cases prevented them from sleeping, feeling safe, doing homework at home, or having a place to study. Children and youth in the United States absorbed much of the anxiety mothers had.

Every dollar counted toward the children. This point was driven home to me by my experiences with Violeta's family, as described in my field notes:

We were walking from Violeta's house to school to pick up the children. Tatiana, Violeta's mother, had called Violeta to say, "If you don't send money your boy can't go to school." Violeta entered a lottery store and used $10 to buy lottery tickets. She held the tickets in her hands and prayed. After a few minutes she started scratching each ticket. As she scratched each ticket she asked for the Virgin of Guadalupe to help her. Finally one ticket seemed promising.

Violeta won $120. I was in disbelief. She turned to me and said, "Now I can feed the kids and send $20 to Andrés so he can buy his books and enroll in school." Violeta owed money to different "loan sharks" and she had to cover for her sisters who were part of the loan group but were not paying back the loans.

The fact that Violeta took a chance on a lottery ticket meant that she was pursuing financial reward in every way that she could. Just like that, Andrés received money to buy books and pay enrollment fees. It was astounding to me how public schools requested so much paperwork and extra fees from children and youth for things such as new pictures, renewed documents, fees for books and uniforms, donations for class-room materials, after-school programs, etc. Even though Andrés would have been able to go to school without the $20, he would not have newer books or uniforms that fit, or been able to go on field trips. Violeta could not help but compare this reality with that of her children in New York City, who had all of those things and opportunities, which was the con-text for her anxiety about remitting money for Andrés's school expenses.

Relationship with Partners

The second component of stability for mothers was a positive relation-ship with their partners in New York City. Financial and emotional support were interrupted or fragmented every time women were in a relationship that was abusive or negative in some way. Maria Fernan-da's partner, Armando, was the father of Mariana and Rosa. Armando described himself as a "functioning alcoholic." He worked long hours at a factory and needed to drink a few beers in order to fall asleep. That was the case of at least five other families in my study. In the bedrooms, fam-ily size bottles of beer were kept on shelves. The men in these families described feelings of anxiety regarding work and paying bills and thus counted on the help of alcohol to relax. In the case of Maria Fernanda and Armando, he was not violent or abusive. Rather, Armando was mellow and caring. He never opposed Maria Fernanda's goal of send-ing money to Joaquín and from the beginning treated Florencia like his own daughter. He had two other daughters from a previous marriage who lived in New Jersey. Maria Fernanda also got along with them and the half-siblings were always happy when their half-sisters would come from New Jersey for sleepovers. Even though Maria Fernanda seemed to be in a happy union and have stability, that had not always been the case. As I mentioned previously, Maria Fernanda had tough years when she first arrived in New York City and her relationship with Florencia suffered from the anxieties that came with unstable work, housing, and relationships. It is important to mention that the narratives were predominantly coming from the women about their husbands, as their work schedules precluded my ability to spend any extended time with them.

Camila, a mother in Brooklyn, was married to Ezequiel, a man she met after she migrated to New York City to be with her first husband. In her first two years in New York City, Camila stayed with her first husband, Fred (the father of three daughters she had left in Mexico), who had been living with another woman already and she was pregnant. Camila lived with them in the same house and experienced high levels of depression and anxiety. Even though Fred was the father of her three daughters in Mexico, he did not send any money to the children. At the same time, it was hard for Camila to save money and send any money back home. The living arrangement in which Camila had to share her husband with a pregnant woman was incredibly tough on her and, according to Camila, part of the reason she could not keep a job for long. Two other mothers in this research experienced similar situations. Camila described those two years as "lost" for her girls in Mexico. She worried that she could not support them and that lack of support would impact the rest of their educational lives. Her older daughter did stop going to school for a year in order to help her grandmother-caregiver who sold chicken at the main plaza of the town. Ana, her daughter, eventually went back to school, but dropped out when she became pregnant at sixteen. Ezequiel, Camila's second husband, supported her commitment of sending money to her daughters, but his priority was making sure their three children in New York City had everything they needed.

Ezequiel was from Guatemala. He worked 18–20 hours a day from the moment he arrived in New York City 12 years prior. His boss, an older Jewish man in the neighborhood who owned multiple stores, always encouraged Ezequiel to open his own bodega. Ezequiel did just that with the money he had saved and that's where Camila worked before and during her pregnancies. After she had all three children Ezequiel opened another bodega closer to their home, where Camila assumed the manager position and was able to work flexible hours in order to be with her children. According to Camila and her daughters, as soon as Camila got together with Ezequiel, they thought their mother was "breathing better," that she was more relaxed and confident about working and saving money. As Ana described, "She felt balanced."

Eleven of the 20 mothers who were part of the core transnational constellations had been married at least twice in their lives. Seventeen of them reported suffering some kind of verbal or physical abuse from their first partners, and four of the 20 reported suffering sporadic abuse from their current partners. The women who had non-abusive relationships with their husbands tended to save more and remit more money to their children in Mexico. Seven women out of the 20 did not have partners. They worked longer hours and were able to send less money to Mexico. The women who did not have partners had to share their apartments with more people on average in order to make ends meet. The four women who had only married once and had all their children with the same partner had fewer discussions about the importance of sending money to Mexico and were able to be more consistent. It is important to mention that the amount of money varied from US$50 per month to more than US$1,500 per month. The families in Mexico were more concerned with the consistency of remitting money than with the amount. Very quickly, caregivers in Mexico started to count on the money that came in every month; interruptions thus represented major changes in household spending in Mexico.

Even though all mothers in this study aimed to provide all their children with emotional and financial support, if they themselves did not experience stability at home, caregivers in Mexico would be the first to feel the difference. However, in interviews with them, all caregivers but one told me they did not share with the children the fact that their mothers would stop sending resources from time to time. Instead, children and youth were constantly told that they had to do well in school in order to receive gifts or money. Even though grandmothers did their best not to pass along the difficulties mothers would experience in New York City, as they got older youth started to inquire about financial support and emotional presence in the form of phone calls and gifts. They wanted to know if their siblings in New York City were receiving more attention and care than they were.

Caregivers in Mexico, with the exception of Aruna's mother, tried to hide the fact that there were issues with remittances on occasion. Thus, even when there was financial instability for mothers in New York, caregivers were able to remedy the situation by selling animals or requesting family loans in the small Mexican pueblos.

That created tensions for caregivers in Mexico, but did not necessarily affect the material resources available for them in the house. Nonetheless, children and youth in Mexico felt a lack of emotional support and attention from their mothers in New York City. Families in Mexico owned their homes and had a network of family support.

Almost all the families in Mexico were able to invest some of the money received into small stores and animals that guaranteed children's livelihoods for a period of time. The consequences of mothers' stability (or instability) were more evident in availability of school-related items—field trips, additional books, and school supplies. The activities and materials were sometimes restricted because of lack of remittances, so if mothers in New York City were laid off from their jobs or separated from their husbands, children in Mexico felt the lack of financial support almost immediately. There was not much room for savings and no families in this study had bank accounts.

Schooling Experiences

On both sides of the border the external environment where children were being raised either aided in or added stress to finding work and attending and/or staying in school. I argue that there was more variation in the quality of the education children and youth experienced in New York City than in the towns researched in Mexico. In this section I compare the schooling experiences of separated siblings in Mexico and in New York City and their expectations with regard to social opportunities where they lived.

Schooling in Mexico

According to a 2012 OECD report, Mexico has achieved one of the highest enrollment rates of four-year-old children among OECD countries since making pre-primary education compulsory. The country still faces challenges such as high student-teacher ratios in early education. In the last decade the country watched its graduation rates at the upper secondary level increase by 14 percent. Still, less than half of all students are expected to graduate. Out of the 64 children I observed and interviewed in Mexico, 11 dropped out in high school. This number is high; there were only 19 high school age youth in the sample.

All the children and youth in Mexico who participated in this study lived in houses where their own mothers had grown up. These houses, in most cases, had been refurbished—a floor was added, rooms were built, bathrooms were installed inside the house. The outside of these homes remained the same—large backyards with animals. The towns where I conducted research in Mexico ranged from rural to urban. There was variation in the landscape, labor conditions, politics, and economics within each of the states. However, the point here is to address how children and youth interacted with the surroundings of their hometowns as well their schools and how those interactions, coupled with their relationships with caregivers and migrant mothers, impacted their opportunities and experiences. In the places I worked, finishing eighth grade was the goal of children, youth, and caregivers. "If he continues after that, what a blessing!" Clarisa, a grandmother caregiver, told me. In these small towns, finding a job or migrating to the United States sometimes seemed like a better investment of time than going to school.

Children and youth in Mexico missed classes for reasons such as helping grandparents at home with the animals, going to visit family far away, or having visitors [like me] in the house. Sometimes they just did not want to go to school. Caregivers were lenient and did not enforce school attendance like mothers in New York City. There was also not much accountability in terms of grading homework, providing feedback, and involving parents in curriculum discussion. In the eight constellations I spent the most time with in Mexico, I was able to observe children in school and at home. Their textbooks often contained incomplete answers for homework and some of the teachers did not check the books to see if the tasks were done. During my three years of research I never heard participants describe meeting with guidance counselors, attending career fairs, or receiving information about ways to get financial support to attend university. There was interest from the families, but it was unclear if schools provided space or information about higher education or work opportunities.

Schoolteachers interviewed in different schools in Mexico reported that the academic performance of children dropped steeply in three situations that stem from migration issues: (1) when there is a rupture and a parent migrates; (2) when children in Mexico hear about parents who are in the United States getting a divorce or separating and starting new families; and (3) when one parent returns and the children have to adapt to new realities. However, four teachers and the principal at one school in the state of Morelos observed a difference in children's academic performance when the mother was the one who migrated, especially among children who were originally raised by a single mother. Maria Fernanda, the principal of one school, told me: "I don't know how many children who have migrant mothers drop out, but what I do know is that the ones who have their mothers as migrants talk more about trying to cross [migrate to the United States]." Schoolteachers reported that children and especially boys between the ages of 11 and 14 who had recently been separated from their mothers could have two very distinct reactions: (1) "shut down" and not speak to anyone in class; or (2) "rebel," that is, start fights, behave rudely, and skip classes.

Teachers also reported that children with one or both migrant parents often exhibited classroom behavior that was "spacey" or "not engaged." Teachers did not differentiate behavior among boys and girls, but they did note a difference in the impact of paternal and maternal migration. One middle school teacher described a class, "when we asked about the occupation of their fathers, children [with a migrant father] raised their hands and said, 'my dad is in El Norte,' but when I asked about mothers' occupation, no one from those who had migrant mothers wanted to talk about it." When I asked this teacher what he thought was the reason the children were not talking about the occupation of their mothers, he continued, "I think there is something to do with feeling abandoned . . . see, in this town it is normal and it has been normal for fathers to leave to el Norte, not for mothers, do you understand?" This insight was reinforced during a focus group I conducted with children who had recently experienced maternal separation. The majority of the children were quick to talk about their father's occupation in the United States. Some were proud to tell stories of their fathers riding bikes in streets of some big city in the United States doing delivery services. However, the tone and excitement changed when children talked about their migrant mothers. I asked them why it was not as exciting to talk about their mother's occupation. Seven-year-old Lila told me, "The mamás are the ones who feed us, take care of us, hug us . . . I didn't want her to go."

Teachers reported that maternal migration instigates migration aspirations among children. Ernestina, a teacher with 22 years of experience, seemed worried about children's futures: "The problem is, children with fathers living in the United States already think about moving there . . . but then when the mamá leaves, *por Dios*, their desire to go be with their mothers is even stronger!" Franco, a physical education teacher, also shared his thoughts: "It's a combination, there is not much to aspire to be in this town and then there are all the stories about the North and some kids have almost all of their family members living there! Can you blame them [for wanting to migrate]?" These quotes suggest that maternal migration provokes migration aspirations among children, with potential consequences for children's investment in schooling; this possibility deserves further research.

The children in Mexico also had to negotiate complex relationships with their caregivers. Dreby (2007) showed that migrant parents did not always perceive the caregivers in Mexico to be active or invested in the academic performance of children. Even though I have found parents' perspective in New York City to corroborate Dreby's findings, my research suggested that each relationship had its own dynamic. Some grandmothers required children to attend school, reminding them of their mother's sacrifice; however, working grandmothers had little time to support the children academically and non-working grandmothers often lacked the cultural and social capital to feel comfortable doing it. According to one teacher, "We don't know what to do, because sometimes you see that they [the children] are putting effort into learning, but when they go home they have no support, especially if the grandparents run a farm or have a job where they are all day."

Indeed, in my study, most of the caregivers had full- or part-time jobs, which limited their ability to be home with the children. Another teacher complained, "Not only do they not do their homework, but they come to school wearing filthy uniforms, their nails are dirty, their feet are dirty . . . that's when you see the impact of the mother's absence (*como hace falta la mamá*)!" It is interesting that the teacher blamed the absence of mothers rather than the lack of funds for multiple shirts, dirt floors in the homes, or the dirt road leading to the school.

Tensions between students and teachers in Mexico did seem intense when children's caregivers were older grandparents who worked all day, did not read or write, and felt intimidated going to school and talking to teachers and principals. Principals and teachers seemed to have very little patience and willingness to help. They would set up appointments with grandparents, who were the caregivers, but would not see them or offer no help filling out papers and forms. There was a perception that grandparents lacked "education" to comprehend the demands of youth and children in school.

Schooling in New York City

The varied socioeconomic and educational backgrounds of immigrant families can affect a child's opportunities and experiences in different ways. Parents with more resources can settle in more affluent and integrated neighborhoods that typically offer better schools for their children. Conversely, parents of more limited means will tend to gravitate to poorer neighborhoods where they are likely to find inferior schools. The neighborhood shapes the lives of immigrants' children in many ways. Concentrated poverty is associated with chronic underemployment or unemployment and youth must look for work somewhere else. Other factors, however, play important roles. Even though I conducted research in four boroughs in New York City, I will focus on the experiences of children and youth in preschools and kindergarten through fifth grade schools in Sunset Park, Brooklyn and in the South Bronx.

Schools and space. In different interviews with community members of Sunset Park, the word *revival* came up multiple times. Even though it was hard for members of the community to pinpoint when this revival started, other government documents suggest that it was in the 1970s. It is estimated that about half of Sunset Park's 100,000 residents are Hispanic (Natrella, 2013). They include a large number of Dominicans, as well as Ecuadorians, Nicaraguans, and Puerto Ricans, and, recently, many Mexicans from the state of Puebla. I spent time at the Center for

Family Services in Sunset Park, which provides assistance to immigrants regardless of their legal status, job placement, filing taxes, and making school choices. According to the New York City Department of Housing Preservation and Development, Sunset Park is bounded by 65th Street to the south, Prospect Expressway to the north, Eighth Avenue and Greenwood Cemetery on the east, and New York Bay on the west.

Maria Fernanda lived in Sunset Park. Her daughters attended a public elementary school close to their home and she had a very positive outlook on their schooling experiences. Both Mariana and Rosa woke up excited to go to school, had pictures with their teachers on the refrigerator, and looked forward to attending school functions. Gemma's children, Yazmin and Alejandro Jr., who also went to school in Sunset Park, had great relationships with teachers and school staff and participated in weekend activities. Gemma served as field trip chaperone, coordinated a bake sale, and was extremely vocal at parents' meetings about her safety concerns.

The families in this study who resided in the South Bronx had a very different reality from the families in Sunset Park. Emilia, Violeta, and Aruna, among other South Bronx–based families, struggled not only with housing, work, and safety in their neighborhood, but also with overcrowded schools with limited resources and teachers who generally did not seem to care about the learning process of the children.

None of these three women had a steady job. During the time of my research they swapped jobs a few times and ended up selling Herbalife products or Mary Kay makeup on a door-to-door basis. This type of business required acquiring debt in the beginning in order to buy the products. These women tried to host "meetings" in their homes so that they would not need to travel with the merchandise and their children in the subway. They also tried to time their sales when their children were in school. A common place to be in the afternoon was the Herbalife office. Dozens of women gathered with their children as they consumed the company's products and sold other products to one another. Children would do school work in this office. During a normal day, moving from home to school to the Herbalife offices and then back home was part of the routine. Children and youth complained about feeling "locked in," as Ramiro (age 12) described:

I am not allowed to go to the park because there is violence and my mom will slap me if she finds out I went. In the house my father decides what is on TV and I don't like the movies. In school . . . there is some time to play, but the P.E. teacher is always angry and cuts our time short. Sometimes I just want to run out, because I am always locked in.

Bartlett and Garcia (2011) observed similar phenomena with Dominican youth in Washington Heights. In their study the youth described their perceived limitations in terms of public space, time, interpersonal trust, personal mobility, and safety with the expression of *tranca'o* meaning *trancado*—"locked up." Even though US-born children and youth were not "missing" the freedom they once had (because the current reality was all they remembered), they wanted to be able to go out and play. In many instances I watched children sitting by the window looking out and begging their mothers and fathers to be allowed to go out. For the families in the South Bronx, the answer was always no. Emilia explained to me,

One day I told Alonso he could go up and down the stairs of our apartment because he was driving me crazy. One of the neighbors got angry at his noise and screamed at him. He started crying so loud . . . I tell you it was so loud I didn't know what to do . . . next thing I know there is a police officer in the building . . . I froze. I thought: "They are going to take him from me." The police wanted to know why this child was screaming and if I was mistreating him. They gave me a warning! I didn't understand anything.

This situation was a common complaint of mothers in the South Bronx, Violeta told me: "If you leave your children in the care of others, the cops will show up and take them from you." Lack of trust in neighbors and fears about safety outside kept children and youth inside crowded apartments.

I accompanied mothers and their children on their trips to and from their schools. Parents sometimes used those moments at dismissal to ask the teachers a question and check in. In the two schools there was a clear divide between migrant mothers and teachers. One day I went with Aruna, Pablo (four-month-old baby), and Santino (age 4) to pick up Carlito (age 7). As we approached, we saw Carlito running toward us, crying and upset. Aruna rolled her eyes and commented, "This boy, again." I asked Carlito what had happened and he told me he had gotten into a fight with another boy and the teacher blamed him for starting the fight. For a multitude of reasons, it was hard to understand who had started the fight and the teacher's position. Aruna approached the teacher to ask her what had happened and the teacher, who was Puerto Rican, said, "Ai mami, you know, everything is a problem with this boy . . . he is so dramatic and cries for no good reason." Carlito was indeed very sensitive and he absorbed much of the stress he witnessed from his parents. The situation Carlito described to me was the following, "We were in class and then we went to bathroom and then they locked me in there and turned the lights off . . . I was in the dark, I was left there in the dark [tears coming down his cheeks]." Another boy approached us and said, "We were all playing, we always play like that, he wasn't alone!" As we started walking home, I asked Carlito if he thought he was alone in the bathroom and he told me, "My mom says that if I do something wrong she will give me to the police and I will never see her again." Aruna then turned to him and said, "It's true, if you don't do well in school and behave yourself I'll call the police and you know what they do with you here . . . they take you. Maybe then you will stop complaining about being locked in and start studying."

This situation illustrates a lack of trust in the school, teachers, police officers, and family. The idea of a "threat" was a constant trope in the lives of children and youth of these three families in the South Bronx. At the dinner table, conversations involved children and youth asking about news they had heard of people being stabbed locally and stories of violence in Mexico. Violeta, Aruna, and Emilia complained about the prejudice they felt, especially from African Americans. Children and youth contributed to the portrait their mothers presented by telling stories about school peers that were "mean." As I explained in chapter 3, context is paramount in order to understand why these narratives of prejudice were present in the lives of these families in the South Bronx. Families had witnessed violence between Latinos and African Americans in the playgrounds, streets, bars, and grocery stores. Out of the seven constellations that lived in the South Bronx, six reported some sort of negative interaction with an African American neighbor, teacher, boss, or with unknown people in the streets. These interactions were discussed at length at home and children were involved in these conversations.

Finally, even though families in Sunset Park and the South Bronx faced similar issues with regard to being unable to assist their children with homework and feeling the pressure of work and money, mothers in the South Bronx were unable to consistently enroll their children in after-school programs. Even though the city government assigned free tutors, these professionals did not show up, stayed for a shorter number of hours, and ultimately did not help children with homework. One day I called the tutor from a company called Champion Learning Center and told him that Aruna's family had been waiting for him for four days in a row and he did not call to say he was not coming. The tutor profusely apologized to me and promised that it would never happen again. He told me he thought the parents did not care so it made him not care. Obviously that response aggravated me, since this man was just not doing his job. Aruna did not know if the man could speak Spanish so she did not call him. She also said, "I don't want to cause problems or bring attention to my family, you know?" Teachers were constantly asking parents to be more involved in children's homework, especially in the English language, but offered little to no assistance in terms of how to go about doing it. The South Bronx has great centers and organizations, but these families simply do not get around to finding them. Mothers reported that schools did not help them with referrals. I asked teachers about referrals and they told me they had given mothers plenty of lists.

Mothers also learned to use the welfare system to qualify for child support, even though they all lived with their partners. Before social services came to check on the accuracy of the information, mothers told their children to tell the social service person that they did not have a father and that they were starving every day. Because children were US citizens, they had social security numbers and qualified for food stamps and subsidy for rent from the government. This was a reality for almost all families I interviewed in the South Bronx. In Sunset Park it was different. Mothers reported not wanting to seek help from the government as they found it to be "embarrassing." Gemma explained to me, "If you work hard and you have work ethic you go far." Micaela also told me,

"The people that rely on government help make us look bad and give us the reputation of being bums and lazy." Instead of receiving government help, constellations based in Sunset Park used non-governmental organizations and church-based organizations to assist them with finding work and caring for their children. In addition, families were actively working with pro bono and paid lawyers to attempt to regularize their undocumented status. Gemma's husband told me: "I'm not afraid, I paid taxes, I paid bills, I'm not afraid."

The Assistance and Education Center based in Sunset Park provided families in the neighborhood with a range of social services. They had cooperatives led by women who were nannies, cleaning ladies, or assisted the elderly. They provided them with training and reference letters so they could get hired. In Sunset Park I accompanied women to pediatrician appointments, school, work, grocery shopping, and cooperative meetings. Their daily interactions with other members from the neighborhood were constant. Women who were part of the cooperatives housed by the Assistance and Education Center offered to cook food for each other when someone in the family was ill, helped care for children, and made leisure plans like lunch after church or play dates. Sunset Park showed me a distinct reality from the South Bronx that influenced how children perceived their own lives and opportunities.

Conclusion

Who is better off in their education trajectories—Joaquín, in Mexico; Florencia, undocumented in the United States; or US-born Mariana and Rosa? There is no easy answer to this question. What is clear is that neighborhoods and schools, gender, family income at different phases, and stability influence the kind of educational trajectory children and youth have. In fact, Maria Fernanda's constellation shows us that equating left-behind children with abandonment is not always accurate, though the three sets of children in her constellation face completely different options for their future.

Micro-contexts of reception documented throughout this ethnography make a qualitative contribution to community studies and census data available in each neighborhood. This sustained and close ethnography shows the importance of using a transnational lens and long-term research to better understand the paths families follow. While larger sociological studies are helpful to identify general patterns of adaptation of immigrants in the United States, they fail to focus on the local micro-context these families experience every day. In addition, responses and reactions from the other side of the border are just as important when parents make decisions about how to prioritize children and youth's education involvement. Transnational care constellation structures matter when children and youth go through schooling experiences. Financial and emotional stability of mothers is important to the type of assistance and help children and youth receive in schools both in New York City and in Mexico. Thus, to focus solely on the lives of the so-called first, 1.5, and/or second generation is to ignore a much larger familial structure that works across borders and shapes the social and education trajectories of separated siblings. If we focus on Maria Fernanda's story in New York City without knowing of her family needs in Mexico and how her partner, neighbors, and local schools have assisted her, what can we say about the path of assimilation she went through? Did Maria Fernanda and Florencia experience limited assimilation and are Rosa and Mariana fully integrated? Maybe, but this analysis does not help us understand why that has happened and how it influences Florencia, Rosa, and Mariana's lives and choices.

To summarize, Mexican migrant women in New York City were able to provide for children in Mexico and in the United States only if they were able to experience stability in their homes. Children and youth in New York City had much more varied experiences regarding schooling experiences than their siblings in Mexico, also because micro-contexts matter in this case. Teachers and schools in the Mexican pueblos where I conducted research are not equipped with many books and suffer from lack of resources and lack of teacher training. In New York City, families in the South Bronx experienced crowded schools where they felt there was very little space for parents to participate.

INTERLUDE 5

Camila and Stella

Camila lived with her partner Ezequiel in Sunset Park, Brooklyn. Ezequiel was from Guatemala. As previously mentioned, they owned a grocery store in the neighborhood and lived in a two-bedroom house with their three children. Camila also had three daughters, Ana (age 18), Lilly (age 16), and Stella (age 14), whom she left in Mexico when she migrated to New York in 2000. Camila described herself as a "friendless" person and told me she did not trust people easily. She wanted to talk about her story nonetheless. During my first interview with Camila I asked her to tell me why she left Mexico 12 years before. Camila had a tough life. Her husband, 20 years her senior, left her with the three girls in Mexico and came to the United States. A few years later he sent enough money for her to cross into the United States. He promised her they would go back in a year to be with their three daughters. However, when she arrived in New York City he already had a new partner and asked Camila if the three of them could live together. Camila said she felt ashamed and terrible about the situation. She went to a friend's house and asked her if she could stay there until she had enough money to go back to Mexico. It was not the first time her husband had been disloyal. He had an affair with Camila's mother when they lived in the same house in Mexico. Camila told me she had forgiven them both. What she worried about was the shame of returning home "with nothing." Camila explained to me, "I could not take the shame of not being able to send money back home . . . after leaving my children with my mother . . . can you imagine coming back with nothing: no husband, no money?"

Camila worked as a cleaning lady and at a laundry services shop; she also became part of a cooperative at the Assistance and Education Center in Sunset Park. Through a friend Camila met her husband Ezequiel and together they had three children, Antonio (age 10), Natalia (age 7), and Nina (age 5). The three children attended school and Antonio was in the process of applying for a private school because of his strong grades. Camila, like other mothers in Sunset Park, was able to secure private tutoring for her children and she was an active participant in school-related activities. Antonio told me his mom was always watching him and he thought that if he did not do well in school he would get in trouble. Natalia told me that she wanted to be like her big brother and earn good grades. Antonio was promised a new video game if he got into the private school he was applying to. Even though Antonio did well in school, Camila did not feel she helped him with homework or even to be a better student. The three children spoke English to each other in the home. Camila constantly interrupted them and said, "*no te entiendo*" (I don't understand you) when they spoke in English to her. Like in other households, children spoke to each other purely in English and mothers felt excluded from conversations.

The academic achievement of her daughters in Mexico was very important to Camila. Camila told me multiple times how she always thought her daughters in Mexico were very smart and capable of so much. "The problem," she told me, "is that I can't be there to enforce and discipline them." Camila blamed herself for everything that went wrong in her daughters' lives back in Vera Cruz. Her 18-year-old daughter Ana had two children already and from different fathers. Ana was a great student but since she had her first baby she was no longer attending school. Her other daughter Lilly was pregnant but had a scholarship for high school at a private school in Jalapa, the main city in Vera Cruz. Camila worried about Lilly dropping out of school, but above all she worried that her daughters in Mexico did not love her anymore. She told me:

> I have love reserved for my daughters in Mexico. I feel guilty to give all my love to the children here, so I save some for the kids there. I know deep down that my children there don't love me as much . . . *yo no puedo reclamar es mi culpa, yo fui quien las deje . . . no es culpa de ellas* (I can't complain, it's my fault, I was the one that left them, it's not their fault). Camila continued, They say to me, you left us, abandoned us, and then I stop them and I explain to them that I am helping them and they say "I want to be like you" mamá, someone that works hard.

Camila has had dreams about reuniting with her daughters. She said that in her dreams she cries and hugs each one of them and they talk for hours. It was almost a last piece of hope she hung on to. One day Camila told me she was going to try to bring her daughter Stella to the United States. Camila worried that Stella, like her sisters, would also find a boyfriend and become pregnant. She told me she needed to act fast. A few months later Camila sent me a text message telling me that Stella was indeed en route to New York City. She hired a "coyote" that a friend of hers knew well and paid him half of the total price, US$2,500 in the beginning of Stella's journey. It took Stella three weeks to cross into the United States and another week to arrive in New York City. Stella took a bus from her town in Vera Cruz to the border of Tamaulipas and Texas and attempted to cross several times. She was caught by border patrol twice, but because she was a minor she was not charged with any criminal activity. Stella was put into a temporary government foster home until her grandmother signed an authorization for release. Camila was on the edge of her seat for these weeks as Stella tried to cross. She worried that she had put her daughter in potential danger and she told me, "If anything happens to her I will never be able to live with myself." Stella eventually succeeded in crossing and Camila paid the rest of the money to the coyote. Stella was put in a van that brought her to New York City.

"When I saw her, I cried and cried and hugged her and thanked the Lord for her safety. I was so happy to see my baby girl." Stella told me that day, "I was happy to see my mamá, but I'm so tired and it was so tough." The day they were reunited I attended a small party at Camila's house. Stella stood in the corner and asked her mother several times if she could just go to sleep. Camila was disappointed from the start and was upset that Stella was not into the party she had arranged. Antonio, Natalia, and Nina were fascinated by Stella and wanted to talk to her, play with her, and show her things. Stella struggled with English, but her siblings made an effort to speak in Spanish.

A month later I visited them again. Even though I had wrapped up my fieldwork at that point, Camila told me she needed to talk. Since her daughter Stella arrived in New York, her husband was having privacy issues and had essentially moved out the week before. What she meant was that her husband did not feel comfortable in his two-bedroom home with a teenage girl. Camila said that he liked walking around in shorts with no shirt on and watch television and did not feel he could do that with Stella at home. Camila felt pretty strongly about her children coming first. "If he tells me it's my daughter or him, I will take my daughter no question." I asked if he had given her that choice. She responded, "No, but I am ready. I can sense in his actions that's what he means. She [Stella] feels really bad and she cries. But I tell her not to cry, it's not her fault."

Stella was working at the grocery store Camila opened and was dating one of the boys who worked there. Esteban was not pleased with the fact that Stella was dating another employee. She also did not speak any English yet and could barely communicate with her siblings. Stella told me she felt really anxious and she got headaches and intense chest pains that prevented her from breathing from time to time. She wanted to go back to Mexico. Stella said that because she felt good in the home where she grew up, she didn't really focus on why her mother left. Her sisters, on the other hand, "*siempre quejábanse porque la mamá no esta*" (always complained about their mother's absence). Camila interrupted her and said, "I have given more financially to them in Mexico than to the kids here! I always gave them money for birthday, school, *dia de los niños*, there are many women that come here and don't send money to their children. I wasn't one of them."

Months went by and school started in September. Camila did not enroll Stella in school, she told me, because of a vaccine requirement. After speaking to Camila again it became clear she didn't have the patience to help Stella and felt that school would not be good for her, since she was undocumented. Camila told me,

> You know that saying we make plans and God laughs? I think that's what is happening . . . I got Stella out of Mexico so she could be someone and have opportunities, then she gets here doesn't go to school . . . she told me she can't find her papers from school in Mexico, so I can't enroll her . . . and she has a boyfriend, she put an earring on her eyebrow. Maybe she was better off in Mexico! This is very confusing to me. I try to talk to her about taking care of herself sexually, I want to be her friend.

Stella told me she felt intimidated by school and worried about not having papers. She liked school in Mexico, she said:

> I was a good student there, I was doing well and I was going to do *prepa* (high school) at the best school in Jalapa. Since I got here my stepfather is always leaving because of me, my mamá cries a lot, my siblings speak English among themselves, and I feel like I have no future because I don't have papers. I really like my boyfriend. I was promised a better school, a better life, better education here. I decided to come because they told me my degree in Mexico was not as good as a degree in the United States.

5

For My Mother

Gendered Education Experiences

In this chapter I explore why girls in Mexico performed better academically when compared with boys left in Mexico and their siblings in the United States. By "performing better academically" I mean a combination of academic performance indicated by grades, homework completion, in-class behavior, and the overall educational experience that feeds aspirations for the future. Ethnographic data for this chapter stem from interviews with 30 children in Mexico whose mothers were in New York and part of the 20 transnational constellations I followed in-depth over a period of 18 months.

Half of them were female; their age ranged from seven to eighteen years old. In New York I observed and interviewed more than 37 children who were sons and daughters of migrant Mexican mothers in three New York City neighborhoods. Twenty were girls and seventeen were boys; their age ranged from four months to seventeen years old, though I only interviewed children age three and up.

The fifteen girls observed and interviewed in Mexico had consistently better grades—they averaged above the 90th percentile within their class—when compared to the boys, who averaged a little above the 60th percentile of their class. These percentiles were obtained through interviews with teachers who talked to me about these children's performance within the two previous years and disclosed grades for my analysis. The grades I obtained were from the 2011/2012 academic year only. In comparison, in New York City there was much more variability and in many cases boys performed better than girls in terms of academic achievement. Nonetheless, the girls in Mexico consistently outperformed the boys in Mexico and all the children in New York.

Isolating the impact of maternal migration on the migration aspirations of children left behind is a difficult task in a country with such long-standing migration ties to the United States as Mexico. To find out how maternal migration affects school experience as well as education aspirations of boys and girls in Mexico, I carried out surveys with 225 children and youth between the ages of seven and sixteen in four schools in the municipality of Tlapanalá in the state of Puebla, Mexico. Surveys were conducted in three *secundária* or junior high schools (185 students) and one *primária* or elementary school (40 students) in the month of June 2012. Out of the 225 surveys administered, 131 respondents were female versus 94 (42 percent) male. An overwhelming majority of participants reported having at least one family member living in the United States (93 percent). In addition, 33 percent of the children and youth reported having one or more parent(s) living in the United States. In a state like Puebla with long-standing ties to the United States, male migration has always been the norm. Thus, even though most participants had a father migrant, the percentage of participants who had only a mother migrant represents the trend of feminization of migration: 18 percent of respondents had a mother who migrated within the last decade.

The two factors I used to look at education experience are homework completion and a desire to continue studying in the future. During this extensive ethnographic research in Puebla I found children and youth's education aspirations to be influenced by parental migration. Children and youth took pride in showing me their homework and showing homework assignments to parents who were away, as well. In order to assess education aspirations of participants with migrant mothers and fathers, one of the questions asked was about homework completion. The results showed a gendered finding: 81 percent of girls with migrant mothers reported always doing their homework, compared to 23.8 percent of girls with mothers at home. Boys reported not finishing their homework regardless of their mothers being migrants or not (9 percent with mothers at home and 12.5 percent with migrant mothers did homework regularly).

Why do girls in Mexico outperform the other groups of children in this research? Even though I found both boys and girls to experience feelings of resentment and love for their mothers, they responded differently when the issue at stake was academic performance and schooling experiences. However, previous studies have discussed the links between gender and schooling. Skinner and Holland (1996) stated that getting an education has "gendered dimensions." Bartlett's work with literacy (2003) discussed the narrative that exists in young women's minds regarding education as a space for liberation. Similarly, Murphy-Graham (2012) argued that the participation of women in a secondary education program in Honduras increased women's gender consciousness, which in turn heightened their desire for change in the domestic sphere. She found that in many instances women were able to negotiate a new sharing of responsibilities with their spouses. Based on ethnographic research in a secondary school in Amman, Adely (2012) posited that young women in Jordan saw education as making them more marriageable, thus enhancing their future prospects. In addition, the literature on gender inequality regarding educational achievement has found that boys under-perform relative to girls in schools (Legewie & DiPrete, 2012). As described by Legewie and DiPrete,

> Some see the gender gap as largely biological in origin. Others blame schools for an allegedly de-masculinized learning environment and a tendency to evaluate boys negatively for fitting into this environment less well than girls. Yet, the true impact of school context on the size of the gender gap in academic performance remains controversial. (p. 463)

To this complex discussion I add the analytical layer of the consequences of maternal migration on the educational trajectories of girls and boys.

In Mexico, national statistics show that girls outperform boys in academic achievement. It is useful to consider that four out of every ten working-age Mexican immigrants in the United States have less than 10 years of formal education, according to the Pew Hispanic Report (2012): Mexican-born immigrants on average are less educated than other immigrants. Among Mexican-born immigrants age 25 and older, 60 percent have less than a high school education, compared with a fifth (21 percent) of other immigrants. Only 5 percent of the Mexican-born hold a college degree, compared with more than a third (36 percent) of other immigrants (Passel et al., 2012).

In Mexico, 36 percent of adults age 25 to 64 have earned the equivalent of a high school degree (OECD, 2012). According to statistics from the same OECD report, girls outperformed boys in the whole country.

The OECD report states that in the last 50 years there was a tenfold increase in the number of enrolled students in Mexico, from 3 million to 30 million, which means that almost every child between the ages of 5 and 14 is enrolled in school. As a comparison, in the year 2000 a little more than 40 percent of the student population finished high school.

In the context of this research I argue that girls' superior educational performance is linked to the following narratives: (1) education attainment as a path to reunification with mothers; (2) overachieving in school to live up to the expectations of mothers and hoping that academic performance would bring them together; (3) performing well in school with the expectations of receiving material gifts; and (4) school as a space to forget about problems. It is important to mention that these narratives are not mutually exclusive, as they are fluid and sometimes overlap. I also address the realities girls face in their homes in terms of gender role expectations, which show correlations between transnational gossip, gendered division of housework, and school performance. Maternal expectations and gender role expectations sometimes complicate notions of performing well in school, thus creating different experiences for boys and girls. To gain a more complete picture of how and why girls in Mexico are performing better in school, I present examples of boys in Mexico and also compare children in Mexico and the children born in or living in the United States.

Education Expectations for Children "Here" and "There"

My mamá left three years ago. I remember crying a lot because I am the one that is the closest to her. I did everything with her . . . so I miss her. Did she ask about me? Did she talk about me to you? Did she say I do very well in school? I do it for her, for my mother. (Ailyn, age 12, daughter of Brianna)

All I want to know is if she is doing well in school and thinking about her future. (Gemma, age 37)

The expectations of mothers and caregivers are a combination of their expectations regarding gender roles and their expectations regarding their desires "for a better life" for their children. Ideologies of gender sometimes change expectations.

Mothers reported that the main reason for leaving their children back home is their hope for "*mejores oportunidades*" (better opportunities). Sara, a mother of two, told me, "I came to this country so I could provide better opportunities for him [son]." When I inquired what "better opportunities" were, all mothers gave me the same initial answer "*para la escuela*" (for school) or "*por la educación*" (for education). Mothers emphasized schooling and linked education with the hope of a better life, placing tremendous expectations on their children left behind. Horton (2008) found similar narratives in her study with Salvadorans and Mexican families in California. She states:

> Parents often used the popular idiomatic expression, "*para que salgan adelante*," to explain their motivations in settling in the United States. Some mothers used even more powerful language to emphasize the forceful "pushing" required to propel and sustain their children's forward momentum, employing the phrase, *para sacar los niños adelante*" (literally, "to push them forward"). (p. 930)

* * *

Caregivers in Mexico generally reinforced these ideas, conveying to the children their mothers' expectations. Almost all caregivers interviewed were maternal grandmothers. At times, however, caregivers of boys had a harder time disciplining them and conveying the value of education and schooling.

In contrast to mothers' and caregivers' education expectations, the boys I interviewed in Mexico expressed challenges associated with schooling, whereas girls seemed to be academically engaged with school. Grades and school behavior were better among girls, and girls often explained that they worked hard so they could find better jobs, receive gifts, and please their mothers. In contrast, boys reported not necessarily seeing school or a degree as a pathway to better jobs. I observed boys cutting school and asking their caregivers if they could stay home many mornings. As a result, at times there was significant mismatch between maternal expectations and male children's experiences. The expectations mothers in New York placed on their US-born children differed as well. As I explained in chapters 3 and 4, mothers in New York City were less involved in the academic lives of US-born children and had generally lower education expectations of sons and daughters they brought to the United States who were undocumented.

Boys did not respond to pressure to stay in school. Agustín, Clarisa, and Sara were part of a constellation I observed and got to know for more than three years. From ages 13 to 16, I saw that, Agustín showed respect and love for his grandmother, Clarisa. He used to call her mamá when I first met him at age 13, but then he switched to *abuela*. Clarisa tried to do what she could to discipline Agustín. She did not allow him to bring his girlfriend home, she tried to enforce school attendance, and she had him working at their corner store and feeding the animals early in the morning.

Agustín did all the work his grandmother asked him to do, but he dropped out of school. Clarisa told me,

> I wish he would stay in school, but his mother calls and talks to him and all they do is yell at each other. They fight all the time because she doesn't know him . . . she doesn't know his plans and his priorities. I understand him. He asks me, "*abuela estudiar para que?*" (study for what?) And I know that even with a degree it is hard to find work . . . but I tell him, if you want to go to El Norte you are better off with a high school diploma!

Agustín had little motivation to study; he did not feel it would provide more economic opportunities, nor would his degree be respected if he chose to migrate to the United States.

On the other hand, mothers' expectations with children and youth in New York City proved to be different. As discussed in previous chapters, mothers in New York City understood the education of their children to be taken care of by society and the government. Guillermina, mother of Heloisa (age 5) and Yessenia (age 3), who were both born in New York City, explained to me,

> Here in America your children go to school. There is no arguing, no questioning, no option, no excuse that it is too far . . . they go, there are buses! I know I don't have to worry about enforcing that, because it's just like living and breathing. If they [children] don't want to do well in school, then it's their loss. But in Mexico we have to impose, otherwise they [children] think they can choose.

Guillermina continued by stating that her daughter Pilar (age 13) in Mexico did well in school in part because she kept her in check. Weekly interactions with Pilar were about grades and school-related activities. Guillermina was proud to say that she was the one who made sure Pilar was making a life for herself. Pilar, on the other side, tried to match her mother's expectations, but was curious as to whether Guillermina was as "strict" with her sisters Heloisa and Yessenia. Her curiosity was not unfounded. Guillermina explained to me,

> My children in Mexico have to deal with the fact that I am not there every day. They have to think about that. They also think their siblings are better off here. But my children here have no idea what hard work is, so I can't expect them to work as hard. They just have a different life.

In addition, as explained in other chapters, mothers felt they had little power or knowledge of school policies, English language, and homework content in New York and felt that their influence in the academic lives of their US-born children was minimal. An interesting fact also arose from all 20 transnational mothers' interviews. They explained that children in Mexico were "left" there, thus mothers expected children in Mexico to know what suffering and sacrifice felt like and have it in them to thrive because of that sacrifice. In New York City, children were born and raised already exposed to heightened consumerism and large schools, without the "trauma" of ever being left behind. Gemma, a mother from Puebla who lived in Sunset Park, explained to me how much she loved school and wanted to be in school when she was young. The condition her mother gave her was, you may stay in school, but you cannot find a boyfriend. She met her first husband in nursing school. All she ever wanted growing up was to be free, "*estar libre* . . . until Satan [ex-husband] crossed my path." She was going to do her residence in Puebla, but they did not have space at the hospital and she ended up getting pulled back to the smaller town of Izúcar de Matamoros, where she met him.

She told me about her two US-born children:

> Alejandro Jr. and Yazmin are spoiled rotten, they have everything exactly how they want. I loved going to school, because staying at home meant

housework and I never once said NO to my mamá, so I hated doing housework. But they [Alejandro Jr. and Yazmin] don't have housework and they go to school, so they don't care, they can't see the value of school. They want to watch TV.

Aruna echoed similar sentiments:

My sons are not being taught to do housework because we don't live like I lived in Mexico, having to do so much physical work. They did not learn that discipline of working. So what happens now, they take everything for granted. My daughters in Mexico have to do work at home and go to school, they have responsibilities they learned since they were young.

Gender ideologies shape much of the interactions between caregivers and children at home. For example, in many transnational maternal-child relationships, conversations with both sons and daughters often center on schooling and education. Mothers' first questions to caregivers and children were always "how is s/he doing in school" or "is s/he obeying you and doing homework?" I found this to be true across gender of children and length of separation. As Karina, a mother in New York told me, "It has to be worth it." For these mothers, the expected returns on migration for their children were: good academic performance, willingness to do well in school, and ambition to stay in school and pursue a college degree (see Smith 2005). The irony, however, is that in some cases the very expectations that motivated mothers to depart (providing better schooling and education) are the one boys left behind had most trouble with. The stronger school performance of girls was consistently motivated by their desire to not disappoint their absent mothers.

I address the realities girls face in their homes in terms of gender role expectations using the concepts of *mujercitas* and *hombrecitos* to explain how maternal expectations and gender role expectations sometimes complicate notions of performing well in school, thus creating different experiences for boys and girls. I begin the following section with a detailed story of the Osorio constellation. With this story I show how even though education expectations of mothers in New York and gender role expectations of caregivers in Mexico complicate children and youth's experiences of education, females in Mexico managed to have better grades in school and were motivated to finish *la prepa* (high school).

The Osorio Constellation

At the time of our interview, Brianna had been in Jackson Heights, New York City for three years. Brianna left three daughters Fernanda (age 14), Ashley (age 12), and Tina (age 8) in San Bernardo, Puebla when she moved to New York. Ronald, her husband, had been going back and forth between Puebla and New York for 15 years. Ronald was undocumented, so crossing the border was always costly and dangerous. For this reason, in his first 11 years he went back to Mexico to see his wife three times. Each of the times Ronald went to Mexico, Brianna became pregnant with one of their three daughters.

During her first pregnancy, Ronald brought Brianna to the United States to establish their family in California. Fernanda, the oldest daughter, was born in the United States, but at five months Brianna took her back to Mexico, where Fernanda lived until her fifteenth birthday. Brianna decided she needed support from her extended family to raise her daughter since Ronald was working all day. Ten years and two pregnancies later, Brianna returned to the United States, this time leaving their three daughters behind so she could join Ronald in New York City. Brianna described her life since she migrated to the United States as "lonely" and "without a main purpose." When I asked her what the main purpose of her life was she said, "Raising my children, taking care of them, making sure they have an education."

Though I found these responses to be somewhat normative and part of an appropriate narrative, they shaped the dynamics between mother and child. Prior to migrating, she lived in San Bernardo, Puebla, with her mother Leila, her sister Leti, her niece Lesley, her sister-in-law Marcia, and Marcia's daughter Cece. Brianna explained to me,

> I only left San Bernardo because Ronald and I thought that we had to try to live as husband and wife . . . it's so hard being apart for so long and since the buildings fell [September 11 terrorist attack] Ronald kept saying

that it would only get harder for us to see each other. So we thought, I will go for one or two years and then come back for my children. You know . . . a strong marriage is very important to children's development as well.

Brianna's daughters all attended the local public school in their pueblo. Fernanda went to the high school in the village about 15 minutes' walking distance from her home, and Ashley and Tina walked about five minutes to their elementary and middle schools. The three daughters have grades that correspond to being in the top 20th percentile or higher in the United States. While the girls in this constellation performed well in school, it did not come without pressure from their families. During many meals at their home in Puebla, Leila told the girls how "shameful" it would be if they were not good students. "Your parents are there, and especially your mother, to provide for you, to dress you, to buy you books and shoes for you to go to school. Remember that when you are being difficult and annoying." The sisters rolled their eyes, complained, and fought with each other, as they felt they were being "lectured" by their grandmother. At the same time, they understood the pressure of performing well in school because teachers and principals acknowledged their grades and efforts. Their motivations and experiences with education, however, were very different, and will be described in subsequent sections of this chapter.

Gendered Education Expectations for Children in Mexico

Girls between the ages of 13 and 18 had different ideas regarding the purpose of doing well in school, but a pattern emerged in which they saw education as a pathway for reunification with their mothers and as a possibility to find better opportunities elsewhere, as illustrated with the case of Brianna's daughter Fernanda. Fernanda was disengaged in school and she was waiting for her parents to arrange her trip to the United States. Fernanda, who was actually born in the United States but returned to Mexico when she was a baby, went to school from morning until 2 p.m. When she came home, she watched television for hours as she battled her own sleepy eyes. When on the phone with Brianna (her mother), Fernanda only responded "yes" or "no" and repeatedly asked the question: "When are you going to take me to New York? You only make promises . . . stop making promises you can't keep. I do *every-thing* [emphasis added] you ask me." Fernanda's grades in Mexico were good, even though she showed little enthusiasm for school, except for English classes. She had downloaded all of Justin Bieber's songs onto her smart phone and practiced saying the words and translating the meaning from English to Spanish. Her teachers and principal commented on how much potential Fernanda had and how her writing abilities were among the strongest in her class. Fernanda told me that her main goal was to keep her grades up so her parents would take her to the United States sooner. One of the teachers explained to me, "she is that kind of student who is very cooperative and easy to get along with. She is kind and follows rules. However, she has no interest in going beyond that and becoming the best student in her class. She is content with being good." The principal of Fernanda's school described youth who had parents living in the United States as "spacey" and said they lived in "a limbo" where a person physically lives in one place, but daydreams about being elsewhere.

Other girls interviewed showed the same approach toward education. Girls responded that they expected to apply for a student visa or a work visa in the United States so they could reunite with mothers as soon as they finished *la prepa*. One of them explained: "I know that they [US Consulate] don't give visas to people that don't have a high school degree. So I am trying to get all my documents in order."[1] Camila's daughter Stella, who was in Mexico, also discussed the fact that she "would not be able to get a good job" in Mexico City or in the United States if she did not earn a high school degree. She was preoccupied with "ending up" like so many people in her own pueblo. The group of girls interviewed saw education and schooling and above all good performance as a "way out" of the lives they were living in their hometown. Ultimately, they also discussed the idea of education as a way out as part of what their mothers wanted for them. In many cases, girls wanted to migrate to the United States since parents had promised they would help them only if they did well in school; in other cases girls discussed the job market and the fact that, in order to be successful nurses and teachers, a person "needs to go to school and the person needs to do well" (Lilly, age 16). Their narratives matched their mothers' narratives in terms of equating finishing high school with good grades and a better future. Unlike the boys, girls had no interest in going to the United States illegally; they believed that with their degree they would be better candidates for legal entry into America.

The boys I interviewed did not have the same understanding of education as a way out; in fact, it was precisely the opposite. Dropping out of high school and becoming unemployed were common phenomena among the older male teenagers in this research study. In San Nicolas in Hidalgo, the principal estimated that as many as 70 percent of all boys in grade 9 would not return to finish high school. Among the participants in my study, only one boy in Hidalgo, Agustín (age 16), had dropped out while still in obligatory schooling. The other boys were enrolled in middle school but were not performing as well as the girls. Joaquín, Maria Fernanda's son, finished high school and was about to start university. Andrés, who was in grade 8, performed well in school—in the 70th percentile. The other 12 boys of the transnational care constellations had average grades that put them between the 60th and 65th percentiles in their classes.[2]

Girls seemed to be more amenable to their mothers' education expectations and most sought to nurture their relationships with their migrant mothers by making them proud of their educational achievements. Nine-year-old Emilia described her conversations with her mother in the United States as being about how well she was doing in school. Emilia said, "I always tell my mom that I am doing really well in school. She likes it." Before her mother's departure, Emilia had a complicated relationship with her. Her grandmother caregiver reported that when Emilia was only three years old, her mother would try to force-feed her and was aggressive toward her. Emilia knew about this story and as her grandmother finishing telling it to me, Emilia said, "I don't want her to get mad at me ever again, so when I say I'm a good student, she gets happy, she asks more questions, we talk longer on the phone, it's fun." Ashley's story was similar. She was the best student in her class, won prizes, taught math and science to children who were older, and she was calm and respectful in class. She explained to me: "If I do well in school my mother gets happy and I think oh maybe now she will come back, you know? Because she is proud of me." Of Brianna's three daughters, Ashley was the one with whom establishing a relationship based on trust took the longest. She told me: "I'm sorry I didn't talk to you in the beginning when you got here . . . I don't like the idea that people come and go . . . and I am always here." Ashley did not say that she wanted to go to school and do well in order to "leave" her pueblo. Quite the opposite. She explained to me that her effort was based on the premise that her mother would come back to see her graduate and maybe decide to stay. Ashley was the one who spoke on the phone the longest with Brianna and gave her detailed information about her routine in school. Brianna, in return, felt more invested in Ashley's educational future, as evidenced when Brianna interfered by having her daughter moved to a different classroom (see chapter 3).

According to Dreby (2006), aside from reported behavioral problems, a more widespread difficulty for families with migrant parents was in-school performance. In her research she found that more than 40 percent of children interviewed dropped out of school in the middle of their studies. Dreby (2006) found that the pattern of problems contradicts the expectations of most parents who have migrated. Similarly, I found that that the expectations of migrant mothers do not always match the actual performance of male children in Mexico. However, the expectations mothers have for their sons were more flexible than those they had for their daughters. As Sara said of her son Agustín, "Of course my priority for him is to go to school and finish his studies, but he is also a man that has to be able to make his own choices, there is very little I can do." On the other hand, Camila explained with regard to her three daughters she left in Mexico, "The problem is that if my girls drop out of school I know it's because of a man . . . pregnancy, moving to another town for a man, to serve him . . . and I think they are too young for that."

In the cases described here, girls understand that getting a formal education may provide a way out of the reality they live in. In many interviews girls alluded to the idea that they did not want to "end up" being dependent on a husband and they needed to be able to support themselves. In part this thinking is the result of the analysis of the labor market that the children and the mothers do. These claims were usually followed by ideas of a stable and happy marriage and children. Like many teenagers around the world, these girls had conflicting ideas of what their future aspirations looked like. They knew what they did not want, though, and that usually meant not having a violent, "drunk husband" who would not take care of them. Mothers and caregivers used their academic expectations to control and "keep an eye" on girls and prevent them from making decisions they thought to be bad; in this way, mothers created a narrative that implied that if their daughters performed well academically, their chances of going to the United States to find good jobs and their prospects for a good life would increase.

Much of the conversation that took place on the phone and via Skype between mothers in New York and their daughters in Mexico started with comments much like those offered by Gemma to Daniela in one conversation I witnessed: "*Hija*, you need to make a life for yourself, you need to do things that I wasn't able to do." When mothers talked to their sons on the phone, the conversation was slightly different and had more to do with ideas about being a *hombrecito*, a "good" and "respectable man." Grandmothers in Mexico were raising all of the boys in this study, and mothers in New York worried about what Sara expressed as "the lack of a male figure to teach him the value of work." Mothers also regularly instructed their sons not to impregnate their girlfriends. Mothers were concerned with alcoholism and with the idea that their sons would end up having a child or children while they were still teenagers themselves.

Gender Role Expectations for Children in Mexico

Girls discussed the difficulties of arriving home and having to clean, cook, and wash their uniforms before dinner every day. They complained about the lack of time to do homework and about the disparity of treatment between girls and boys. Even though I found girls did better in school, the girls accumulated more housework because the mothers were gone, which impacted their academic performance. They spent less time doing homework and finishing assignments. Other scholars have explored the idea of the double burden for girls. Results from the survey administered in three schools in Puebla show that trend as well: on average girls have 1.8 jobs at home and boys have 1.2. Housework included in the survey encompassed cooking, cleaning, taking care of siblings, feeding the family, helping with homework, and feeding the animals.

These tasks were chosen after two pilot surveys on housework division and qualitative interviews with more than 60 participants in which people described what the primary jobs within a household entailed. For male respondents, housework increased significantly only when both parents were gone (3.3 jobs versus a little over 1 job when mothers were home). Even though the number of chores also grew for female respondents when both parents migrated, girls performed significantly more chores even when only the mother had migrated. My observations show that girls take over many of the roles of their mothers when a mother leaves home and there are changes in the division of household chores.

The household arrangements of the children in Mexico and the tasks that come along are important indicators of how their lives are shaped by the migration of their mothers. All 20 caregivers interviewed reported that girls take over the tasks their mothers would be responsible for if they were home. Tami, Pilar's grandmother, explained to me, "Ever since Guillermina left I tell Pilar (age 13), 'Listen (Pilar) you will have to do your Mamá's job, do you understand that?'" They did not mention boys taking up any of the tasks of mothers who left. Tami continued, "I tell Pilar every day, *hija* your Mamá is gone, you better grow fast into a *mujercita* and do her job." When I inquired what a mujercita was, Pilar and Tami told me the three key duties of a female in these households in Mexico: *lavar, limpiar, y cocinar* (to wash, clean, and cook). Pilar told me,

> Well, all the *Mamás*, the ones that stay-at-home, say household duties never, never end. Because you might clean one place and then it gets dirty, because the kids came in all dirty, and you need to clean again. And the dishes that we use to eat, you need to wash again and again . . . like every time you eat, because you can't end without plates to eat. Then you have to wash your uniform before you go to school . . . then if there is someone visiting—an uncle or another *señor*—you have to prepare him food and then clean. They say, "you need to work a lot to have this place clean."

The caregivers interviewed told me that boys do little in the house. As Agustina (age 52) pointed out, "there is not much for boys to do," regardless of having a migrant mother. According to Agustina, Brian's grandmother, girls need to be *mujercitas* (little women) from as early as seven years old, when they start making tortillas, cleaning the house, and washing clothes. I observed girls as young as three years of age helping to cook by using knives to slice tomatoes, onions, and avocados. Girls in Mexico learn to care for others from a young age: They learn to serve their brothers, fathers, and uncles or to help their mothers and grandmothers. Even though this is not a generalized finding of an entire society, gendered division of labor was prevalent in the families researched.

Fifty-six percent of the girls reported cleaning the house as their primary responsibility within the household, whereas boys reported feeding the animals (48 percent) as their primary duty. The only housework boys overwhelmingly reported not doing was cooking. Thus, there is a gendered division of labor within the house. Many girls were having trouble completing their homework assignments. Alondra told me, "If I had as much time as some of these other boys have I would be the best in school!" Boys were, however, involved in extracurricular activities: swimming lessons, martial arts, and soccer were part of their afternoon routines. Andrés, age 13, was taking swimming lessons at a nearby community pool. Agustín, age 15, was taking jujitsu classes in the afternoon.

It is also possible that the discipline and responsibilities girls assume at home influence their school achievement. Mirna, a caregiver and grandmother, told me, "Learning to be a *mujercita*, you know, a good girl, is about obeying rules . . . is about obedience. I think Carolina [her granddaughter] obeys me, her teacher, her mother . . . she is a good girl." During my observations it became apparent that girls were indeed obeying their caregivers more regularly than boys. However, the girls explained that obedience was coming, in part, from a place of appreciation of the caregiver. In many instances, girls said that the one person who took care of them, helped them, took them out, and fed them was their grandmother caregiver, therefore girls felt that "the right thing to do" was to take care of their grandmother.

In contrast, none of the boys strived to excel in their academic pursuits. They were interested in going to school if that meant that they could play sports. This is not to say that they necessarily underperformed, but to illustrate how even though mothers had expectations of all their children being successful in school, it was acceptable for boys not to perform well. Levinson 1997) found that, in Mexico, dominant norms of masculinity stipulated modest involvement with academics, and excessive attention to studies was occasionally stigmatized as effeminate, mainly because of the assumption that to do a lot of after-school *tarea* (homework) means spending more time in the domestic, feminine space of the home (p. 10).

Transnational gossip and stigmatization, a phenomenon observed by scholars like Joanna Dreby and Robert C. Smith, influenced children's schooling experiences in this research. Seven-year-old Brian was disinterested in school. He reported being teased by peers about being raised by his grandmother or, as he described, "having many mothers." Brian's grandmother caregiver Agustina reported that, one day on returning from school, Brian pointed to her stomach and asked, "Did I come from here?" She told him that he did. She did that to comfort him and, as she told me, to show him love and protect him from the "ugly truth." When she talked to me about enforcing school attendance, Agustina expressed feeling "guilty" and being willing to let Brian stay home from school to avoid being hurt:

> If he doesn't want to go to school, he won't go to school. The poor baby already went through so much with his mother leaving him and he doesn't like it when other children make fun of him for having two mothers, I feel guilty.

Avoiding discussions that were difficult (where he came from) and situations that were hard (peers at school teasing him) seemed to be Agustina's way of dealing with Brian's emotional reactions to his mother's absence. Though Agustina wanted to defend her daughter and justify her departure to Brian, she did not want Brian to feel that he was the reason his mother left. Agustina explained, "It's hard for my daughter, I know . . . but it is harder for Brian, so I might change the story to him a little bit, but it is out of love."

Brian's mother did not know about any of these challenges. She told me she had not called Brian in a while because she was embarrassed that she had not been able to send money for uniforms and books, which were at the top of her priority list when sending money home.

Brian's grandmother worked hard to provide for him. With her own husband incarcerated in Texas, accused of human trafficking, she took a job selling peanuts and corn in order to make ends meet. She was also going through their savings to support her own two daughters and Brian.

School Performance Incentives: Gifts from the United States

Tina (age 8), the youngest of the sisters in the Osorio constellation, loved to dance, and she had the most outgoing personality in the family. She liked to tell jokes and perform for the camera. Her interest in dance and performance accrued costs for Brianna and Ronald, as Tina needed new tutus, skirts, and entire outfits depending on the dance she was going to perform in school that week. Tina had no problem picking up the phone and calling Brianna or sending her text messages to ask for costumes for plays and school performances. Brianna told Tina multiple times: "*hija,* I will send you clothes, but you know what I need from you, right?" Tina rolled her eyes and said "*Si, si* . . . I know . . . but my reports are good *mamá*." Tina took pride in going to school wearing her bright pink Dora the Explorer T-shirt and her matching backpack.

Other children in her class asked her how she was always so well dressed and had the best costumes for the dance performances in school. Tina answered, "I have a rich mamá that sends me gifts all the time." A girl asked her, "Really, you don't need to do anything for her to give you all these gifts, with my *mamá* here I have to clean the entire house!" Tina replied, "I tell her about my grades and how the professors here love me . . . right *maestro* Felipe, don't you think I am a good student and deserve all the gifts and more?" The teacher looked at me and whispered under his breath, "That's not the way to bring up your daughter."

Brianna and Ronald worked hard to provide financial stability for their children, and proof of that was sending gifts and money. The three sisters became accustomed to receiving gifts. The last time I visited them, I brought with me a suitcase with tennis shoes, t-shirts, dresses, and toys from their parents. The three sisters went through the suitcase and picked out the things they liked and the things they did not like. After a few minutes looking at all the gifts they started arguing with each other:

> TINA: My mother told me she sent me an orange shirt, she told me that just yesterday on the phone.
> ASHLEY: This orange shirt doesn't even fit you; it's for older girls not a baby like you.
> TINA: I don't care! I go to school and I need the clothes to dance at my next performance. It's mine! She told me. She told me!

Tina ended up with the orange shirt and as she sobbed and sat on her grandmother's lap, she said:

> I don't understand mamá Leila (grandmother), my mamá Brianna promised me that if I went to school and was a good student she would give me everything . . . does that mean that she won't give me the doll house? *Yo hice mucha tarea, mamá Leila, mucha* (I did so much homework, so much).

There was anxiety on Tina's part to know whether or not her "efforts" would be compensated. Tina was only seven years old and she was focused on the almost weekly reward she would receive because she was a "good" student. On the other side of the border I accompanied Brianna many times as she rushed through streets to find what Tina had asked her for. Brianna's worry was clear, "She will not trust me anymore and worse than that she will use it [not receiving gifts] to blackmail me and she will start missing school, because her grandmother feels bad about forcing her!"

Boys were also materially compensated for performance, but the effect was not necessarily as positive, as illustrated by the case of Agustín. Then 14-year-old Agustín lived with his maternal grandmother, Clarisa, in a small village in the state of Hidalgo. His mother, Sara, lived in New York City with her 4-year-old son, Felipe, and worked as a nanny, as previously described. Sara left Agustín in 2002, when he was six years old. After four years she returned to Hidalgo for six months. She then left Agustín behind once again. Agustín lived in a big renovated house built by his mother and her siblings, who continued to maintain it through monthly remittances. One day, as I was visiting, Agustín locked himself in his room in the morning and said he did not want to go school.

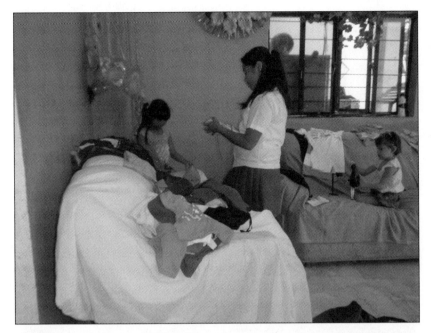

Figure 5.1. Tina, Fernanda, and their cousin Cece opening gifts sent by Brianna and Ronald.

From the other side of the door, his grandmother told him, "*Hijo*, how can you waste your future like this? Don't you want to make your mother proud? Remember, *hijo*, that's why she left." Minutes later Agustín opened the door in his uniform and was ready to go. As we got to the school his teacher, who was also the principal, called him into her office.

She told him that he was going to fail eighth grade. Agustín turned to his teacher and asked her, "How am I going to explain this to my *mamá*?" Later, during a meal, Agustín told me, "She [Sara] doesn't know me. I want to stay home and watch movies. She is not here . . . she only wants to know about school." Indeed, school performance was Agustín's currency with his mother. To discipline him, Sara withheld gifts like tennis shoes, video games, DVDs, etc. Therefore, upon talking to the principal, Agustín quickly thought about how his mother would be disappointed in him and also about how he would not receive the gifts he looked forward to. Though Sara threatened to withhold gifts from Agustín, she ended up sending him all of them regardless of school performance. Sara's expectations of school achievement were pushed back by her "idea" of what a young man should be able to do.

In the cases of Tina and Agustín, school performance was rewarded with gifts sent from the United States. Tina was frustrated because she felt that she did what was asked in terms of school achievement, but she did not receive what was promised. In contrast, Agustín knew that Sara would send the gifts even if he did not do well in school, something that Tina was not sure about—perhaps because of her younger age. Also, a pattern emerged through the different stories of Brian and Agustín. Though they were different ages and had different relationships with their mothers, their mothers wanted them to be successful at school. However, these boys were aware of their power within the relationship with their mothers and grandmothers and knew they could "get away" with not doing well in school.

Positive Schooling Experiences in Mexico: Daniela and Carolina

According to a 2006 UNICEF report about Latin America and the Caribbean, boys generally have higher repetition rates and lower academic achievement levels than girls, and in some countries, a higher rate of absenteeism. Some have argued that girls, even in their most vulnerable situations, tend to perform better academically since the school functions as a space for liberation, as illustrated by Daniela's case. At the time of our interview, she was 15, had been separated from her mother for more than a decade, and had a difficult relationship with her grandfather, who was reported to be an alcoholic.

Daniela told me that in the past he had hit her and her grandmother. I asked Daniela if she had ever tried to speak to Gemma, her mother in New York, about the incidents. Daniela replied to me, "Yes, she calls and talks to him about it and then has to change topics because he starts to say ugly things to her . . . like . . . 'who do you think you are? You left the father of your daughter and now you live far away.'" Daniela described her last few years and put emphasis on how school helped her "forget" about her feelings of abandonment and rejection: "It feels good to be good at something . . . everyone compliments you . . . doing homework and going to school get my mind off of thinking about bad things." I asked Daniela what those bad things were:

G: What do you mean by "bad things"?

D: I was really depressed when I was 11 years old. I couldn't even bathe myself . . . I felt worthless. I know my grandmother was thinking about putting me in a place for crazy people.

G: Why do you say that?

D: Because I heard her talking to Gemma on the phone and telling her that I didn't do anything around the house, that I wasn't independent. So I thought my *mamá* . . . I mean Gemma, also did not want me.

G: How did you feel then?

D: I was very confused and I reached out and started talking to my father and his family . . . I wanted to go live with him. I wanted to be with one of my parents and my own mother was so far away with a different family and different husband . . . I felt very depressed. I don't . . . I mean I didn't understand why my mother would leave and not want me.

G: Do you understand now why she left?

D: Now I kind of do . . . she is busy there in El Norte. She works, works, works all the time. I know she doesn't have an easy life and she helps me a lot with school stuff.

A few minutes later Daniela told me,

> I finally feel like . . . like I am worth something. I like that if I put effort into something I do well . . . and I know Gemma and my *mamá* are proud of me, they talk about it all the time. And when I am reading books and learning English I think about all the things I want to do in my life and when I'm in school even though girls gossip so much and talk about me not having a real father and mother I get to think about me.

Fifteen-year-old Carolina (who lived in Puebla), daughter of Lucia (who lived in South Bronx), resisted going with her mother to the United States because she wanted to stay in Mexico and at least finish eighth grade. Carolina told me her mother wanted her to go to the United States because her mother believed that schools were better there. She said, "She doesn't understand that I like school here. I like to study, I like math, social studies. I get good grades too. Ask my aunt!"

In this case there was a match in the educational expectation between mother and daughter, although there was a difference of opinion regarding where that should occur.

Conclusion

The expectations mothers in New York City develop about their children in Mexico are a direct result of their migration. In their minds, they rationalize migration as a way to provide for their children and to give them better lives. On the other hand, once they have children in the United States they assess it as a country that will "take care" of their children's education. They do not expect as great an achievement from children in the United States because, according to them, they do not have to perform extremely well to succeed in life, since they already have the chance of success because they live in and are citizens of the country. In addition, parents do not think they are apt to help and assist their children in the American school system. As in the cases previously explored in the book, parents struggle with language, legal status, work schedule, and an overwhelming feeling of being impotent when facing a teacher at a New York City public school.

Different motivations informed the educational expectations held by mothers and grandmothers. Mothers in New York wanted their daughters to excel not only because of their justification of why they left Mexico in the first place, but also so they could experience a life that they themselves did not have.

> When I was growing up I had to beg my father to let me go to school, he did not let me. I don't know how to read and write. Since my daughter went to the United States she talks more about making sure my granddaughter Daniela not only finishes school, but go on to college . . . I think she sees how in El Norte there is a lot more money and I think it's because people go to school.

Though grandmothers reinforced the message conveyed by mothers, they did so to show allegiance and loyalty to their own daughters in New York. As I have mentioned before, all but one caregiver did not compete with mothers for the post of central decision-makers in the lives of children and youth. Grandmothers used school and education also as a way to "keep an eye" on and have more control of girls' whereabouts.

The education and schooling expectations of mothers in New York City were gendered with regard to their children in Mexico, but not with regard to their children in the United States. Caregivers in Mexico held on to gender ideologies: They believed in a specific division of labor in the house and they believed that there was a difference in the physical freedom boys and girls should enjoy, but in all cases grandmothers protected their grandsons, while enforcing a curfew and mobility rules for their granddaughters. Caregivers and grandmothers were extremely careful with girls. Curfews were enforced and there were clear boundaries regarding boyfriends. Mothers constantly warned against pregnancy; as Ester, a grandmother, explained, "People already think she will find a boyfriend in school and get pregnant and drop out. Not on my watch!"

Such issues have been discussed in the literature on gender and schooling. In many ways mothers and grandmothers vouch for schooling as a direct stepping stone to finding "better opportunities" or jobs that will eventually pay their children more than what they themselves have earned. There is a mixed effect of the different ideas discussed in this chapter: gender ideologies associated with what is masculine and what is feminine, expectations from migrant mothers fueled by the motivation behind their departure in the first place, and the ideology behind what is "good" and "advanced" related to finishing high school and ideally moving on to college.

Girls interacted with their migrant mothers on a daily and weekly basis and the fact that they belonged to a care constellation that is structurally organized across a transnational terrain contributed to their efforts and motivations related to school achievement. Adely (2012) shows in her work that education is central to the narratives of young women. Even though in Jordan much of the discourse around education is tied to economic progress, Adely shows that the schooling experience for young women is less attached to economic benefits and more aligned with ideas about living a pious life and appropriate and respectful gender roles. Bartlett (2003) describes education for young women as a space of deliberation in their lives, as part and parcel of the national and local ideals of a developed woman, and as a project with substantial material implications.

Murphy-Graham (2012) explains that education, for women, can be a way of recognizing one's own worth and the importance of the individual. According to Murphy-Graham, this process of empowerment makes women believe they have the ability to contribute to personal and social betterment.

Most of the girls in this research had intense domestic work chores, so the fact that mothers in New York placed such expectations on their academic performance gave them something tangible to work for and provided caregivers and mothers with the constant subject of academic achievement; this context made a difference in terms of the academic achievement of girls in Mexico. I observed conversations between mothers and daughters via Skype, telephone, Facebook, and text messages that would always start and end with discussions about school. It is also true that conversations between mothers and their sons included topics related to school performance; however, the effect that school performance expectations had on girls and on boys was different. Differences also existed across age groups, with teenagers being keen on finding ways "out" of the small pueblo they lived in and younger girls wanting their mother's approval and support.

Measuring academic performance of girls and boys around the world has been the mission of different international agencies as well as local and federal governments. Much of education policy comes from the type of "hard data" produced by elaborate regressions, large samples, and longitudinal studies. In this chapter my aim was to discuss what these reports do not assess: the particularities of these constellations and how relationships across borders have consequences not only on how boys and girls experience schooling, but also on how they fare academically. My choices of having a child- or youth-centered approach and focusing on the narratives that girls and boys use to describe their education experiences was not by chance. Educational attainment helps to bond (for better or for worse) the pieces of the constellation. If care is what holds a constellation together in their everyday lives, education and schooling are the topics of conversation that give mothers, caregivers, and children hope for a future together.

INTERLUDE 6

Letter to Carlitos

During my very first fieldwork visit to Mexico in the summer of 2010, I arrived at the house where I would be staying in the suburbs of the city of Puebla and shared my first meal with my "host" family. I described what I wanted to study in Mexico. In addition, I told them I wanted to look into the role of caregivers and the relationship of these children with their mothers. Julio, my host, went to his library and came back with a letter, dated 1972, from his sister to her son, then a five-year-old boy. His sister Yuli, age 24 at the time, was part of the student revolutionary movement that had begun in 1968 in Mexico. This movement was still fighting against the government army in 1972 and Yuli left her son, Carlitos, to participate in the armed fight that year. Reading this letter on that first day of fieldwork, I noticed how similar this mother's narrative was to my research findings about caregiving and school expectations.

The letter read (translated from Spanish to English):

Dear Carlitos,
It will make me very happy if you receive this letter and if with this letter you can feel how much I love you. Always remember that while I'm alive wherever I am I think of you. And if I'm not with you right now, please know that it makes me sad. I want you to live in a different environment from what exists right now, where all people are good and love one another. I want you to be happy and surrounded by happy people, and to achieve this for you and for other kids I need to be working far away from you.

My *hijito* (little boy) I know that you may suffer sometimes because you are not with me, but always remember this: Tere and Julio are my parents, they took care of me when I was a little girl and now they are taking care of you, my son, and because of that you must love them like you love me. Be obedient to them, don't do bad things, don't be rude. Please be a good boy and you will see how everybody is going to love you, because everyone likes the good boys and you are a very good boy.

When people fool you and tell you that you are a bad kid, don't believe them because you are a noble little boy. What is happening is that life has put you in a different condition than of other kids. And this should make you a *hombrecito* (little man). I know you love me a lot, and because of this love you should pay attention to what I tell you. I also want you to be the best in your class. I know you can because you are very intelligent and it won't be hard for you. Just put a little effort every day and do your homework. Be neat with your notebooks, ask your grandparents to cut your fingernails and toe nails. Be organized and you will see how your teachers will appreciate you more and you will like school every day more. For me it is extremely important that you study. For you to come work with me you need to be a very good student.

I don't want you to be a troublemaker or selfish, but at the same time don't ever let people treat you unjustly. Don't let the older kids treat you bad and at the same time don't ever treat the young ones bad.

Always remember that you are the person that I love the most in my life, you are my treasure and I wish you all the best. It hurts me too to be away from you, but we don't always have the life we want, sometimes you have to fulfill duties and right now our country needs people working to make this society a new one, and just like you there are many little boys that have their parents away and some of them don't even have the grandparents and they are sad. Think that you are OK because you have Julio and Tere, you have my sisters that I know are always going to be there for you.

Be really good in school so that one day you can write me telling me about how you are doing and even if I don't receive these letters know that every day that I live is dedicated to you. You will see that your mother will never lie to you and one day you will clearly understand why it is worth for us to be separated now.

I send you a lot of kisses and a big, long hug.

Tu *Mamá*,

Yuli

Conclusion

Millions of people in the world today live as part of transnational care constellations. In order to understand children and youth's care and education experiences in Mexico and in the United States, researchers must view them as part of these transnational care constellations. If children have difficulty learning or speaking the host country's language, if parents or caregivers don't seem enthusiastic about children's schooling, or if children with immigrant parents are performing well in school, teachers, researchers, and policy makers must ask themselves—who is involved in the care of these children and youth? Who is making the decisions regarding their education trajectories? And how does the other side, where part of the family remains, influence behavior, decisions, and experiences? I have posited that immigrant Mexican women with children in both Mexico and the United States remain a part of their offspring's lives, especially with regard to education and schooling. As a central figure in these constellations, mothers along with caregivers link separated siblings and their different realities in a way that makes children and youth interact with the other side. In a world where people are constantly on the move, we still have a lot to learn from how communication across borders takes place and what kind of influence these distant realities have on one another.

In the African proverb made so popular by Hillary Clinton, "It takes a whole village to raise a child," the village becomes blurred and borderless when we try to understand who is involved not only in raising the child, but also in educating the child. Where is the village in a transnational perspective? It becomes the transnational care constellation where separated siblings are connected through their mothers and their imaginaries, where migration and the narratives that come with it are a latent topic in children's everyday lives and contribute to how they perceive their schools, their homes, and their families.

This book has explored the ways in which maternal migration shapes the lives of children who are part of transnational care constellations divided between Mexico and the United States. It focused on the re-configuration of family relationships in the wake of maternal migra-tion; each chapter describes how these changes have shaped children's lives on both sides of the border. Levitt and Glick-Schiller have argued that central to the project of transnational migration studies and to the scholarship on other transnational phenomena is a reformulation of the concept of society:

> Our analytical lens must necessarily broaden and deepen because mi-grants are often embedded in multi-layered, multi-sited transnational social fields, encompassing those who move and those who stay behind. As a result, basic assumptions about social institutions such as the family, citizenship, and nation-states need to be revisited. (2004: 4)

Through the use of transnational care constellations I have "broadened" and "deepened" our analytical lens on migration. I broadened it in the sense that I looked at both sides of the border where families are, and I deepened it as I focused on the people involved in the micro-contexts of caring for the children here and there. This book has aimed to revisit assumptions of motherhood, caregiving, and family structure by looking at how transnational practices shape and influence the lives of children.

This volume has shown that the influence of migration cannot be un-derstood by looking at only one side of the border. Children's lives and experiences are an important, yet often overlooked, part of migration phenomena. Indeed, when we examine their lives, we find that care-giving practices and arrangements that derive from maternal migration particularly shape and influence children's experiences of education and schooling. Mothers' expectations and educational investments vary according to children's location and mothers' financial and emotional stability. In addition, the gender of the child plays an important role in how expectations of education and schooling unfold. As we have seen, academic achievement and education experiences differ for sep-arated siblings in Mexico and in New York City, and assumptions of "better" schooling systems are complicated when we look at the micro-interactions and everyday practices of families. By focusing on the lived and relational dimensions of maternal migration as experienced by members of "transnational care constellations," this research contributes to the existing migration scholarship by illuminating how transnational migration and people's mobility shape the lives of children and youth "left behind," "brought over," and "born here." By arguing for the importance of attending to children's lived experiences of familial separation and participation in care constellations, this research provides a nuanced analysis of migration's many facets.

I focused on micro-contexts "here" and "there" in order to show how everyday realities are shaped by these transnational relationships. For example, economic and sociological arguments of migration build on assumptions of why people migrate and leave out important distinctions that are not just anecdotes or caveats, but rather the reality in which millions of people live and organize their family structure—transnational care constellations. Transnational families face many of the same challenges as immigrant families: adapting to a new culture, learning a new language, locating suitable affordable housing, seeking jobs, and adjusting to the educational and larger societal systems. In addition, transnational families face physical separation accompanied by communication facilitated by technology. As Schmalzbauer states:

> Although transnational families are not a new phenomenon, there are critical differences between the transnational families of the late 20th and early 21st centuries and earlier forms. Contemporary transnational families survive in a world in which communication and transportation technology makes it easier for families to stay connected. (2004: 1318)

My data show that even though some things may be easier, communication is also strained by filters in social media and expectations that are built around what is shown to the other side. Transnational care constellations are unique in a sense that separation exists alongside the desire to maintain family ties through this system. Part of the definition of transnational motherhood is the idea that women have of "being here" and "being there" simultaneously. Mothers in this research showed how they operated outside the here/there dichotomy by crossing the border with their care, fully acknowledging their positions within the care constellation, and using Internet and Communication Technology (ICT) to fulfill their roles. Migrant mothers were constantly faced with challenges regarding how to negotiate care and educational investments for all of their children. They understood children in Mexico to be the beneficiaries of their sacrifice and thus expected more from them.

Ideas and Practices of Transnational Motherhood

Women borrow emblems and ideas of motherhood from Mexico, their home country, as they become transnational mothers in New York City. The ideal of motherhood, as others have noticed, is deeply associated with ideas of sacrifice for one's children. However, women have other desires and motivations to migrate that appeared to be hiding behind the justification considered legitimate by family members and themselves: providing for the children.

In a review of the literature of migration, it becomes clear that the primary reported motivation for people to leave their homes and go to a different country is economic: migration as a personal and sometimes "household" decision to increase economic gains through family separation. Even though from a rational choice perspective this may be a feasible explanation, migrant mothers not only had particular economic reasons for migration, but also focused on being able to provide in order to further their children's education. As demonstrated in chapter 2, the economic explanation does not fully account for the stories of migrants who are women and mothers who have children on both sides of the border. Discussing push and pull economic indicators for why people move is inadequate, as it does not question the motivation of this group of individuals and consequently how mothers' mobility shapes the lives of children and youth on both sides (beyond the impact of remittances for those who stay and being first- or second-generation for those who are in the United States). I focused on how intergenerational relationships among women have contributed to constructions of the ideals behind caregiving and thus transnational motherhood. The ideas of "the good mother" influenced how women in this study took care of their children. Justifying migration as an act of sacrifice provided a comforting explanation for many women. Personal desires fed motivations to migrate; however, they were quickly suppressed by the perceived duty of how a mother should care for a child. Women were not contradicting ideas of motherhood learned from their mothers in Mexico; they were using those concepts to create new forms of mothering from afar.

As we have seen, one of the ways parenting from a distance is enacted relates to education and schooling-related decisions. Migrant mothers took on the role of decision-makers in school-related decisions for their children "here" and "there" while—in almost parallel experiences—caregivers on one side and mothers on the other side struggled to participate in the lives of children they physically cared for.

Women, even when separated from their children for a number of years, continue their mission to provide for them and keep their bond alive. Many women considered themselves less capable of assisting children in schools where they were present, in New York City, and thus their presence at parent-teacher conferences and school events was minimal. Transnational motherhood is a more complex and nuanced practice than just having children here and there. Transnational mothers are constantly making decisions and choices that affect the lives of their children in Mexico, their children in New York City, and caregivers in Mexico. On the other side, in Mexico, caregivers struggled with similar issues. Feeling out of place to assist their grandchildren with homework and school, grandmothers described not knowing much about how school worked and did not think they could improve children's performance or help them in any way. The co-presence of caregivers and children in the same country, city, and home did not necessarily mean that more support would be provided. We saw how and when women borrowed from ideas of what a mother "should" do and put them into practice regardless of distance.

Children and Youth Perspectives: A Transnational Comparative Lens

A major task of this research has been to address the experiences of children and youth in migration contexts. Coe et al. (2011) have described children and youth as under theorized "key players" in globalization and transnational processes. Few scholars (see Dreby, 2010, 2015) have been able to overcome the barriers of doing research with children who are affected by the migration of their parents. There is little documentation on the communication between separated siblings or whether their experiences differ in transnational contexts. This book has addressed not only how mothers relate to the different groups of children in their lives, but also how children and youth relate to one another. Focusing on siblings allows us to understand how kinship travels across borders and how these relationships are formed and questioned.

Children and youth used a transnational comparative lens to form their thoughts and impressions about migration, separated families and their siblings on the other side, inequality within the family, and their sense of belonging in the family. Physical resemblance was important when children and youth discussed their siblings, grandmothers, and mothers. In addition to their emotions, children and youth on both sides of the border imagined their siblings in different times and spaces, almost as if they were "stuck" in these imaginaries. Describing the other side, children and youth started with an economic perspective of how the "rest" of the family lived and used those ideas to build character concepts of these family members and their lives. Using inequality as a lens to analyze how siblings lived on the other side was a common practice among children in this study. Siblings in New York City worried about the well-being of their siblings in Mexico and considered Mexico a "harder" or "tougher" place to live. At the same time, there were examples of children in New York City who used the situation of their siblings in Mexico as leverage to demand more material gifts from their mothers.

Siblings Separated by Migration

Members of the transnational constellation have also come to expect mothers to assist them with remittances, material gifts, and emotional support. Mexican migrant women in New York City were able to provide for children in Mexico and in the United States only if they were able to experience stability in their home. Children and youth in New York City had much more varied experiences regarding schooling experiences than their siblings in Mexico. The varied socioeconomic and educational backgrounds of immigrant families can affect a child's opportunities and experiences in different ways. Migrant mothers with more resources may find ways to settle in more affluent neighborhoods with better schools. Migrant mothers with fewer resources may have to settle where housing is cheaper, and send their children to overcrowded, low-quality schools.

Mothers often justified migration by saying it would lead to better opportunities. However, as we have seen, boys and girls in Mexico reacted differently to the educational expectations of their mothers. There was a mismatch in terms of expectations when it came to mothers and their sons, as boys tended to underperform academically and drop out in the middle of their studies. Children born in the United States were significantly influenced by the quality of the school they attended. Even though mothers in Sunset Park and the South Bronx faced similar issues with being unable to assist their children with homework and feeling the pressure of work and money, children in the South Bronx had a harder time at school. Mothers in the South Bronx felt that there was very little space for them to participate in their children's schooling, and the living situation in the neighborhood contributed to the lack of trust mothers had in teachers at the school and vice-versa. Further, mothers in the South Bronx were consistently unable to enroll their children in after-school programs and felt that there was little help from principals or school staff regarding opportunities for their children. Even though the city government assigned free tutors, the professionals did not show up, stayed for a shorter number of hours than expected, and ultimately did not help the children with homework. Also, families in the South Bronx relied on government assistance like food stamps and child support. They made substantially less money than the families in Sunset Park and Queens. Sunset Park was also different in that there was a large, supportive Mexican population, whereas families in the South Bronx experienced challenges with violence, racial/ethnic tension, and poor housing.

There is a narrative of struggle and sacrificed lives in transnational mothers' worlds, but I observed them working on building different types of practices as a way to remain present in their children's lives in Mexico. The child-rearing practices in New York City varied significantly, depending on these mothers' location and financial situation. The pressure of being the provider when women owed money to loan sharks, had unstable partners, or lived in cramped, small apartments had enormous influence on how they treated their US-born children. Violence and poverty exacerbated the already tenuous situations of women who worried about their legal status and lack of English knowledge.

Gender, Migration, and Education

Girls' superior educational performance may be linked to narratives of possible reunification with mothers and hopes that academic performance would bring them together. Girls also discussed their expectations of receiving material gifts. In addition, "doing well" in school allowed girls to use school as a space to forget about problems. It is important to mention that these ideas are not mutually exclusive; instead, they are fluid and overlap at times. I have argued that maternal expectations and gender role expectations sometimes complicate notions of performing well in school, thus creating different experiences for boys and girls.

Different motivations informed the educational expectations of mothers and grandmothers. On the one hand, mothers in New York wanted their daughters to excel not only to reinforce their justification of why they left Mexico, but also so they could experience a life that they themselves did not have. On the other hand, even though grandmothers reinforced the message conveyed by mothers, they did so to show allegiance and loyalty to their own daughters in New York. A final gendered pattern that emerged was that grandmothers used school and education also as a way to "keep an eye" on girls and have more control of their whereabouts.

Policy and Practice

Under the Obama administration, the United States saw an increase in removals of undocumented immigrants instead of returns. The goal was to prevent multiple attempts by the same person to enter the country. Even though the Obama administration removed more than 3 million people[1] (Chishti, Pierce, & Bolter, 2017) during its tenure, the number of apprehensions was much lower than during the Clinton or Bush administrations. In early 2017, President Donald Trump signed two executive orders promising wide-ranging expansions of the enforcement system, including priorities that focus on removing not only noncitizens with criminal records, but also those who have committed potentially criminal acts or who have abused public benefits. It will not be possible, however, to assess how different the administrations will be until we have numbers to compare.

Under this auspice, parents and families are once again faced with the imminent threat of separation, but now from those who were born in the United States. In *Everyday Illegal* (2015), Joanna Dreby describes the "sudden single mother" phenomenon where targeted undocumented men are being detained and deported, leaving women to care for their children on their own in the United States. Many of these men are unable to return to the United States or to send "reverse remittances" from the Mexican side, since they cannot secure jobs that pay as much. This reverse rupture is causing families to have to address illegality inside the home and discuss measures and action plans with their children. As I continued to visit the families who participated in this research, I witnessed numerous conversations and instructions that parents were giving their children if something were to happen to them. During one instance, Gemma tried to explain to her daughter what she should do if something were to happen to her and her husband:

GEMMA: *Hija*, do you know why we can't travel to Mexico to see your grandparents and your sister?

YAZMIN: Because it's dangerous there.

GEMMA: No, not really. The reality is that we don't have the paperwork to travel. Like the papers that the government gives you that says "this person is *free* [emphasis added] to travel to one side and to another side . . . understand?

YAZMIN: Why don't you have these papers? Do I have these papers?

GEMMA: You do . . . because you were born here. But I don't and your father doesn't because we weren't born here . . . it's complicated . . . but we have been trying to get these papers for a long time, *hija*.

YAZMIN: Why can't you get it? [PAUSE]

GEMMA: Because of politicians . . . and now the president. He doesn't want to let more people "be from here." But when you're older you will be able to travel to Mexico and come back without a problem. But I want to tell you another thing . . . because the politicians and the police don't want more people to be from here they can ask us to leave.

YAZMIN: Move out of the house?

GEMMA: No . . . leave the country. Go back to Mexico once and for all. And if that happens . . . if they take us, the first thing you

will do is call and stay with Aunt Frida. She will take care of
you and your brother until we can take you guys with us. OK?

At that moment, panic set in for Yazmin. Her face was flushed and
her eyes got teary. She asked her mother to explain how long that separation would last and why would this happen to them. Gemma calmly told
her that there was no need to be upset because they already had a plan,
and that it would probably be two to three weeks until they would all be
together. In fact, there is tremendous variation in the length of time to
reunification for a family taken by law enforcement. Gemma was doing
her best to keep her daughter in the loop, without expecting her to react
as an adult.

> GEMMA: *Hija*, please know that our separation would be brief, would
> be quick. I want you to be prepared. And specially to take care of
> your brother.
> YAZMIN: But mamá, what about his skin disease and all the doctors
> and creams and medicine. How am I going to do that?
> GEMMA: Aunt Frida will help you and it will be quick. I make you a
> promise. A life promise. *I will not abandon you* [emphasis added].

Transnational care constellations are shaken up once again and potentially broken up only to find themselves having to reorganize care.

From an education policy perspective, this book shines light on the
complex issue of school performance and the education experience of
Latinos, especially Mexicans. The list of education-related outcomes in
which Latinos, but especially Mexicans, trail other ethnic groups is strik-
ing. It includes achievement test performance at age five and younger;
performance in reading and math at grades 4, 8, and 12; high school
grade point average; and rates of high school graduation, college attendance, and college degree completion. I designed this research in such
a way that I was able to move from homes to schools in both countries
and understand the challenges and hardships these families face in both
Mexico and New York City. I observed children and youth coming home
after school in a small village in Puebla and finding their grandparents
unable to help them with homework, while their US-born siblings experienced similar difficulties as their mothers were not able to understand

enough English to help them with homework. Teachers on both sides of the border described the relationships at home as an issue for the academic achievement of children and youth. I found girls in Mexico to have four times more housework than boys, leaving them little time to do homework and readings. Grandmothers explained to me that since the girls' mothers had immigrated, their daughters had to "step up" and take on their mothers' "jobs."

In addition, this ethnography contributes to the development of a research agenda and topics to be explored regarding larger immigration reform. Migration has been constantly associated with development (Glick Schiller, 2012). This nexus needs to be untangled as we assess not only who the participants are in migration movements, but also with whom they remain connected. This book contributes to debates on immigration, education, and gender while also adding to the discussion and the debates on how the United States and Mexico will deal with the effects of a broader immigration policy, mixed-status, and mixed spatial families in the coming years.

What's Next?

It is perhaps fitting to close this book by discussing an instance of family reunification. By 2013, Brianna and Fernanda, who had been apart for more than three years, were finally sharing the same apartment in Jackson Heights, New York City. Based on the longing I knew each had for the other, when I arrived at their apartment two months after Fernanda had moved to New York City, I expected to see very loving interactions. Contrary to my expectations, I found both women wanting to vent about the experiences of living together. Brianna had lost weight, and when I asked her what she was doing differently, she told me, "Zumba!" I distinctly remember Brianna while she was pregnant and after she gave birth. She had little energy and told me she felt extremely depressed and missed her daughters in Mexico. She also developed type II diabetes during her pregnancy. After enduring a traumatic birthing experience, she had experienced postpartum depression. "Now," she explained to me, "I have her [pointing to Fernanda] . . . she helps me with everything . . . I mean she helps me when she is not upset and complaining. That is all she does, complains and gets sad . . . I don't know why. Do you?" I did not have an answer for Brianna; I had one too many guesses.

Fernanda told me how her crossing went. She was born in the United States, so she did not have to worry about her legal status when she was crossing into the country. Ronald and Brianna did not have enough money to pay for air fare, so they trusted friends to bring Fernanda by car from Puebla all the way to New York City. It took almost two weeks for Fernanda to arrive in New York, as they went to Chicago first. She told me she slept in the car every day and developed a chronic pain in her neck. Fernanda was still upset as she walked me through her journey. At the end of her story she had tears in her eyes and asked me, "Why did they bring me here?" Brianna overheard Fernanda saying that and quickly responded: "Your sisters would die to be here in your place, don't be so ungrateful."

Eventually, Fernanda grew fond of her new American school in Jackson Heights. As an English Language Learner student, she picked up English faster than other students in her class and showed tremendous versatility and adaptation when using slang and new vocabulary while interacting with friends. She became an instant fan of American pop music and an avid user of online social networks. She was already a good student in Mexico, but she was even better after she moved to New York City. Her grades were consistently in the 90th percentile and she was proud to show me her assignments. Like the transnational students described by Hamann et al. (2008) from their study in Nuevo León, Fernanda seemed to have figured out how to move between the two systems.

Fernanda and Brianna's relationship continued to be challenging. Fernanda was left to care for her baby brother for hours every day. Brianna was working again, making decorations for parties in the neighborhood, and Ronald continued to work seven days a week, almost 18 hours a day. Fernanda sent me text messages asking me to visit when I had a chance. She told me that because of her baby brother she could not get out of the house much to hang out with her friends. During one of my visits, I asked Fernanda what her favorite thing was about being in the United States and she told me: "School, I love school here. We use computers all the time, the teachers are nice, and I am making new friends. I really like learning English, but I wish I had more time." When I asked Fernanda what she meant by that, she said, "My mother treats me like her little slave . . . not even mamá Leila [her grandmother caregiver] did that to me. It's almost like I have more chores here and my mamá is trying to teach me a lesson or something. Doesn't she know I already cleaned a lot in my life?"

This reunification story represented yet another facet in the transnational care constellation. After being separated for a few years, what happens to mothers and their children when they reunite? I noticed that Brianna continued to have high expectations in terms of academic achievement for her daughter. Brianna constantly asked Fernanda if she had done homework and how well was she learning English; she pressured Fernanda to stay in the United States and pursue higher education. Fernanda's response to her mother was: "I still want to be in Mexico for my *quinceñera* (equivalent of a sweet sixteen), you promised." All of her previous thoughts on reunification with her family were no longer prevalent in her responses. Fernanda reportedly felt "split" between Mexico and the United States. She loved her new friends and school in Queens, but she felt that she was accumulating more household tasks in her new home. Brianna, on the other hand, developed a new narrative of sacrifice; she said to Fernanda more than once, "I brought you here, I saved all this money to bring you here and give you more opportunities and this is how you react? I'm tired of the complaining."

The chain reactions unleashed by transnational migration are bigger than what we know. The story of reunification between Brianna and Fernanda only begins to scratch the surface. How is Fernanda going to fare in school in the future? Will she eventually want to go back to Mexico? And now that Brianna's romanticized ideas of reunification have not played out, will she want to return to Mexico or bring her other daughters to New York City? When she was pregnant, she told me over and over that as soon as he was born and was allowed to travel, she would pack her bags and go back to Mexico to be with her daughters and help her mother. In my last formal interview with Brianna, she told me she did not know if it was a good idea to be in the same physical space as all her other daughters, because they have grown used to the distance. She also wondered aloud, "What if they start hating me . . . like Fernanda? . . . Isn't it better for us to stay like this? I send them money and gifts and they *need* me [emphasis added]. If I'm there are they going to need me? Are they going to forgive me?"

ACKNOWLEDGMENTS

This book would have been impossible without the generous time and the openness of the incredible families I was lucky to work with in the last five years. The women in these families presented me with strength, perseverance, and love. The children and youth in both Mexico and New York City showed me flexibility, wit, and good humor. I am forever thankful for their trust and for letting me into their homes, their hearts, and their stories.

First and foremost, I would like to thank my advisor, mentor, teacher, and inspiration, Lesley Bartlett. It is truly impossible to thank her enough for her constant support, infinite edits, and insights that not only changed the way I look at research, but also changed the way I look at life. She taught me how to teach, how to read critically, how to write better, how to present at conferences, how to present myself and my ideas, and she encouraged me to persist every step of the way. It has been an honor to work with her as her advisee and colleague.

To Lila Abu-Lughod, whose work and teachings inspired me from my very first week in graduate school when I begged her to be in her class. She pushed me to follow people's stories and engage in an in-depth ethnography. She read multiple drafts and commented on almost every page of each one of them. She showed me tireless support even when life was challenging. Her work inspired me to write with women and about women without losing track of ideas about gender roles throughout the world. To Claudio Lomnitz, a renaissance man with whom I spent hours discussing each part of this book. From theory to practice, Claudio always helped me figure out how to analyze the data I had. From Mexico to New York City he always found time to talk to me and enlighten me with his never-ending knowledge. He believed in me and in my work and pushed me to make bolder conclusions and take risks while writing. To Hervé Varenne, who taught me my first ethnography class and supported me through the very tough first two years of this program. Always encouraging, but with hard questions, he made me a better researcher and ethnographer. To Joanna Dreby, who has always been incredibly available and who helped me clarify and streamline my thoughts, think through my data, and reflect on the contribution of my work. Her work represents the very research that has inspired me to do my own.

I would like to thank my colleagues and friends who did more than support me throughout this time. Their work has inspired me every day. They listened to me, gave me constructive feedback, and encouraged me to keep going. I was lucky to be in your company, Jennifer Van Tiem, Michael Scroggins, and Scott Freeman.

Throughout the years, friends and colleagues have inspired me and cheered me on when I was feeling unsure. Thank you, Juliette De Wolfe, Karishma Desai, Diana Rodriguez, Roshan Shah, Casey Ehrlich Rollow, Jill Williams, Katherine Brown, Mila Burns, Marina Mansur, Ana Sarkovas, and Mariana Oliva. To mentors who read my work and gave me incredible feedback, Charles Harrington, Sonya Michel, Yasmine Ergas, Deborah Boehm, Ted Hamann, Grey Gundaker and Dan MaCintyre, I am so thankful. To Tawnya Fey for helping me get my verbs in order. To Marjorie Faulstich Orellana, who motivated me and worked with me in important moments during the writing process and with whom I had some of the most meaningful conversations about immigrant experiences. To the students I taught in the last decade, thank you for challenging me every day.

To my friends in Mexico who welcomed me into their homes, connected me to people, and allowed me into their field sites so I could recruit participants. First, to Regina Cortina, who introduced me to Valentina. To Valentina Glockner, a great friend and researcher who made my research possible and introduced me to the best researchers in Puebla. To Julio Glockner (and the entire Glockner family) and Antonella Fagetti, my Mexican family, who fed me, gave me a place to stay, allowed me to use their car, treated me like a daughter, and shared their wisdom about Mexico with me. To Brenda Stephany Ramírez, Monica Perera, and Claudia Axel Ramírez for all your help with the workshops and surveys in Puebla and for giving me a home away from home.

Without funding, I would not have been able to complete my fieldwork or write this book. Thank you to the Institute of Latin American

Studies at Columbia University Grant which allowed me to start my fieldwork in Mexico. To the Provost Research Grant at Teachers College, to the Myra Sadker Foundation, and especially to the National Academy of Education/ Spencer Foundation Grant for allowing me the time to write this book and for providing the best environment for me to discuss and workshop my work. To Shirley Brice Heath and Stanton Wortham, my mentors at Spencer Foundation and my cohort who helped me focus as I was writing.

My sincere thank you to Jennifer Hammer, editor at NYU Press, who believed in the project and provided some of the most helpful reviews I could ask for. Thank you to Amy Klopfenstein, who was so patient and diligent throughout the whole process. To all the external reviewers who were so generous with their time and advice—Especially to Alyshia Gálvez. Her writing is a work of art, and she was so giving and open-minded about my project and provided me with extremely detailed feedback. I would also like to thank colleagues at the Lynch School of Education at Boston College for their encouragement and excitement about my work. To Andrés Castro Samayoa and Jon Wargo, thank you for the most genuine support I could have asked for.

The most generous support has come from my parents, Newton and Blenda. They have always encouraged me to pursue my dreams and goals, even when that meant traveling to uncertain places with little communication available. I thank them for their unconditional support, for teaching me about family and love. I only hope to make them as proud of me as I am grateful for them. I am also thankful for my wonderful sisters Caroline and Michelle and my brothers-in-law Lee and Renato. Even from afar, Carol (in Los Angeles) and Mica (in São Paulo) made sure I knew how they felt about my work, always encouraging me and letting me chat away about immigration. We built our own transnational care constellation. I am also thankful for my godson Martin, who only encourages me to fight for a better and more just world. To Francina who taught me so much about love and care. To Nancy and Greg and the entire Thome and Backes family for being my strongest cheerleaders and always being so interested and excited about my work.

Finally, I would like to thank my partner and superhero husband, Alex Thome. This was a family project in a sense that he gave me infinite love and support for me to travel, do fieldwork, talk about my work, and write for hours straight without ever asking for anything in return. I have learned so much from his generosity. I am blessed to have him by my side. We've had millions of conversations about my work at every stage, he helped recruit participants, he did fieldwork with me on the weekends, he helped me design surveys, he formatted all my documents, he read everything I have ever written, and he probably knows my research better than I do. I can say with confidence that I would not have made it this far without him.

I am more thankful than ever for having the privilege of having learned so much about motherhood from so many incredible women and children in this research. My son Jack teaches me about family, love, and sacrifice every day and I will try to be as good of a mother to him as the women who are participants in this research try to be to their own children. As I sit here and hold my baby Noah, I am in awe of the women and children around the world who make it work through love, sacrifice, and dedication. We need this strength today more than ever.

APPENDIX A

Transnational Care Constellations

Appendix A table appears on the following three pages.

Level of Engagement	Transnational Mother	Marital Status	Residence in NYC	Origin in Mexico	Occupation	Description of Children (name, age, gender, and location)	Caregiver in Mexico
3	Gemma Govela	Married (2 marriages)	Sunset Park, Brooklyn	Puebla	Elderly care	Daniela, 15, female, Mexico Yazmin, 11, female, NYC Alejandro Jr., 10, male, NYC	Lupe (maternal grandmother)
3	Maria Fernanda Bernal	Married (2 marriages)	Sunset Park, Brooklyn	Puebla	Nanny	Joaquin 18, male, Mexico Florencia, 17, female, NYC Mariana, 8, female, NYC Rosa, 6, female, NYC	Cecilia (maternal grandmother)
3	Violeta Mora	Married	South Bronx	Mexico	Cook	Andrés, 13, male, Mexico Ramiro, 10, male, NYC Leah, 8, female, NYC Nicole, 6, female, NYC Kimberly, 3, female, NYC	Tatiana (maternal grandmother)
3	Emilia Cárdenas	Married (2 marriages)	South Bronx	Vera Cruz	Sells Herbalife products	Esperanza, 17, female, Mexico Yago, 13, male, Mexico Juan Pablo, 12, male, Mexico Alonso, 4, male, NYC Alondra, 4 months, female, NYC	Ester (maternal grandmother)
3	Aruna Lozano	Married (2 marriages)	South Bronx	Morelos	Sells Herbalife products	Kaia, 10, female, Mexico Elvira, 9, female, Mexico Carlito, 6, male, NYC Santino, 4, male, NYC Pablo, 4 months, male, NYC	Clara (maternal grandmother)
3	Sara Blanco	Single (2 previous marriages)	East Harlem	Hidalgo	Nanny/Cleans homes	Agustín, 15, male, Mexico Felipenardo, 6, male, NYC	Clarisa (maternal grandmother)

3	Camila Ramos	Married (2 previous marriages)	Sunset Park, Brooklyn	Vera Cruz	Works at a grocery store owned by husband	Ana, 18, female, Mexico Lilly, 16, female, Mexico Stella, 14, female, Mexico/NYC Antonio, 10, male, NYC Natalia, 7, female, NYC Nina, 5, female, NYC	Francisca (maternal grandmother)
3	Brianna Osorio	Married	Jackson Heights, Queens	Puebla	Stays at home	Fernanda, 14, female, Mexico/NYC Ashley, 12, female, Mexico Tina, 8, female, Mexico Ronald Jr., newborn, male, NYC	Leila (maternal grandmother)
2	Gloria Fuentes	Single (1 previous marriage)	South Bronx	Puebla	Cleans homes	Carlos, 16, male, Mexico Julito, 10, male, NYC	Itzel (maternal grandmother)
2	Betty Marcondes	Single (1 previous marriage)	South Bronx	Puebla	Cleans homes	Yenny, 16, female, Mexico Jean, 10, female, NYC Isabel, 7, female, NYC	Filo (maternal grandmother)
2	Nancy Palmares	Married (2 marriages)	South Bronx	Vera Cruz	Sells Herbalife products	Marcos, 12, male, Mexico Anthony, 6, male, NYC Wendy, 3, female, NYC	Merina (maternal grandmother)
2	Mayra Consuelo	Married	Sunset Park, Brooklyn	Hidalgo	Cleans homes	Rodrigo, 14, male, Mexico Ruiz, 9, male, NYC Lucy, 7, female, NYC	Laura (maternal grandmother)
2	Allison Matar	Single (3 previous marriages)	East Harlem	Puebla	Salesperson at jewelry store	Brian, 7, male, Mexico Andina, 4, female, NYC Luis, 1, male, NYC	Agustina (maternal grandmother)

(continued)

Level of Engage-ment	Transnational Mother	Marital Status	Residence in NYC	Origin in Mexico	Occupation	Description of Children (name, age, gender, and location)	Caregiver in Mexico
2	Julia Campos	Married (2 previous marriages)	Sunset Park, Brooklyn	Puebla	Cook	Mia, 13, female, Mexico José, 6, male, NYC	Maria (paternal grandmother)
2	Micaela Valles	Single (1 previous marriage)	Sunset Park, Brooklyn	Puebla	Nanny	Yuri, 15, male, Mexico Regina, 12, female, Mexico Dino, 7, male, NYC	Rita (maternal grandmother)
2	Angela Mendoza	Single (1 previous marriage)	Jackson Heights, Queens	Puebla	Nanny	Marcia, 16, female, Mexico Cece, 6, female, NYC Mariano, 4, male, NYC	Sandra (aunt, father's sister)
2	Esther Campos	Married	Sunset Park, Brooklyn	Mexico	Nanny	Esteban, 17, male, Mexico Mickey, 16, male, Mexico Gina, 10, female, NYC	Lina (maternal grandmother)
2	Guillermina Cortez	Married (2 marriages)	Sunset Park, Brooklyn	Puebla	Cleans homes	Pilar, 13, female, Mexico Heloisa, 5, female, NYC Yessenia, 3, female, NYC	Gloria (maternal grandmother)
2	Lucia Martinez	Single (1 previous marriage)	South Bronx	Puebla	Cleans homes	Carolina, 15, female, Mexico Keanu, 12, male, Mexico Jennifer, 3, female, NYC	Mirna (maternal grandmother)
2	Karina Castellanos	Married (2 marriages)	Sunset Park, Brooklyn	Puebla	Cleans homes	Henrique, 15, male, Mexico Katarina, 6, female, NYC	Nari (maternal grandmother)

APPENDIX B

Schooling Systems Here and There

	Mexico	United States
Curriculum	National	National
Systemic organization	Jardin de los niños (kindergarten): ages 3–5.	Universal Preschool; Preschool: Not mandatory; operated by independent organizations and not part of the state education system.
	Primária: grades 1–6, ages 6–14, compulsory. Students older than 15 who have not finished their primary education may attend primary school classes for adults.	Primary or Elementary school is comprised of seven levels/grades (kindergarten to grade 6) for children ages 5–12.
	Secundária: Grades 7–9, compulsory since 1993, it is designed for students ages 12–16 and takes three years to complete. Secondary education also provides learning opportunities for students older than 16 and working adults. Completing this level of education is required for students who want to advance to preparatória.	Middle or Junior High School: Depending on the organization of the school district, the next level of education is called either "middle school" or "junior high." These schools are composed of two or three school years for children ages 12–15. Students must finish elementary school before advancing to middle school. Completion of this level of education is mandatory.
	Telesecundaria: Can be found in rural areas and is equivalent to grades 7–9 in junior high schools in the US. Every hour the students are given 15-minute televised lessons followed by 45 minutes to complete assignments in their national text book with support of a teacher or para professional.	
	Preparatória: Students in preparatory school have three educational options. They can take general education classes, complete technical or vocational training (Bachillerato), or obtain a degree that prepares them for higher education.	High school includes four years of courses and is required for students ages 14–18. Students are prepared to transition to various types of subsequent education or training. Upon completion of high school, students receive a diploma and can then enter into technical training or university. A high school diploma is required for most jobs in the United States.

(continued)

	Mexico	United States
Hours and schedules	Until preparatória or bachillerato there are two shifts: one in the morning and one in the afternoon.	Usually from morning to afternoon.
Grading practices	Number system: "10" is the best grade, "6" passing poorly, "5" failed course/subject.	Letter system: "A" is the best grade, "D" passing poorly, "F" failed course/subject. Number systems are also available.
Types of schools	Public and private schools	Public and private schools
Expectations of parent involvement	Parents are not part of the governing boards of schools; legal mandates don't require parental participation. Parents are invited to school with the expectation of monetary or in-kind support. Parents are expected to help in physical aspects of the school (painting, building, etc.). They are also expected to attend parties and celebrations.	Parent-teacher conferences, chaperons, positions within the school, fund-raising.
Classrooms and facilities	Varied according to location.	Varied according to neighborhood.

APPENDIX C

Mexican Migration to the United States by State and Sex, 2010

Entidad federativa	Total	Men	Women
Estados Unidos Mexicanos	1,112,273	832,441	279,832
Aguascalientes	17,057	12,239	4,818
Baja California	18,432	10,912	7,520
Baja California Sur	2,966	1,477	1,489
Campeche	2,155	1,450	705
Coahuila de Zaragoza	14,795	10,459	4,336
Colima	7,118	4,522	2,596
Chiapas	21,797	18,115	3,682
Chihuahua	30,313	18,941	11,372
Distrito Federal	50,281	32,556	17,725
Durango	18,808	13,171	5,637
Guanajuato	119,706	100,952	18,754
Guerrero	43,111	31,173	11,938
Hidalgo	40,659	33,992	6,667
Jalisco	86,152	60,641	25,511
Mexico	75,694	57,995	17,699
Michoacan de Ocampo	85,175	65,207	19,968
Morelos	20,898	14,984	5,914
NaYazmint	15,585	11,654	3,931
Nuevo Leon	16,448	9,839	6,609
Oaxaca	58,913	45,975	12,938
Puebla	73,458	57,898	15,560
Querétaro	26,424	22,546	3,878
Quintana Roo	4,401	2,961	1,440
San Luis Potos	34,044	26,594	7,450
Sinaloa	15,427	10,565	4,862

(*continued*)

Entidad federativa	Total	Men	Women
Sonora	18,243	10,068	8,175
Tamaulipas	21,671	14,882	6,789
Tlaxcala	12,947	10,441	2,506
Veracruz de Ignacio de la Llave	62,720	50,488	12,232
Yucatan	6,909	5,300	1,609
Zacatecas	31,205	24,615	6,590
No especificado	52,954	35,272	17,682

Note: Migration according to place of residence five years before, between June 2005 and June 2010. Figures for June 12. *Source:* INEGO Censo de Poblacion y Vivienda 2010. Cuestionario ampilado.

APPENDIX D

Demographic Profile of Research Sites in New York City

	Poverty Rate	Total Population	Percentage of Mexican-born
Queens			
Jackson Heights	20.1	25,919	14.31
Western Astoria	12	2,343	11.61
Long Island City	18.5	749	14.04
Brooklyn			
Bushwick	29.9	8,975	13.45
Brighton Beach	25.7	3,095	15.81
Sunset Park	24.5	13,000	14.00
Manhattan			
East Harlem	33.6	6,239	12.45
Bronx			
Long-Wood-Stock	44.2	1,659	9.78
Mid-South Bronx	35.3	1,974	12.07
South Bronx	44.8	2,846	10.84
Belmont	43.7	3,095	15.81
South West Bronx	41.8	3,017	11.49
Staten Island			
North East Staten Island	25.1	681	4.36
North West Staten Island	15.5	2,758	11.56
Rest of the City	16.9	101,833	1.33

Source: US Census 2010.

APPENDIX E

A Note on Methods

RESEARCH TECHNIQUES

Transnational ethnography requires a variety of research techniques. Participant observation was documented through detailed field notes. Most families lived in close proximity in the Mixteca Poblana; though I lived with each household for a specific period of time, I was able to interact with the other families at school, public markets, parties, church, and places of work. For the families that lived in different states, I stayed with them for seven to ten days each time I went to Mexico. In New York I participated in teacher-parent conferences, observed after-school programs, and interviewed teachers, principals, and nurses at the schools. In New York City my time was split between the South Bronx, Sunset Park, East Harlem, and Jackson Heights, where I conducted research for a period of 12 (16 families) to 24 months (four families). I visited families in the different boroughs every day and took one day off during the week. I was able to be part of families' weekday routines as well as weekend activities.

Interviews with children under the age of ten in Puebla and in New York were less structured and centered on the elaboration and explanation of drawings of (a) their families and their communication with relatives in Mexico/New York; (b) their school; (c) their ideal school; (d) how they imagine the school their siblings attend in the other country; and (e) where they would like to be living in the future. Interviews with immigrant children in New York who were older than age ten included topics such as: their thoughts on school and education; their perceptions/memories of school in Mexico; their future aspirations; their thoughts on high school and college; their performance in school; their behavior in school; language barriers; their involvement in extracurricular activities; and their relationships with their mothers, siblings, peers, teachers, and school staff. The same topics were discussed when interviewing US-born children living in New York who were older than age ten, except the topics related to schooling experiences in Mexico.

As I interviewed children and youth older than age ten in Mexico, topics included: their educational experiences, including the quality of education and social relationships with peers; thoughts on immigrating; how the mother's absence influences the migration plans and educational investment of girls and boys; chores boys and girls have at home; their thoughts on high school and college; their performance in school; their behavior in school; their involvement in extracurricular activities; and their relationships with their mothers, caregivers, siblings, peers, teachers, and school staff. I accompanied the focal children to school, where I observed classrooms and informally interviewed teachers and administrators. I observed gender roles in the home and assessed the academic climate at school. When I interviewed caregivers in Mexico, the topics included: their involvement in the children's schooling activities; their ability to help the children with homework; their idea of the value of schooling; and their relationships with the biological mothers of these children. Almost all caregivers in my study were grandmothers (17 maternal, two paternal, and one aunt).

Many anthropologists who work with children have developed specific techniques that take into account children's attention spans and daily activities. Some of these techniques involve interpreting children's paintings and drawings, which allows younger children to participate in research (Montgomery, 2009). Many scholars (Dreby, 2010, 2009a, 2009b; Glockner, 2002) have used child-friendly methods when talking specifically about separation from parents in migrant families. Inspired by the work of Dreby (2010), I used drawings as a child-friendly method because drawings were part of their everyday lives. Sometimes children did not respond well to one-on-one interactions and visual aids were often helpful. Punch (2002) points out, though, that drawings are not necessarily a simple, "natural" method to use with children, as drawing depends on children's actual and perceived ability to draw. Punch (2002) notes that some children, particularly older children, are more inhibited by a lack of artistic competence, and may not consider drawing to be a fun method. The methods I used looked at children as actors and "pivotal points" in the construction of a transnational field (Orellana et al., 2001). Using this strategy, I asked children to engage in pictorial representations when I interviewed them in their homes. I also held art workshops while in Mexico where more than 20 children participated each time. Each workshop lasted two to three hours and each child would draw two to three pictures in one session. Each was asked with minimal instruction to first draw a picture of his or her family, then a picture of how the child imagined New York or the United States, and last, to draw his or her house. I used these drawings as tools for children to narrate their experiences of separation and migration and to understand when and where mothers and fathers showed up in these pictorial representations.

As previously mentioned, I also collected data from cell phones (such as text messages and pictures) and content from social networks websites like Facebook. The most common communication between mothers and their teenage children in Mexico took place through these two vehicles. I had a Facebook account where I was able to chat and see the exchange of messages through the network even from a distance. The text messages were shown to me and I wrote them in my notebook. I was also able to witness and document phone conversations between mothers and caregivers, mothers and children, and separated siblings. Most of the time, the families would put the call on speaker mode (if it was not a land line) and I was able to hear both sides. In addition, I observed separated siblings interacting over Facebook and playing video games remotely from a small town in Mexico to an apartment in the South Bronx. These siblings interacted with each other, talked, cursed at the game, and laughed together.

In order to analyze my data, I embraced an iterative approach to qualitative research and data analysis (Maxwell, 2005). Each interview and observation was documented through intensive field notes completed on the same day as the research. After completing half of the interviews in each category, and again after completing all interviews, I repeatedly reviewed interview transcripts and notes, modified (when needed) the interview protocol, and coded the interviews inductively and then deductively. I treated children's explanations of their drawings as interview data, but I also analyzed the visual products to look for recurring details, especially in relation to representations of mothers, schooling, and migration. After completing the observation phase, I started coding, seeking discrepant data, and looking for recurring patterns in the experiences of the children, especially related to education, academic achievement, and social opportunities. As I finished transcribing interviews and organized my data, I developed a thematic analysis and coded the data. I worked on an outline to answer each of my research questions. Then, when I completed coding, I looked for discrepant data and for recurring patterns related to education, migration, and transnational motherhood. I reduced and combined codes, documented relations between codes, and developed visual displays of the data, which included giant white boards covered in post-its. I developed an outline to answer each of the research questions, checking the outline against memos and original data, and from there I developed research reports. A large part of my time was spent writing portraits of families and transcribing recorded dialogues. Interviews and observation were done in Spanish and English. Interviews were translated to English with the exception of some words.

This research design required a great deal of flexibility. I attempted to engage in "real time" research by going back and forth from New York City to Mexico often. My observations were "quicker" since I was able to ask a mother something that had happened within recent months or weeks. I wanted my observations and interviews to have the flexibility of organization that these constellations have in their own way of structuring.

NOTES

INTRODUCTION

1 In some cases, women are victims smuggled into the United States and other wealthy countries to be exploited as sex workers (Dwyer, 2004).

INTERLUDE 1. PARALLEL LIVES

1 Herbalife is a nutritional company.

CHAPTER 1. IDEALS AND PRACTICES OF TRANSNATIONAL MOTHERHOOD AND CARE

1 The 1986 Act legalized undocumented immigrants who had entered the United States before January 1, 1982 and resided there continuously with the penalty of a fine, back taxes, and admission of guilt. About 3 million undocumented immigrants were thus granted legal status.

CHAPTER 2. TRANSNATIONAL MOTHERS AND SCHOOL-RELATED DECISIONS

1 "Listen," she told me later when I was in Mexico, "I love my girls and my daughter, but I am tired. Brianna has to come back. I have to enroll the girls in different classes, I have to go talk to the government for oportunidades (cash transfer program), I have to buy them clothes, take them to the doctor, and the worst part: deal with school and the people at the school!" Leila did not enforce school attendance; she found it difficult to coordinate the different times each granddaughter had to be in school and to make breakfast for the girls before they left for school. She said many times, "I am tired."

2 In the previous year the police had made four arrests in their previous building, all regarding selling and dealing illegal drugs. In addition, the structure of the building had been causing leaks and ruptures on the walls. There were many rats and cockroaches getting into the walls and the city considered the building a safety hazard.

3 See Varenne and McDermott (1998) for a discussion of how American schools are successful at failing students and for case studies of students' interactions in educational settings.

CHAPTER 4. EDUCATIONAL ASPIRATIONS AND SOCIAL TRAJECTORIES OF SEPARATED SIBLINGS

1 In Mexico, basic education is usually divided in three steps: primary school (primária), including grades 1–6; junior high school (secundária), including grades 7–9; and high school (preparatória), including grades 10–12.

2 Jenny Ye, John Keefe, and Louise Ma / WNYC Data News Team Median Income, NYC Neighborhoods; available at: www.project.wnyc.org.

CHAPTER 5. FOR MY MOTHER

1 After many interviews with the consul at the Mexican Consulate in New York, I found that statement to be true only if youth wanted to pursue formal education in the United States and if they were not applying for any refugee or asylum type of visa.

2 I was not allowed to hold on to grade documents from the students. Teachers and principals allowed me to look at spreadsheets in the schools and they identified the percentiles and let me copy information into my notebook. Percentile calculations were made by the school.

CONCLUSION

1 Fiscal year (FY) 2003–15 data from Department of Homeland Security (DHS), *Yearbook of Immigration Statistics* (Washington, DC: DHS Office of Immigration Statistics, 2015), available at: https://www.dhs.gov.

FY2016 data from DHS, "DHS Releases End of Year Fiscal Year 2016 Statistics" (press release, December 30, 2016), available at: https://www.dhs.gov.

BIBLIOGRAPHY

Abrego, L. (2009). Economic well-being in Salvadoran transnational families: How gender affects remittance practices. *Journal of Marriage & Family* 71(4): 1070–1085.

Abu-Lughod, L. (1991). Writing against culture. In *Recapturing Anthropology: Working in the Present*, 137–162. Seattle: University of Washington Press.

Adely, F. J. (2012). *Gendered Paradoxes: Educating Jordanian Women in Nation, Faith, and Progress*. Chicago and London: University of Chicago Press.

Aguilar, F. V., Jr., Penalosa, J., Estanley, J. Z., Liwanag, T., Cruz, R., & Melendrez, J. M. (2009). *Maalwang Buhay: Family, Overseas Migration and Cultures of Relatedness in Barangay Paraiso*. Quezon City: Ateneo de Manila University Press.

Añonuevo, E. D., & Añonuevo, A. (Eds.). (2002). *Coming Home: Women, Migration and Reintegration*. Balikbayani Foundation, Inc. and Atikha Overseas Workers and Communities Initiatives, Inc.

Anzaldúa, G. (1987). *Borderlands/La Frontera: The New Mestiza*. San Francisco: Spinsters/Aunt Lute.

Appadurai, A. (1996). *Modernity at Large Cultural Dimensions of Globalization*. Minneapolis: University of Minnesota Press.

Asis, M. (2006). Living with migration: experiences of left behind children in the Philippines. *Asian Population Studies* 2(1): 45–67.

Asis, M., & Ruiz-Marave, C. (2013). Leaving a Legacy: Parental Migration and School Outcomes Among Young Children in the Philippines. *Asian Pacific Migration Journal* 22, 3 (December 1): 349–376.

Baldassar, L. (2007). Transnational families and the provision of moral and emotional support: The relationship between truth and distance. *Identities: Global Studies in Culture and Power* 14(4): Special Issue: Emotions and Globalization.

———. (2008). Missing kin and longing to be together: Emotions and the construction of co-presence in transnational relationships. In Svasek, M. (ed.), *Transnational Families and Emotions, Special Issue, Journal of Intercultural Studies*, 29(3): 247–266.

———. (2014). Guilty feelings and the guilt trip: Emotions and motivation in migration and transnational caregiving. *Journal of Emotions, Space and Society* 13: 152.

Baldassar, L., Vellekoop Baldock, C., & Wilding, R. (2007). *Families Caring Across Borders: Migration, Aging and Transnational Caregiving*. London: Palgrave MacMillan.

Barban, N., & White, M. J. (2011). Immigrants' children's transition to secondary school in Italy. *International Migration Review* 45: 702–726.

Barth, F. (1969). *Ethnic Groups and Boundaries: The Social Organization*. New York: Little, Brown Series in Anthropology.

Barthes, R. (1972). *Mythologies: Roland Barthes.* New York: Hill and Wang.

Bartlett, L. (2003). World culture or transnational project? Competing educational projects in Brazil. In Kathryn Anderson-Levitt, ed., *Local Meanings, Global Schooling: Anthropology and World Culture Theory.* New York: Palgrave Global Publishing. Pp. 183–200.

———. (2007). Human capital or human connections? The cultural meanings of education in Brazil. *Teachers College Record* 109(7): 1613–1636.

Bartlett, L., & García, O. (2011). *Additive Schooling in Subtractive Times: Bilingual Education and Dominican Immigrant Youth in The Heights.* Nashville, TN: Vanderbilt University Press.

Basch, L., Glick-Schiller, N., & Szanton-Blanc, C. (1994). *Nations Unbound: Transnational Projects, Postcolonial Predicaments and De-Territorialized Nation-States.* London: Gordon and Breach Science Publishers.

Battistella, G., & Conaco, M.C.G. (1996). Impact of migration on the children left behind. *Asian Migrant* 9(3): 86–91.

Baubock, R. (2010). Studying citizenship constellations. *Journal of Ethnic and Migration Studies* 365 (May): 847–859.

Bernard, R. (2006). *Analyzing Qualitative Data: Systematic Approaches.* Sage Publications.

———. (2011). *Research Methods in Anthropology: Qualitative and Quantitative Approaches.* 5th edition. Lanham, MD: Altamira Press.

Bernhard, J., Landolt, P., & Goldring, L. (2005). Transnational, multi-local motherhood: Experiences of separation and reunification among Latin American Families in Canada. *Early Childhood Education Publications and Research.* CERIS Working Paper No. 40. Ryerson University.

Bhandari, R., Mullen, K., & Calderon, S. (2005). Immigrant mother's involvement in their children's education at home and at school in 1999–2000. MPR Inc., Draft Working Paper, December. Available at: www.mprinc.com.

Boehm, D. A. (2001). "From Both Sides": (Trans)nationality, citizenship, and belonging among Mexican immigrants to the United States. In Elzbieta M. Gozdziak and Dianna J. Shandy, eds., *Rethinking Refuge and Displacement, Selected Papers on Refugees and Immigrants,* Volume 8. American Anthropological Association, Committee on Refugees and Immigrants. Pp. 111–141.

———. (2004). Gender(ed) migrations: Shifting gender subjectivities in a transnational Mexican community. Working Paper No. 100. Center for Comparative Immigration Studies, University of California at San Diego.

———. (2011). Here/not here: Contingent citizenship and transnational Mexican children. In Cati Coe, Rachel R. Reynolds, Deborah A. Boehm, Julia Meredith Hess, and Heather Rae-Espinoza, *Everyday Ruptures: Children, Youth, and Migration in Global Perspective.* Nashville, TN: Vanderbilt University Press.

Brettel, C. (2003). *Anthropology and Migration: Essays in Transnationalism, Ethnicity and Identity.* Walnut Creek, CA: Altamira Press.

Brettel, C., & Hollifield, J. F. (2000). *Migration Theory: Talking Across Disciplines.* New York: Routledge.

———. (2008). *Migration Theory: Talking Across Disciplines*. New York: Routledge. 2nd edition. Includes "Introduction" by Caroline B. Brettell and James F. Hollifield, and "Theorizing Migration in Anthropology: The Social Construction of Networks, Identities, Communities, and Globalscapes" by Caroline B. Brettell.

Brick, K., Challinor, A. E., & Rosenblum, M. R. (2011). Mexican and Central American immigrants in the United States. Migration Policy Institute, June.

Capps, R., Fix, M., Ost, J., Reardon-Anderson, J., & Passel, J. S. (2004). *The health and well-being of young children of immigrants*. Urban Institute. Available at: www .urban.org.

Capps, Randy, & Fortuny, Karina. (2006). "Immigration and Child and Family Policy." Low-Income Children Paper 3. Washington, DC: Urban Institute.

Carandang, M.L.A., & Sison, B. A. (2007). *Nawala ang Ilaw ng Tahanan: Case Studies Of Families Left Behind by OFW Mothers*. Manila: Anvil Publishing.

Carling, J., Mejívar, C., & Schmalzbauer, L. (2012). Central themes in the study of transnational parenthood. *Journal of Ethnic and Migration Studies* 38, 2 (February): 191–217.

Castles, S. (1999). International migration and the global agenda: Reflections on the 1998 UN Technical Symposium. *International Migration* 37, 1, (March): 5–19.

Cerrutti, M., & Massey, D. (2001). On the auspices of female migration from Mexico to the United States. *Demography* 38(2): 187–200.

Chaney, E. (1979). The world economy and contemporary migration. *International Migration Review* 13: 204–212.

Chang, Leslie. (2009). *Factory Girls: From Village to City in a Changing China*. New York: Random House.

Chishti, Muzaffar, Pierce, Sarah, & Bolter, Jessica. 2017. The Obama record on deportations: Deporter in Chief or not? Migration Policy Institute. Available at: www .migrationpolicy.org.

Chodorow, N. (1978). *The Reproduction of Mothering*. Berkeley: University of California Press.

Coe, C., Reynolds, R. R., Boehm, D. A., Hess, J. M., & Rae-Espinoza, H. (2011). *Everyday Ruptures: Children, Youth, and Migration in Global Perspective*. Nashville, TN: Vanderbilt University Press.

Cohen, J. (2004). *The Culture of Migration in Southern Mexico*. Austin: University of Texas Press.

Collier, J. F., & Yanagisako, S. J. (1987). *Gender and Kinship: Essays Toward a Unified Analysis*. Stanford, CA: Stanford University Press.

Cortés, R. (2007). *Remittances and Children's Rights: An Overview of Academic and Policy Literature*. UNICEF, Division of Policy and Planning, Working Papers, New York, January.

Crul, M., & Schneider, J. (2009). Children of Turkish immigrants in Germany and the Netherlands: The impact of differences in vocational and academic tracking systems. *Teachers College Record* 111 (6): 1508–1527.

Dreby, J. (2006). Honor and virtue: Mexican parenting in the transnational context. *Gender & Society* 20: 32–59.

———. (2007). Children and power in Mexican transnational families. *Journal of Marriage and Family* 69: 1050–1064.

———. (2009a). Negotiating work and family over the life course: Mexican family dynamics in a binational context. In N. Foner, ed., *Across Generations: Immigrant Families in America*. New York: New York University Press.

———. (2009b). Transnational gossip. *Qualitative Sociology* 32: 33–52.

———. (2010). *Divided by Borders: Mexican Migrants and Their Children*. Berkeley: University of California Press.

Dreby, J., & Schmalzbauer, L. (2013). The relational contexts of migration: Mexican women in new destination sites. *Sociological Forum* 28: 1–26.

Dreby, J., & Stutz, L. (2012). Making something of the sacrifice: Gender, migration and Mexican children's educational aspirations. *Global Networks* 12, 1 (January): 71–90.

Dreby, Joana. (2015). *Everyday Illegal: When Policies Undermine Immigrant Families*. Berkeley: University of California Press.

Drummond, L. (1978). The transatlantic nanny: Notes on a comparative semiotics of the family in English speaking societies. *American Ethnologist* 5, 1 (February): 30–43.

Dwyer, J. (2004). Illegal immigrants, health care, and social responsibility. *Hasting Report* 34(5): 34–41.

Ebaugh, H. R. F., & Saltzman Chafetz, J. (2002). *Religion Across Borders: Transnational Immigrant Networks*. Walnut Creek, CA: Altamira Press.

Ehrenreich, B., & Hochschild, A. (2002). *Global Women: Nannies, Maids and Sex Workers in the New Economy*. New York: Metropolitan Books.

Fagetti, A. (1995). Relaciones de Genero y Transformaciones Agrarias. In Soledad Gonzalez Montes y Vania Salles, eds., *Estudios sobre el campo mexicano*. El Colegio de Mexico.

Fernández-Kelly, M. P. (2008). Gender and economic change in the United States and Mexico, 1900–2000. *American Behavioral Scientist* 52(3): 377–404.

Forbes Martin, S. (2003). *Refugee Women*. Lanham, MD: Lexington Books.

Fresnoza-Flot, A. (2013). Cultural capital acquisition through maternal migration: Educational experiences of Filipino left-behind children. In L. Bartlett and A. Ghaffar-Kucher, eds., *Refugees, Immigrants, and Education in the Global South: Lives in Motion*. New York and London: Routledge Research.

Fry, R., & Gonzalez, F. (2008). *One-in-Five and Growing Fast: A Profile of Hispanic PublicSchool Students*. Pew Hispanic Center, August 26. Available at: www .pewtrusts.org.

Gálvez, Alyshia. 2010. *Guadalupe in New York: Devotion and Struggle for Citizenship Rights*. New York: New York University Press.

———. 2011. *Patient Citizens, Immigrant Mothers: Mexican Women, Public Prenatal Care, and the Birth Weight Paradox*. New Brunswick, NJ: Rutgers University Press.

Gamburd, M. R. (2000). *The Kitchen's Spoon Handle: Transnationalism and Sri Lanka Migrant Households*. Ithaca, NY: Cornell University Press.

Garcia-Zamora, R. (2006). Un pasivo: Mujeres y niños en comunidades de alta migración internacional en Michoacan, Jalisco y Zacatecas, México. In Las remesas de los migrantes Mexicanos en Estados Unidos y su impacto sobre las condiciones de vida de los infants en México. Unpublished UNESCO field report.

Gardner, K. (2012). Transnational migration and the study of children: An introduction. *Journal of Ethnic and Migration Studies* 38(6): 889–912.

Gindling, T. H., & Poggio, S. (2009). Family separation and the educational success of immigrant children. UMBC Policy Brief no 7. Baltimore: Department of Public Policy, University of Maryland.

Glick Schiller, N. 2012. Unravelling the migration and development web: Research and policy implications. *International Migration* 50(3): 92–99.

Glick-Schiller, N., Basch, L., & Szanton-Blanc, C. (1995). From immigrant to transmigrant: Theorizing transnational migration. *Anthropological Quarterly* 68, 1 (January): 48–63.

Glockner, V. (2002). *De La Montaña a la Frontera: etnicidad, representaciones sociales y migración de los niños mixtecos de Guerrero*. Mexico: El Colegio de Michoacán.

Gomberg-Muñoz, Ruth. 2016. The Juárez Wives Club: Gendered citizenship and US immigration law. *American Ethnologist* 43, 2 (May): 339–352.

Gonzalez-Barrera, A., & Lopez, Hugo, M. (2013). *A Demographic Portrait of Mexican-Origin Hispanics in the United States*. Statistical Profile. Pew Hispanic Center. Available at: www.pewhispanic.org.

Grasmuck, S., & Pessar, P. (2005). *Between Two Islands: Dominican International Migration*. Berkeley: University of California Press.

Gutmann, M. C. (2007). *The Meanings of Macho: Being a Man in Mexico City*. Berkeley: University of California Press.

Haas, H. (2008). Migration and development: A theoretical perspective. International Migration Institute, Working Paper 9.

Hamann, E. T., & Zúñiga, V. (2011). Schooling and the everyday ruptures transnational children encounter in the United States and Mexico. In Cati Coe, Rachel R. Reynolds, Deborah A. Boehm, Julia Meredith Hess, and Heather Rae-Espinoza, *Everyday Ruptures: Children, Youth, and Migration in Global Perspective*. Nashville, TN: Vanderbilt University Press.

Hamann, E. T., Zúñiga, V., & Sánchez García, J. (2008). From Nuevo León to the USA and back again: Transnational students in Mexico. *Journal of Immigrant and Refugee Studies* 6: 60–84.

Hays, S. (1996). *The Cultural Contradictions of Motherhood*. New Haven, CT: Yale University Press.

Heymann, J., Flores-Macias, F., Hayes, J. A., Kennedy, M., Lahaie, C., & Earle, A. (2009). The impact of migration on the well-being of transnational families: New data from sending communities in Mexico. *Community, Work & Family* 12: 91–103.

Hirsch, J. H. (2003). *A Courtship After Marriage: Sexuality and Love in Mexican Transnational Families*. Berkeley: University of California Press.

Hochschild, A. R. (2013). *So How's the Family?: And Other Essays*. Berkeley: University of California Press.

Hondagneu-Sotelo, P. (1992). Overcoming patriarchal constraints: The reconstruction of gender relations among Mexican immigrant women and men. *Gender & Society* 6: 393–415.

———. (1994). *Gendered Transitions: Mexican Experiences of Immigration*. Berkeley: University of California Press.

———. (2001). *Domestica: Immigrant Workers Cleaning and Caring in the Shadows of Affluence*. Berkeley: University of California Press.

———. (Ed.). (2003). *Gender and U.S. Immigration: Contemporary Trends*. Berkeley: University of California Press.

Hondagneu-Sotelo, P., & Avila, E. (1997). I'm not here but I'm there: The meanings of Latina transnational motherhood. *Gender and Society* 11: 548–560.

Horton, S. (2008). Consuming Childhood: "Lost" childhoods and "ideal" childhoods as a motivation for migration. *Anthropological Quarterly* 81(4): 925–943.

———. (2009). A mother's heart is weighed down with stones: A phenomenological approach to the experience of transnational motherhood. *Culture, Medicine, Psychiatry* 33(1): 21–40.

Jensen, B., & Sawyer, A. (2012). *Regarding Educacion: Mexican-American Schooling, Immigration, and Bi-national Improvement*. New York: Teachers College Press.

Kandel, W., & Kao, G. (2001). The impact of temporary labor migration on Mexican children's educational aspirations and performance. *International Migration Review* 3: 1205–1231.

Kandel, W., & Massey, D. (2002). The culture of Mexican migration: A theoretical and empirical analysis. *Social Forces* 80(3): 981–1004.

Kearney, M. (1986). From the invisible hand to visible feet: Anthropological studies of migration and development. *Annual Review of Anthropology* 15: 331–361. Reprinted in *Theories of Migration*, ed. Robin Cohen. Cheltenham: Edward Elgar.

———. (2004). *Changing Fields of American Anthropology: From Local to Global*. Boulder, CO: Rowman & Littlefield.

Kearns Goodwin, D. (2005). *Team of Rivals: The Political Genius of Abraham Lincoln*. New York: Simon & Schuster.

Lahaie, C., Hayes, J. A., Markham, P. T., & Heymann, J. (2009). Work and family divided across borders: The impact of parental migration on Mexican children in transnational families. *Community, Work & Family* 12: 299–312.

Legewie, J., & DiPrete, T. (2012). School context and the gender gap in educational achievement. *American Sociological Review* 77(3): 463–485.

Lévi-Strauss, C. (1995). *Myth and Meaning*. New York: Shocken Books.

LeVine, R. A., LeVine, S. E., Schnell-Anzola, B., Rowe M. L., & Dexter, E. (2012). *Literacy and Mothering: How Women's Schooling Changes the Lives of the World's Children*. Oxford: Oxford University Press.

Levinson, B. (1997). Masculinities and Femininities in the Mexican Secundaria: Notes toward an Institutional Practice of Gender Equity. Paper prepared for delivery at the 1997 meeting of the Latin American Studies Association, session on "Gender and Education in Latin America," Continental Plaza Hotel, Guadalajara, Jalisco, Mexico, April 17.

Levitt, P., & Glick-Schiller, N. (2004). Conceptualizing simultaneity: A transnational social field perspective on society. *International Migration Review* 38, 3 (September): 1002–1039.

Lewis, O. (1959). *Five Families: Mexican Case Studies in the Culture of Poverty*. New York: Basic Books.

Lionnet, F., & Shih, S. (2005). *Minor Transnationalism*. Durham, NC: Duke University Press.

Lomnitz, C. (2005). *Death and the Idea of Mexico*. New York: Zone Books.

Lutz, H. (2012). Care workers, care drain, and care chains: Reflections on care, migration, and citizenship. *Social Politics* 19, 1(Spring): 15–37.

Madianou, M. (2012) Migration and the accentuated ambivalence of motherhood: The role of ICTs in Filipino transnational families. *Global Networks* 12(3): 277–295.

Madianou, M., & Miller, D. (2012). *Migration and New Media: Transnational Families and Polymedia*. New York: Routledge.

Mahler, S., & Pessar, P. (2001). Gender and transnational migration. Paper presented to the conference on Transnational Migration: Comparative Perspectives. Princeton University, June 30–July 1.

Marcus, G. E. (1995). Ethnography in/of the World System: The emergence of multi-sited ethnography. *Annual Review of Anthropology* 24: 95–117.

———. (1998). *Ethnography Through Thick and Thin*. Princeton, NJ: Princeton University Press.

Maxwell, J. A. (2005). *Qualitative Research Design: An Interactive Approach*. Second edition. Applied Social Research Methods Series, Volume 42. Thousand Oaks, CA: Sage Publications.

Mendoza, J. E. (2008). Economic and social determinants of Mexican circular and permanent migration. *Análisis Económico* 23: 203–224.

Montgomery, H. (2009). *An Introduction to Childhood: Anthropological Perspectives on Children's lives*. UK: Wiley-Blackwell.

Murphy-Graham, E. (2012). *Opening Minds, Improving Lives: Education and Women's Empowerment in Honduras*. Nashville, TN: Vanderbilt University Press.

Natrella, E. (2013). The contextual rezoning of Sunset Park, Brooklyn, and the decision in *Chinese Staff & Workers Association v. Burden*: The basic principles governing limited judicial review of environmental challenges in New York endure. *Albany Law Review* 76.2: 1239–1273.

Napolitano, Valentina. (2016). *Migrant Hearts and the Atlantic Return: Transnationalism and the Roman Catholic Church*. New York: Fordham University Press.

Nobles, J. (2013). Migration and father absence: Shifting family structure in Mexico. *Demography* 50, 4 (August): 1303–1314.

OECD. (2012). *Mexico Country Note. Education at a glance: OECD Indicators*.

Orellana, M. F. (2001). The work kids do. *Harvard Education Review*. Volume 71, Immigration and Education.

———. (2009). *Translating Childhoods: Immigrant Youth, Language and Culture*. New Brunswick, NJ: Rutgers University Press.

Orellana, M. F., Thorne, B., Chee, A., & Lam, W.S.E. (2001). Transnational childhoods: The participation of children in processes of family migration. *Social Problems* 48(4): 572–591.

Parreñas, R. S. (2001). Mothering from a distance: Emotions, gender and intergenerational relations in Filipino transnational families. *Feminist Studies* 27(2): 261–290.

———. (2005a). *Children of Global Migration: Transnational Families and Gendered Woes*. Manila: Ateneo de Manila University Press.

———. (2005b). The gender paradox in the transnational families of Filipino migrant women. *Asian and Pacific Migration Journal* 4(3): 243–268.

———. (2010). Transnational mothering: A source of gender conflicts in the family. *University of North Carolina Law Review* 88(5): 1825–1856.

Passel, J. S., Cohn, D., & Gonzalez-Barrera, A. (2012). *Net Migration from Mexico Falls to Zero—and Perhaps Less*. Pew Hispanic Center Hispanic Trends, April 23. Available at: www.pewhispanic.org.

Paz, O. (1985). *The Labyrinth of Solitude and Other Writings*. New York: Grove Press.

Pew Hispanic Center. (2012). *How Many Mexicans Live in the USA: Mexican Immigration to America*. Available at: www.pewhispanic.org.

Portes, A., Guarnizo, L. E., & Landolt, P. (1999). The study of transnationalism: pitfalls and promise of an emergent research field. *Ethnic and Racial Studies* 22(2): 217–237.

Portes, A., Lynch, S. M., & Haller, W. (2011). Dreams fulfilled and shattered: Determinants of segmented assimilation in the second generation. *Social Forces* 89(3): 733–762.

Portes, A., & Rumbaut, R. G. (1996). *Immigrant America: A Portrait*. Berkeley: University of California Press.

———. (2001). *Legacies: The Story of the Immigrant Second Generation*. New York: Russell Sage Foundation.

Pratt, G. (2012). *Families Apart: Migrant Mothers and the Conflicts of Labor and Love*. Minneapolis: University of Minnesota Press.

Prins, E. (2011). On becoming an educated person: Salvadoran adult learners' cultural model of educación/education. *Teachers College Record* 113(7): 1477–1505.

Punch, S. (2002). Negotiating autonomy: Childhoods in rural Bolivia. In Leena Alanen and Berry Mayall, eds., *Conceptualizing Child-Adult Relations*. London: Falmer Press.

Redfield, R. (1941). *The Folk Culture of Yucatan*. Chicago: University of Chicago Press.

Rojas-Flores, L., Clements, M. L., Koo, H. J., & London, J. (2017). Trauma and psychological distress in Latino citizen children following parental detention and deportation. *Psychological Trauma: Theory, Research, Practice, and Policy* 9(3): 352–261.

Rosaldo, R. (2014). Vital Topics Forum on Latin@s and the immigration debate. *American Anthropologist* 116(1): 1–14.

Rouse, R. (2011). Mexican migration and the social space of postmodernism. *Diaspora: A Journal of Transnational Studies* 1(1): 8–23.

Ruddick, S. (1983). Maternal thinking. *Feminist Studies* 6, 2 (Summer): 342–367.

———. (1989). *Maternal Thinking: Toward a Politics of Peace*. Boston: Beacon.

Saiz-Álvarez, José Manuel. (2016). *Handbook of Research on Social Entrepreneurship and Solidarity Economics*. Hershey, PA: Business Science Reference IGI Global.

Sassen, S. (2002). Global cities and survival circuits. In A. R. Hochschild and B. Ehrenreich, eds., *Global Woman: Nannies, Maids, and Sex Workers in the New Economy*. New York: Henry Holt and Company. Pp. 254–274.

———. (2010). Strategic gendering: One factor in the constituting of novel political economies. In S. Chant, ed., *International Handbook of Gender and Poverty: Concepts, Research, Policy*. Cheltenham: Edward Elgar.

Sawyer, A. (2010). *In Mexico, Mother's Education and Remittances Matter in School Outcomes*. Migration Information Source, Migration Policy Institute (MPI). March 29. Available at: www.migrationpolicy.org.

Scheper-Hughes, N. (1992). *Death without Weeping: The Violence of Everyday Life in Brazil*. Berkeley: University of California Press.

Schmalzbauer, L. (2004). Searching for wages and mothering from Afar: The case of Honduran transnational families. *Journal of Marriage and Family* 66, 5 (December): 1317–1331.

———. (2005). *Striving and Surviving: A Daily Life Analysis of Honduran Transnational Families*. New York: Routledge.

———. (2008). Family divided: The class formation of Honduran transnational families. *Global Networks* 8: 329–346.

———. (2009). Gender on a new frontier: Mexican Migration in the rural mountain west. *Gender & Society* 23: 747–767.

Scott, J., & Marshall, G. (2009). *A Dictionary of Sociology Oxford*. Oxford, UK: Oxford University Press.

Segura, D. A. (1994). Working at motherhood: Chicana and Mexican immigrant mothers and employment. In Evelyn Nakano Glenn, Grace Chang, and Linda Rennie Forcey, eds., *Mothering: Ideology, Experience, and Agency*. New York: Routledge.

Semple, K. (2011). In New York, Mexicans lag in education. *New York Times*, November 24. Available at: www.nytimes.com.

Skinner, D., & Holland, D. (1996). Schools as a heteroglossic site for the cultural production of persons in and beyond a hill community in Nepal. In B. Levinson, D. Foley, and D. Holland, eds., *The Cultural Production of the Educated Person: Critical Ethnographies of Schooling and Local Practice*. Buffalo: State University of New York Press. Pp. 273–299.

Smith, R. C. (2005). *Mexican New York: Transnational Lives of New Immigrants*. Berkeley: University of California Press.

Sørensen, N. N. (2005). Transnational family life across the Atlantic: The experience of Colombian and Dominican migrants in Europe. Paper presented at the International Conference on Migration and Domestic Work in a Global Perspective, May 26–29.

Stoney, S., & Batalova, J. (2013). Mexican immigrants in the United States. Migration Policy Institute. Available at: www.migrationpolicy.org.

Suárez-Orozco, C. (2002). Latino families. In Marcelo Suárez-Orozco and Mariela Paez, (eds., *Latinos: Remaking America*. Berkeley: University of California Press. Pp. 302–305.

Suárez-Orozco, C., & Baolian Qin, D. (2006). Psychological and gendered perspectives on immigrant origin youth. *Special Issue on the Social Sciences and Migration and Gender of International Migration Review* 40(1): 165–199.

Suárez-Orozco, C., & Suárez-Orozco, M. (2001). *Children of immigration*. Cambridge, MA: Harvard University Press.

Suárez-Orozco, C., Suárez-Orozco, M., & Todorova, I. (Eds.). (2008). *Learning New Land: Immigrant Students in American Society*. Cambridge, MA: Belknap Press.

Suárez-Orozco, C., Todorova, I., & Louie, J. (2002). "Making up for lost time": The experience of separation and reunification among immigrant families. *Family Process* 41(4): 625–643. International Astronomical Union. Accessed: www.iau.org.

Thomson, M., and Crul, M. (2007). The second generation in Europe and the United States: How is the transatlantic debate relevant for further research on the European second generation? *Journal of Ethnic and Racial Studies* 33: 1025–1044.

UNICEF. (2006). *State of the World's Children*. New York: UNICEF.

———. (2011). *The Impact of International Migration: Children Left Behind in Selected Countries of Latin America and the Caribbean*. New York: UNICEF.

United Nations Department of Economic and Public Affairs—Population Division. (2013). *The Number of International Migrants Worldwide Reaches 232 Million*. No. 2013/2 September.

Valdéz, G. (1996). *Con Respeto: Bridging the Distances Between Culturally Diverse Families and Schools: An Ethnographic Portrait*. New York: Teachers College Press.

Valdéz-Gardea, G. C. (2009). Actores de la globalización: reflexiones metodológicas para su estudio. In Gloria Ciria Valdéz-Gardea, ed., *Achicando Futuros*. Hermosillo, Sonora, Mexico: El Colegio de Sonora.

Varenne, H., & McDermott, R. (1998). *Successful Failure: The School America Builds*. Boulder, CO: Westview.

Vertovec, S. (2007). New directions in the anthropology of migration and multiculturalism. *Special issue of Ethnic and Racial Studies* 30: 961–978.

Wallerstein, I. (1980). *The Modern World-System II: Mercantilism and the Consolidation of the European World Economy, 1600–1750*. New York: Academic Press.

———. (1988). *The Modern World-System III: The Second Era of Great Expansion of the Capitalist World Economy, 1730–1840s*. New York: Academic Press.

Yarova, O. (2006). The migration of Ukrainian women to Italy and the impact on their family in Ukraine. In Alice Szczepanikova, Marek Canek, and Jan Grill, *Migration Processes in Central and Eastern Europe: Unpacking the Diversity*. Prague: Multicultural Centre.

Yarris, K. (2011). Living with Mother Migration: Grandmothers, Caregiving, and Children in Nicaraguan Transnational. PhD thesis. UCLA.

Yeates, Nicola. (2005). Global Care Chain: A Critical Introduction. *Global Migration Perspectives*. No. 44. Global Comission on International Migration. Available at: http://www.refworld.org/pdfid/435f85a84.pdf

Yoshikawa, Hirokazu, & Kalil, Ariel. (2011). The Effects of Parental Undocumented Status on the Developmental Contexts of Young Children in Immigrant Families. *Child Development Perspectives*. DOI: 10.1111/j.1750-8606.2011.00204.x.

Zentgraf, K., & Chinchilla, N. (2006). Separation and reunification: The experiences of Central American immigrant families. San Juan, Puerto Rico: paper presented to the Latin American Studies Association meeting, March 15–18.

———. (2012). Transnational family separation: A framework for analysis. *Journal of Ethnic and Migration Studies* 38(2): 345–366.

Zong, J., & Batalova, J. (2014). *Mexican Immigrants in the United States. Migration Information Source Spotlight*. Available at: www.migrationpolicy.org. Migration Policy Institute (MPI).

Zúñiga, V., & Hamann, E. T. (2009). Sojourners in Mexico with U.S. school experience: A new taxonomy for transnational students. *Comparative Education Review* 53: 329–353.

INDEX

abandonment: of children left behind considerations, 16–17, 33, 39, 46–47, 57, 112, 131, 155, 158; grandmothers' in Mexico sense of, 80

Abu-Lughod, Lila, 22

abuse: in caregiver environment, 36, 182; in marriage, 56–57, 61, 125, 127

academic performance. *See* school/ education

African Americans, 78, 153–54

age: of caregivers, 26, 52; of children in NYC (US-born and brought over), 26, 138; of children left behind, 26, 51–52, 138; of migrant mothers, 26, 52; siblings (separated) differences in, 138

alcoholism: with caregivers, 36, 182; concerns about, 175; in marriage, 33–34, 61

anthropology, 218; transnational care in, 18–19; of transnationalism, 10–13

"Approaches from Cultural Analysis in Anthropology to Latin@ Immigration" (Rosaldo), 8–9

assimilation theories, 8, 9, 132, 138, 156

Assistance and Education Center (Brooklyn), 155, 157

asylum, 103, 222n1

Barth, Fredrik, 10

Barthes, Roland, 43

Bartlett, Lesley, 152, 164, 185–86

Baubock, Rainer, 20

Belmont, New York. *See* Bronx, New York

belonging and kinship, 38; children left behind focus on, 120; ICT significance for sense of, 18–19, 28, 89, 115–17, 121, 191; for siblings (separated), 98–99, 112–14, 118–20, 121; transnational care constellation impact on, 98–99

Bergad, Laird, 134

bilingualism, 133, 140

birthing process, 122–24

Boehm, Deborah, 13, 191

border crossings. *See* crossings, undocumented

border militarization, 9

boys. *See* gender

Bracero Program, 6, 45

Brazil, 25, 43

Brighton Beach, New York. *See* Brooklyn, New York

Bronx, New York: research demographics for, 215; research sites and participants in, 23, 24, 30–31, 59. *See also* South Bronx, New York

Brooklyn, New York: research demographics for, 215; research sites in, 23, 24; social services in, 24, 150–51, 155, 157. *See also* Sunset Park, New York

care chains, 4, 42

caregivers (Mexico): abuse/alcoholism with, 36, 182; age range for, 26, 52; on biological mothers role and obligations, 76–77, 85–86; bond with biological mother compared with, 35, 52, 54–55, 65–67, 96–97; children left behind relationships with, 65–67, 149–50, 169, 177, 178–79;

Gabrielle Oliveira is Assistant Professor at the Lynch School of Education at Boston College. She has also taught at Saint John's University, CUNY in New York City and has worked as a Lecturer in the Department of International and Transcultural Studies at Teachers College, Columbia University in New York City. She is originally from São Paulo, Brazil. She received her PhD from Teachers College, Columbia University in Applied Anthropology. She also holds a Masters in International Affairs from Columbia University with a focus in Latin American Studies. Gabrielle Oliveira's research and dissertation have focused on female Mexican migration to the United States, with a specific focus on transnational motherhood, separated siblings, childhood, and education. She was a National Academy of Education/Spencer Foundation Dissertation Fellow. After completing her PhD work, Oliveira was a Post-doc Fellow with the University of Wisconsin's School of Education, working on a research project on immigrant Dominican youth in New York City.